Red Triangle

Fearghal Mac Bhloscaidh is senior lecturer in History at St Mary's University, Belfast, and the author of *Fenians and Ribbonmen* and *Tyrone: The Irish Revolution*. Originally from East Tyrone, he taught for ten years at Coláiste Feirste, the largest Irish-language secondary school on the Island. He was previously a research fellow at the National University of Ireland, Galway.

Contents

The main population centres and villages mentioned in the text

Introduction

In 'The Storyteller', Walter Benjamin claims that every good tale holds a big story inside a smaller one.[1] This book strives to tell the big story of the Irish Revolution through the experiences of ordinary people in one small, problematic corner of the island. I want to capture a fleeting moment when a wave of working-class militancy washed over Ulster, during the years leading up to Partition in 1921. We will see how this militancy raised the tantalising hope of an anti-sectarian and democratic future before crashing on the jagged reality of loyalist counter-revolution and economic depression.

Writing from the Belfast leg of her fact-finding tour of Ireland in late spring 1919, the Chicago journalist Ruth Russell predicted that post-war inflation heralded the 'sickness and death' of Unionist sectarianism by uniting Protestant and Catholic workers in defence of their living standards. As evidence, she pointed to an interview in Belfast with Dawson Gordon, organiser for the Flax Roughers' and Yarn Spinners' Union. From his 'dark little union headquarters', filled with 'shawled spinners and weavers', Gordon first regaled Russell with lurid tales:

> I have heard stories that were so much fuel on the prejudice pile. When I was small, I believed anything I was told about the Catholics. I remember this tale that my mother repeated to me as she said her grandmother had told it to her: A neighbour of grandmother's was alone in her cabin one night. There was a knock at the door. A

> Catholic woman begged for shelter. The neighbour could not bear to turn her back into the night. Then as there was only one bed, the two women shared it. Next morning grandmother heard a moaning in the cabin. On entering, she saw the neighbour lying alone on the bed, stabbed in the back. The neighbour's last words were: 'Never trust a Catholic!' As I grew a little older, I found two other Protestant friends whose grandmothers had had the same experience. And since I have been a labour organiser, I have run across Catholics who told the same story turned about. So, I began to think that there was a hell of a lot of great-grandmothers with stabbed friends – almost too many for belief.[2]

But Gordon, a Protestant follower of James Connolly – executed for his part in the 1916 Easter Rising – then recounted how workers with 'hunger at their heels' were now forgetting the prejudices that had impeded trade-union organisation so often in the past. As evidence, he produced 'a much-thumbed pamphlet on the linen and jute industry'.[3] From 400 members in 1914, union numbers in the Irish Textile Federation had now 'mounted to 40,000', mostly through struggles for higher wages.[4] Gordon described how 'Catholics began to attend meetings in Orange halls; Protestants went along to similar meetings in Hibernian assembly rooms; a small town near Belfast had recently witnessed a labour procession in which one-half of the band was Orange and the other half Hibernian, and yet there was perfect harmony.'[5]

Gordon may have had in mind a large May Day demonstration in Dungannon, County Tyrone, forty miles from the northern metropolis. Dungannon lay on the western tip of Ulster's famed linen triangle – 'the heart of the industry', spanning east to Lisburn and south to Armagh.[6] This book charts the rise and fall of anti-sectarian trade unionism between 1917 and 1920, when ordinary workers briefly turned this triangle red. A cadre of mostly Protestant socialists opposed to partition mobilised thousands of unskilled mill-hands and labourers through the Flax Roughers' and Workers' Unions. Class consciousness briefly trumped an established sectarian dynamic, as Protestant people who had almost nothing stopped looking down on Catholic people who had nothing at all. Remarkably, this solidarity thrived in an area notorious for sectarianism. By the 1970s, the area – once Ulster's linen triangle – became infamous as the 'murder triangle', as documented by Catholic priests Denis Faul and Réamonn Ó Muireadhaigh in their booklet *Triangle of Death*.[7]

As the First World War staggered towards its long-drawn out conclusion, for neither the first nor last time, a significant minority of working-class Protestants embraced egalitarianism. The Orange supremacism deployed to crush this fragile class consciousness relied on material support and deliberate action. Loyalist shock troops led the initial assault, while a discriminatory Northern Irish regime secured its consolidation, its birth pangs echoing to the beat of Lambeg drums.[8] Thus did the Ulster Unionist leadership orchestrate the expulsion of Catholics and Protestant socialists from Belfast's shipyards and engineering works in July 1920, displacing 10,000 workers and eventually driving 24,000 from their homes – an upheaval unmatched elsewhere in revolutionary Ireland. Northern Ireland emerged from this deeply reactionary, sectarian counter-revolution, which came to be enshrined in the very essence of the polity, sowing the dragon's teeth of future conflict.

Unionist leaders could count on unwavering support from an imperial state that preached self-determination for the conquered while expanding its own dominions. In short, the British state intervened politically and materially to uphold Orangeism and suppress democracy. This was perhaps predictable – part of a long tradition stretching back to efforts to suppress the 1798 rebellion. Yet this history from below is striking in revealing the resilience of Protestant socialists and trade unionists, alongside marginalised Catholic agrarian radicals and inheritors of the Fenian tradition, in their shared struggle for a democratic, anti-sectarian and egalitarian future.

Chapter 1 offers a necessary framework for making sense of Irish history over the *longue durée*. The second chapter traces the rise of Belfast as 'Linenopolis' and its hinterland – the famed triangle that lends this book its title. Our 'small story' begins with a group of socialists in Belfast who became the driving force behind trade unionism in mid-Ulster, sparking a wave of militancy that briefly turned local politics upside down. Chapters 3 and 4 chart this movement's rise in the crucible of North Armagh, before moving west to uncover an upsurge of working-class militancy in neighbouring East Tyrone. These chapters expose the rupture opened up by radical labour politics, however fleetingly, in a region notorious (down to the present) for bitter sectarianism, for the pervasiveness of traditional antipathies, for the weakness of class politics, and for the immiseration and poverty suffered by unorganised local workers.

Having charted the rising socialist tide, the narrative then details the methods by which employers, prominent Unionist politicians and the imperial state manipulated sectarianism to defeat the cause of labour and Irish freedom. Chapter 5, on the Caledon Lockout of 1919, provides a case study in rural counter-revolution, followed in Chapter 6 by a detailed account of the notorious pogrom of July 1920, at the core of which lay a series of massive workplace expulsions which decisively broke the red wave. Departing from the familiar story of a liberal Unionist elite bowing helplessly to the bellicose exertions of Protestant workers in the shipyards and elsewhere, this book demonstrates conclusively that the Ulster Unionist elite – and especially its leading lights Edward Carson and Richard Dawson Bates – played prominent roles both in the logistics of fomenting this violence and in supplying it with ideological cover. Furthermore, it outlines how the pogrom drew upon a synthesis of colonial-settler identity and currents of the contemporary British and European extreme right popularised by prominent 'respectable' Unionists.

Chapter 7 examines Sir Samuel Kelly's abortive 'Coalisland Miracle', offering another case study in how sectarianism and discrimination worked in practice in the new Northern Ireland – accurately described as an 'impregnable colonial Pale' by its first prime minister, James Craig.[9]

The book concludes by situating the working-class struggles described in Belfast, Tyrone and Armagh within the wider context of the Irish revolution and counter-revolution, confirming the prescience in Connolly's warning that Partition would inaugurate a 'carnival of reaction North and South'.

This counter-revolutionary dispensation has profoundly conditioned the writing of academic history ever since. In the words of Brendan O'Leary, Irish historiography has largely favoured a perspective that 'tries to erase the legacies of colonialism', thereby suiting 'the interests of the descendants of Protestant settlers and their allies, including British governments'.[10] Or, as Kyla Madden argues in her study of Forkhill, County Armagh: 'much of Irish historical reading rests on an assumed foundation of conflict between Catholics and Protestants, a conflict regarded as constant and essentially unchanging'. As a result, 'sectarianism approaches the status of a historiographical method, characterised by the separation of Irish people into two warring camps, and a historical narrative dedicated to exploring their patterns of confrontation'.[11]

My argument does not seek to marginalise sectarianism's role in the area's history, but it firmly refuses to essentialise it. Sectarianism, like class, is neither a rigid structure nor a category but rather something which in fact happens in human relationships.[12] Many of the real people under study here sold their labour very cheaply in the linen industry. Women had consistently formed 70 per cent of linen factory workers, compared to only half in the Lancashire textile mills. Indeed, women, children and youths together typically made up 80 to 90 per cent of Ulster's linen workforce.[13] In that respect, *Red Triangle* will also fulfil another crucial function of 'history from below', seeking to 'write women back into the historical narrative so they might rightly reclaim the spaces they occupied in revolution, politics, and domestic spheres, as fighters, thinkers, confidantes and breadwinners'.[14]

This struggle for an anti-sectarian and egalitarian future ultimately failed. Indeed, it was defeated by concerted reactionary violence. Nevertheless, for four years, through their own agency and conscious efforts, these workers contributed to the making of history. Too often, as E. P. Thompson wrote, 'the blind alleys, the lost causes, and the losers themselves are forgotten'. This book seeks not only to rescue them from historical oblivion, but to highlight how the lost causes of the women and men of the Red Triangle might help new generations 'discover insights into social evils which we have yet to cure'. I have set out, then, to write a 'history from below', rescuing, if only partially, farm labourers, mill-hands and factory workers from what Thompson famously called the 'enormous condescension of posterity'.[15]

Such history is indispensable if we really want to understand democratic agency, as opposed to castigating and marginalising it. Those who seek to write Irish history 'as it really was' should call to mind James Connolly's injunction in *Labour in Irish History* (1910): 'Were history what it ought to be, an accurate literary reflex of the times with which it professes to deal, the pages of history would be almost entirely engrossed with a recital of the wrongs and struggles of the labouring people, constituting, as they have ever done, the vast mass of mankind.'[16]

1

Land, Linen and Liberty

Three main currents ran through Irish history up to 1921: an anti-imperialist republicanism, a colonised constitutional nationalism, and a colonial loyalism. These did not represent fixed or reified categories, but interacted dialectically. The radical republican tendency – inherited from the United Irishmen of the 1790s – found its most progressive expression in James Connolly's revolutionary socialism. Constitutional nationalism, on the other hand, accepted the sectarian and imperial status quo, seeking only a privileged niche ('Home Rule') for a Catholic middle class within the British system. The third current, colonial loyalism, channelled supremacist loyalism or 'Carsonism' – a modern, paramilitary, colonial-settler identity that defended Protestant privilege and Ireland's dependent link to Britain.

The horrific toll and economic strain of the First World War shattered old certainties across Europe, fuelling a revolutionary mood in Ireland, as elsewhere. During Easter Week in April 1916, republicans hazarded a Rising in Dublin against British rule. The insurrection was suppressed by the British Army, and Connolly and fourteen others were executed by British court-martial. Republicanism surged forward, however, and on 21 January 1919 Sinn Féin MPs declared Irish independence. An anti-sectarian working-class movement directly inspired by Connolly's syndicalist vision saw trade-union membership explode, and a wave of strikes engulfed even loyalist Ulster. Facing this dual threat from labour militancy and the broader democratic mandate for an independent republic, the Unionist elite, with British imperial connivance, moved to crush it. They manipulated sectarian animosities, culminating in the 1920 expulsions, and then partitioned the island through the Anglo-Irish Treaty of 6 December 1921.

In the newly partitioned North, loyalist violence crystallised into the state-funded Ulster Special Constabulary, cementing a reactionary, majoritarian regime. While the North solidified into a discriminatory Orange State, the South coalesced into a conservative Catholic nationalist polity, dominated by a comprador class eager for economic integration with Britain – the same imperial state that sponsored its victory in the Southern Civil War of 1922–23. Both entities excised the revolutionary, socialist potential from the national struggle, leaving Connolly's chair at the table of independence empty.

Colonial Racism and Republican Solidarities

Our story really begins with the fractious birth of modern Ulster, forged in the crucible of conquest and colonisation in the late sixteenth century. This new order granted a Protestant elite land and power, fracturing society along lines of religion and ethnicity. From this contested soil sprang the linen economy, an unexpected engine of change. Fuelled by landlord patronage, the humble flax plant revolutionised Ulster's economy, flooding the region with cash and creating new classes of weavers and drapers. Such ferment, at home and abroad, broke old patterns, stirring ambitions and anxieties that erupted into sectarian conflict between Catholic Defenders and Protestant Peep-o'-Day Boys. Into this volatile world exploded the revolutionary ideals of the 1790s. The United Irishmen's message of a common citizenship found a receptive audience among the weavers of the linen triangle. Momentarily, Presbyterian radicals and Catholic Defenders united, threatening to overturn the colonial order. Their defeat cemented a bitter legacy, setting the stage for the industrial conflicts and unfinished battles over liberty that would define the centuries to come.

This passage by Tudor historian Geoffrey Elton partially describes the early Elizabethan conquest of Gaelic Ulster:

> Shane was permitted to retain the reality of power as captain of Tyrone, while the young heir to the earldom – Hugh O'Neill – was

> taken to England to be educated at court. Of all Elizabeth's Irish opponents Shane was probably the most primitive – a true savage who has been described as 'a drunkard even by contemporary Ulster standards', but a formidable warrior . . . The O'Neill was a great man, as savages go, but his overthrow benefited most of all his own Irish neighbours. The chieftaincy of Tyrone passed to Tirlagh Luineach O'Neill, a man who through nearly thirty years of moderate ambitions and hard drinking proved the wisdom of a cunning policy and the preservative qualities of Irish whiskey.[1]

Elton's tropes echo John Gillingham's characterisation of long-term English commentary on the Irish as the barbarian at work (lazy), the barbarian at war (savage), and the barbarian in bed (animal-like).[2] Elton penned his 'value-free' analysis in the mid 1950s. A decade later, he dismissed the notion that historians carried prejudices and preconceptions into their work as 'pernicious nonsense' leading to an 'extreme relativism'.[3] Indeed, Elton's perspective and practice significantly influenced an extant historiography on early modern and modern Ireland, which too often amounts to an Establishment-liberal defence of power.

Any history of colonisation, however, must also consider the indigenous 'underside', often 'a story of destruction, coercion and endings'.[4] The great theorist of decolonisation, Aimé Césaire, famously proposed an equation – 'colonisation = chosification': a process which produced societies emptied of themselves, vanquished cultures, toppled institutions, confiscated lands, murdered religions, artistic magnificence destroyed, and extraordinary possibilities suppressed.[5] When Césaire spoke of 'negritude', or James Connolly of the reconquest of Ireland, they did not have a reverse chauvinism in mind, but an assertion of the integrity and potentialities of the native culture and civilisation – and, on the further horizon, the 'celebration of [a] universal humanity'.[6]

The universalist republican tendency in the Irish political tradition emerged from the radical humanist current within the Enlightenment. In the words of its Dublin Protestant founder, Wolfe Tone, Irish republicanism sought 'to break the connection with England, the never-failing source of all our political evils', and proposed to establish a republic founded on a civic (rather than ethnic) conception of the Irish nation – one based on universal rights that would 'substitute the common name of Irishman, in place of the denominations of Protestant, Catholic and Dissenter'.[7] The thoroughly forward-facing United Irishmen of the 1790s and their republican successors stood as the most anti-sectarian and egalitarian heirs to Ireland's Enlightenment tradition. 'We have thought little about our ancestors – much of our posterity', they proclaimed. 'Are we forever to walk like beasts of prey over fields which these ancestors stained with blood?'[8] The English colonial state answered forcibly in the affirmative.

The late-eighteenth-century Protestant Ascendancy employed Orangeism as a reactionary check on democracy. As Thomas Knox, scion of the House of Ranfurly, wrote: 'in spite of their licentiousness, on them [Orangemen] we must rely for the preservation of our lives and properties should critical times occur'.[9] Initial colonial racial oppression lingered in Ulster due to Protestant privilege's efficacy as a means of elite social control in industrial Belfast and its hinterland across the long nineteenth century.[10] As C. L. R. James stressed, 'The race question is subsidiary to the class question in politics, and to think of imperialism in terms of race is disastrous. But to neglect the racial factor as merely incidental is an error only less grave than to make it fundamental.'[11] In the case of Ireland, sectarianism served social functions akin to race, and this history from below examines the dialectic between class struggle and sectarianism within a colonial society.

Ireland acted as the laboratory of English racism in the period of conquest and colonisation. This study begins at the source of the 'dreaded spiral': the phase of expansionist mercantilist capital that spawned early European colonialism, when Arthur Chichester, the architect of the Ulster Plantation, 'would have preferred to labour with his hands in Ireland than "dance and sing in Virginia" '.[12] The narrative will then trace the evolution of colonialism, racism and sectarianism, as well as the agency of ordinary people through the growth of local proto-industrial linen manufacture in the run-up to the unsuccessful United Irish revolution, and onwards into the phase of industrial capital and the Act of Union.

Any attempt to write pre-Famine Irish history and history from below must also engage with indigenous language sources, or the resultant analysis remains incomplete. This subaltern consciousness lasted well into the period covered by *Red Triangle*. In his autobiography, the novelist Séamus Ó Grianna (known pseudonymously as 'Máire') related an encounter with *an Gobán*, a native Irish speaker from the Tyrone Gaeltacht on the eve of the First World War:

Sasain, nach í is cúis de? Nach ar chogadh san Eoraip atá sí beo? Sin an saol atá i ndán d'Impireacht na Sasana, go dtí an lá a bheas síocháin san Eoraip . . . Ó, dá hainneoin riamh a chuaigh Sasain chun cogaidh. Ní raibh neart aici air. Sin an chinniúint chruaidh a bhí i ndán di. An solas a lasadh sa dorchadas. Treabha garbha fiáine a thabhairt chun creidimh. Ach ní raibh neart ar sin aici. Ní raibh sa mhaoin ach taisme. Chan ar mhaithe le maoin ná saibhreas a tháinig sé go hÉirinn, nó a chuaigh sé chun na hIndia nó na hÉigipte. Ní hea ar chor ar bith ach de gheall ar Dhia . . . rinne tíortha láidre eile slad is creach ar an laige amanna' . . . 'ach níor thug aon cheann acu iarraidh a chur i gcéill ach Sasain gur ag comhlíonadh aitheanta Dé a bhí siad . . . Agus an chuid is measa de, an dóigh ar éirigh léi a chur in iúl don mhuintir a chuir sé faoi smacht gur lena leas a bhí sí' . . . agus tá siad chomh truaillithe sin ag an daorsmacht is go síleann siad gurb í Sasain réalt eolais an domhain. Nach millteanach an mearadh atá ar mhac Gaeil ar bith a bhfuil an dearcadh sin aige?' . . . 'is é mo chreideamhsa, má tá ionadaí ar bith ar an tsaol ag an diabhal (agus tá) gurb é impireacht na Sasana é.

Isn't it England that's the cause of it? Doesn't she thrive off the back of war in Europe? That is the fate of the British Empire until peace reigns in Europe . . . Oh, it was always despite herself that England went to war. She couldn't help it. For that was her cruel fate – to bring light to the darkness and religion to uncivilised tribes, but she never had any choice in the matter. The resulting plunder was merely coincidental. It was not for the sake of property and wealth that she came to Ireland, or that she went to India or Egypt. Not at all, but in the name of God. On occasion, other powerful countries raped and pillaged the weak . . . but only England ever pretended they were doing God's work. And the worst of it all is the way she convinced the people who she had oppressed that it was all for their own benefit . . . and them so corrupted by oppression that they consider England the font of all wisdom. Isn't it terrible that an Irishman would suffer such madness? It's my firm opinion that if the devil has a representative on Earth, and he does, it's the British Empire.[13]

In September 1914, when John Redmond exhorted Irish nationalists to enlist in the British Army, Máire related another encounter with the broken-hearted *Gobán*. After a chance meeting, *an Gobán* departed: 'agus é ag gabhail ceoil. Amhrán de chuid Thír Eoghain a tharraing sé air agus chonacthas domh go raibh doimhne na síoraíochta sa bhrón agus sa chumha a bhí ann' ('and he sang. He sang a Tyrone song, and it seemed to me that the sorrow and loss in it plumbed the depths of eternity').[14]

Land

James Connolly's *Labour in Irish History*, the country's first materialist history, analysed pre-conquest Ireland, noting that the Irish chief (or taoiseach), 'although recognised in the courts of France, Spain, and Rome . . . in reality held his position upon the sufferance of his people'. In the sixteenth and early seventeenth centuries, the principal area of study in this book, the modern counties of Tyrone and Armagh, lay within Cineál Eoghain, the territory of the Ó Néill dynasty, led by the 'true savage' Shane O'Neill (Seán an Díomais) and his successor, the 'hard drinking' Tirlagh Luineach (Toirdhealbhach Luineach), before the accession of Hugh Ó Néill (Aodh Mór) and the exile, return and defeat of his nephew, Eoghan Ruadh Ó Néill (Owen Roe) in the 1640s, which heralded the ultimate collapse of the Gaelic order.

Here, 'for 400 years after the first conquest (so-called) the English governors could not penetrate except at the head of a powerful army, the social order which prevailed in England – feudalism – was unknown'.[15] As the final bastion of Gaelic civilisation, Tyrone and Armagh represent a case study in Césaire's emptied society, suppressed culture, collapsed institutions, and confiscated lands: in short, the suppression of extraordinary possibilities. All of this began, in part, with the othering of the Gael, since the colonial architect reduces the natives in imagination before he destroys them in reality.

Before the English conquest, Ireland had up to one million inhabitants. While the Gaelic system prevailed across much of the north and west, a sizeable and mostly Catholic 'Old English' or Anglo-Norman community also lived in Leinster and parts of Munster. The area around the English capital, Dublin, held most of the small Protestant 'New English' population in 'the Pale'. The Elizabethan state sought to extend its influence all over the island. In terms of lives lost, the resulting conquest 'must rank as one of the most destructive conflicts anywhere in sixteenth- and early seventeenth-century Europe.'[16] In intent, the English state aimed to 'extirpate' the Gaelic Irish. In 1575, it proposed an early form of apartheid between the Gael (who were beyond the Pale) and the Old and New English: a quarantine to stop the spread of the Gaelic contagion.[17]

In a precursor to innumerable subsequent imperialist tropes, John Davies, the attorney general, believed that the 'common people' would welcome the arrival of English sheriffs and landlords, claiming that 'albeit they were rude and barbarous [they] did quickly apprehend the difference between the tyranny and oppression under which they lived before, and the just government and protection which we promised unto them for the time to come.'[18] While ensconced in Dublin Castle, however, Davies manipulated the system to the natives' disadvantage. In 1610, when Gaelic freeholders in Cavan appealed to the new dispensation, Davies insisted that 'they never had any estates, according to the rules of common law, but only a scrambling and transitory possession, as all other Irish natives within this kingdom.'[19] Here stands the liberal British practice of 'legalised lawlessness' exhaustively detailed, in a much later context, by Caroline Elkins.[20]

Nevertheless, both accommodation and extirpation rested on a supremacist outlook, and when the Gael asserted their own autonomy and cultural legitimacy, the zero-sum implications came into clearer relief: 'extreme violence underpinned anglicisation throughout the early modern period. The Irish theatre of war was one of the bloodiest in Europe.'[21]

The Gael, however, never accepted that the English offered anything approaching a superior civilisation. One Catalan pilgrim, visiting Niall Óg Ó Néill on Christmas Day in 1397, remarked the Irish chief's primitive material culture, but noted how Ó Néill appeared indifferent to contrasts between his own court and those of medieval Europe: 'It appeared to me from his words that they consider their own customs to be better than ours and more advantageous than any others in the whole world.'[22] Over a century and a half later, Richard Stanihurst described Conn Ó Néill's contempt for the English language and culture. Here stood a civilisation secure in its own legitimacy: 'For the Irish man standeth so much upon his gentilitie, that he termeth anie one of the English sept and planted in Ireland, Bobdeagh Galteagh. That is English churle: but if he be an English man borne, then he nameth him, Bobdeagh Saxonnegh, that is, a Saxon churle.'[23]

Tudor attempts to extend dominion over the island provoked a series of revolts, culminating in the Nine Years' War, which cost the English state £2 million and involved 36,000 troops between 1594 and 1603.[24] The war of liberation headed by Conn's grandson, Aodh Mór Ó Néill, began because English colonisation of neighbouring Monaghan sent shock waves across northern Gaelic society. As in Césaire's rendering, Ó Néill was not some ideal character but rather the potentiality of something else. Aodh recognised the process of colonisation and its direct implications for his own civilisation, and looked to deploy all his Machiavellian acumen to counter cultural extinction.[25]

Ó Néill's early opposition remained explicitly Gaelic, but, as the ambitions of his revolt expanded, so too did his ideology. Ó Néill renounced his English title, Tyrone, and had himself proclaimed Gaelic taoiseach, or the Ó Néill at Tullyhogue, in 1593: a gesture replete with symbolism, simultaneously rejecting English authority and asserting Gaelic right.[26] Two years later, the English seized a letter from a priest and emissary of the Ó Néill to the king of Spain. Gaelic Ireland had become a potential backdoor for the invasion of England. The island's military domination remained as a strategic English, and then British, imperative for the next four centuries.[27]

An existential struggle ensued: not between 'civilised' English and 'barbarian' Irish, but between rival elite cultures integrated into the contemporary European mainstream. In April 1600, Ó Néill informed the Pope that he fought 'pro Romana et libertate patriae'. Ó Néill himself internalised commonwealth ideas and civic humanism as a youth in the Pale during the early 1560s and, as an adult, attended the Dublin parliament before his final break with Elizabeth.[28] He therefore synthesised inherent Gaelic culture with derived ideas acquired during his youth and wider Counter-Reformation thinking from the continent's emerging émigré community. Ó Néill attempted to forge the ideology of an early modern Irish nation, but lacked the resources either to fully exert his will militarily or to convince the Old English to throw in their lot with the Gael.

In response, the English, under Mountjoy, defeated Ó Néill's campaign through a genocidal policy of scorched earth, forced famine and mass murder. While accompanying the English Army on expeditions through all four provinces after 1600, Fynes Moryson later recorded: 'No spectacle was more frequent in the ditches of towns, and in the wasted countries, than to see multitudes of these poor people dead, their mouths all coloured green by eating nettles [and] docks.'[29] Arthur Chichester emerged as the conquest's most vicious English soldier of fortune. In 1601, he proudly reported raids across Lough Neagh 'in which journeys we have killed above 100 people of all sorts, besides such as were burnt, how many I know not. We spare none of what quality or sex soever, & it hath bred much terror.' To Chichester, the wild Irish were mere beasts in human form whom he quickly sought to reduce through forced starvation, concluding that 'a million of swords will not do them so much harm as a winter of famine'. Chichester duly set about 'ploughing and breaking up the barbarous Irish nation then sowing the soil with seeds of civility'.[30]

After Ó Néill's defeat at Kinsale (1601) and the Flight of the Earls (1607), Chichester played a significant role in the Plantation, but the basis of English 'good government' found eloquent if unwitting expression from the pen of John Davies, who made a desolation and called it peace:

> Thus had the Queen's army, under Lord Mountjoy, broken and absolutely subdued all the lords and chieftains of the Irish; whereupon the multitude being brayed as it were in a mortar with sword, famine and pestilence, together submitted themselves to the English Government, received the laws and magistrates, and most gladly embraced the King's pardon and peace in all parts of the realm, with demonstrations of joy and comfort.[31]

There is some debate as to the extent and rapidity of the intrusion of the market into Ulster after the 1609 Plantation.[32] There is no doubt, however, that colonisation effectively displaced the indigenous population from the best soil and provided economic, political and judicial preference to the colonisers, as well as grafting market relations onto a pre-existing pastoral economy.

Tyrone, for example, contained between 2,500 and 3,000 Gaelic households before the Plantation. In its wake, 'British settlers were greatly over-represented on land of the best qualities', while the Gael were 'mainly resident on land of medium quality, the only widespread exception to this being in the south-east of the county, where land had been originally allocated to Irish grandees.'[33] In Tyrone, English settlement predominated across the fertile Clogher Valley, while Scottish settlers mostly occupied two fertile tracts in the western Derg Valley and in East Tyrone between the Sperrin foothills and the marshy shores of Lough Neagh.

Anglicans predominated in the north-east corner of Armagh, as English undertakers received Eoghan Ruadh Ó Néill's patrimony in Oneilland. Through a process of 'colonial spread', Presbyterians migrated west into mid-Armagh from established settlements in Antrim and Down. The Catholic native Irish – a large minority everywhere in the county – dominated the population in south Armagh, which arches in a westward crescent between Newry and Keady.[34] Based on an analysis of the Muster Rolls, William Macafee has calculated that, by 1630, Armagh contained 354 English and 462 Scottish households, while the Tyrone figures sat at 298 and 460, respectively. He concludes that, 'if the Plantation had relied exclusively on its initial period of colonisation it is unlikely that by the early eighteenth century the British population in Ulster would even have reached 100,000'.[35]

As I have noted, those Gaelic chieftains who sided with the English also received land as part of the scheme, much of it around Dungannon. Nevertheless, the new dispensation left many indebted and dissatisfied. In 1641, Gaelic nobles, nominally led by Phelim O'Neill, rebelled. The massacre of settlers at places like Portadown that November certainly gained notoriety; but this never approached anything like the earlier genocidal violence deployed to secure the conquest. Rather, 'a gullible [English] public, horrified yet titillated by the gruesome tales emanating from Ireland, accepted uncritically these wildly exaggerated stories of death and mutilation', thereby justifying the Cromwellian Army's genocidal violence at the end of the conflict.[36]

In the meantime, Eoghan Ruadh Ó Néill returned to take up the mantle of his uncle, Aodh Mór, who had died in exile. This time, he promoted a more developed form of Counter-Reformation nationalism. While in exile, Eoghan emerged as the dominant figure in the émigré community in Louvain, which produced the following manifesto in 1627: 'In the name of liberty of the fatherland and of oppressed religion and by establishing as the government a Republic, which should be so called on its flags and its commissions and all other public ordinances should be in the name of the Republic and Kingdom of Ireland.'[37]

For returned Gaelic nobles, this was not about restoring the status quo ante, but setting up a new kingdom or Catholic Commonwealth. We have an excellent insight into Ó Néill's campaign in *Cín Lae Uí Mhealláin*, the account kept by a Franciscan friar. Trained in continental Counter-Reformation ideology, Franciscans, like the Four Masters in Louvain, tried to salvage the remnants of Gaelic civilisation as a means of promoting the Irish case for nationhood. Ó Mealláin described famine, and even cannibalism, in east Ulster during the period; but the most significant sections relate to the Battle of Benburb on 5 June 1646. Ó Néill's exhortation to his troops resonated with the new nationalist discourse forged in the Gaelic émigré community of warriors and scholars in Spanish Europe. The Gael won the battle but lost the war, however, partly because the Old English persisted in their temporal loyalty to the crown.

Eoghan Ruadh's death and Cromwell's arrival in 1649 marked the final rupture of Césaire's great possibilities in a Gaelic context. Between 1649 and 1651, the English parliament sent 55,000 soldiers to Ireland.[38] Cromwell, God's executioner, oversaw 'a war of extermination' in which over one-quarter of the population died – a slaughter rationalised by the assertion that 'the accepted military conventions did not apply in the case of the Catholic Irish.'[39]

The patterns and practices developed in England's first colony spread across the Americas, Asia and Africa. The centuries that followed saw a range of native responses across Britain's sprawling empire, from capitulation to assimilation to decolonisation. It is to the attempt at the latter in an Irish context that attention now turns, in an area that became a cockpit of revolutionary and counter-revolutionary mass politics.

Linen

For Irish Protestants, who supported William of Orange during his three-year campaign in Ireland, victories at the Boyne (1690) and Aughrim (1691) crushed their opponents and heralded a century of Protestant Ascendancy, epitomised by a series of anti-Catholic Penal Laws in the 1690s and early 1700s. Indeed, the Williamite settlement enshrined a Protestant landed interest across the British Isles capable of extracting rents to the extent that 'Irish land now fuelled English expansionism around the world'. After 1690, Ireland 'financed, housed and maintained a standing army of 12,000 men', which, until the 1770s, 'formed the backbone of the British military machine, ready to be deployed across the empire'.[40]

This Protestant Irish nation ruled from its parliament on College Green, but the Declaratory Act (1719–20) confirmed that real power rested with London and the colonial administration in Dublin Castle. While the Penal Laws discriminated against northern Presbyterians as well as Ireland's Catholic majority, they did not do so equally. Similarly, while Gaelic civilisation survived within a subaltern, hidden Ireland, producing poets of the calibre of Art Mac Cumhaigh and Peadar Ó Doirnín, by the end of the eighteenth century, two novel phenomena were convulsing local politics and society: linen and liberty.

By 1712, Ulster contained 270,000 English and Scottish and 330,000 native Irish inhabitants.[41] While the Plantation did not immediately shift the pastoral nature of local agriculture, after the Williamite succession, this area passed through a phase of proto-industrialisation. After the Irish Linen Board was formed in 1711, landlords harnessed local craftsmanship. Using subsidies and regulations, they turbocharged the manufacture of linen. Crucially, unlike wool, linen faced no British tariffs. The result was staggering: exports exploded from 0.3 million yards in 1700 to 18.7 million yards by 1780 – a sixtyfold increase.[42] Nevertheless, Denis O'Hearn forcefully argues that 'the replacement of Irish wool and cotton industries by linen were not trades of like for like, but a replacement of potential leading core industries by dependent semi-peripheral ones'.[43]

Furthermore, this domestic linen manufacture relied primarily on the earlier landed settlement, which acted as the seedbed of indigenous capital accumulation. A close study of William Richardson's estate in Richhill, Armagh, showed that, in the wake of the Plantation, Richardson 'retained some native tenants, on his terms, and attracted suitable English tenants'. In the first half of the eighteenth century, 'land held at low rents for an average [of] 60 years created an environment in which capital accumulation was possible'. Tenants' incomes rose 'as they brought more farmland into commercial production and took on commercial linen-making as well'.[44] In this sense, the landlord's integration into local society and politics helped promote hand-spinning and weaving; the distinctive landlord–tenant relationship typified by the 'Ulster Custom' (or tenant security) mitigated the purely extractive relationship between absentee proprietor and Catholic tenant-at-will typical of large areas across the rest of Ireland.[45] It also further facilitated subdivision and competition for land in what rapidly became the most densely populated region of the island.

Richardson also benefited politically, as his tenants formed an electoral base. As land values rose and forty-shilling freeholders proliferated, the landlord received a small cash payment from tenants for subletting, and 'welcomed the prospect of additional voters'. Indeed, 'not only did the number of the estate's freeholders guarantee the Richardsons a seat in parliament, but it also gave the family the political power to determine the candidate for the other county seat'. Similarly, Richardson 'took advantage of state incentives to promote linen-making', and, as one of Armagh's two MPs, became a trustee of the Linen Board, which distributed spinning wheels, reels, looms and other apparatuses to worthy recipients, giving it a considerable influence in deciding the direction of state policy.[46]

Even at this proto-industrial stage, the development of unified purpose between landlord and merchant sought to exclude the rights of labour. In a 1754 report to the Linen Board, Robert Stevenson, a descendent of planters from Renfrewshire, warned against the dangers of 'combination amongst workmen . . . the tendency of which is such dangerous consequence that, if not provided against by statute', it might endanger the entire linen manufacture. Stephenson railed against how manufacturers, or 'drapers', suffered from the 'terrible effect' of this combination, where they had to consult 'among the weavers to know if they will allow him' to engage in any new branch of the industry. Alluding to agrarian secret societies, Stephenson detailed how 'in the southern provinces they are to a man sworn into a combination to support a bill of prices [wages] they have made'.[47]

The Linen Board quickly nipped this nascent trade unionism in the bud, amending legislation 'to prevent the unlawful combination of weavers and others'. Interestingly, 'improving' landlords who promoted linen manufacture, such as Richardson, William Brownlow (later Lord Lurgan) and Lord Charlemont, also formed the vanguard of the 'Patriot Party' that emerged in the 1780s.[48] This 'Patriot' faction, largely independent of English patronage emanating from Dublin Castle, spearheaded the campaign for legislative independence. In 1757, the same landlords and magistrates had played a key role in fostering the market for linen. As Anne McKernan notes, these 'local notables' backed linen drapers in a clampdown on poor-quality coarse brown linen. Four magistrates, William Richardson (Richhill), Henry Cust (Armagh), Henry Knox (Dungannon) and John Beattie (Monaghan), appointed inspectors to view all cloth exposed for sale in their markets. Armagh quickly became the best coarse linen market in Ireland.[49]

A step further down the social pyramid, a network of entrepreneurs began to consolidate their position. A developing market in fine linens emerged, in which 'male weavers supplied coarse cloth', but also 'sold their better pieces to Ulster drapers for sale further afield'.[50] Stephenson described how 'He who was possessed of a larger capital established a small factory, or purchased or prepared the yarn for the loom, and employed the cottager to weave it. They are now called the manufacturers.'[51] This mutually reinforcing process rested on a novel social base: the tenant-weaver.[52]

As the eighteenth century reached its climax, the processes associated with the domestic manufacture of linen had spread across Ulster, and flax was grown across the province – though in greater concentration in the west, and Donegal in particular. Similarly, scutching mills, which separated the flax and tow for spinning, dotted the entire area, but proliferated in Derry and its hinterland. Further south, the borderland between Ulster and the Connacht and the Leinster midlands became more important for spinning than weaving, the area around Dungannon, Armagh and Portadown producing much of the woven 'brown linen', while a smaller area extending from Lurgan into Lisburn specialised in finer or cambric products.[53] Ironically, manufacturing in Belfast, which grew into the great Linenopolis of the nineteenth century, focused more on cotton in this period.

Hence, while the land settlement operated as the basis for proto-industrial hand-spinning, weaving and the bleaching of cloth, two new social elements appeared – the draper and the weaver – neither of whom had been present in the earlier economic system. At the Lurgan linen market 'nothing but ready money was taken', and Armagh at the time formed a 'hotbed of cash'.[54] This new economy cared little for religion: some of its most successful merchants, like Bernard Coile of Lurgan, were Catholic, defying old divisions. This Catholic entrepreneurial element augmented the pre-existing 'underground gentry', galvanising calls for Catholic relief, as leadership of the Catholic Committee shifted to the rising merchant and professional classes.[55] In an atmosphere of increasing calls among Protestant Patriots for legislative independence, and with Britain's control of its North American colonies on the brink of collapse, the Catholic question again loomed large in Irish political minds.

At the more popular level, one contemporary described an outbreak of sectarian violence at the epicentre of this new economy. North Armagh saw 'the great influx of cash and plentiful markets of provisions among the lower orders of the people'. As a result, 'so many young men take another short apprenticeship to the linen business [that] they get the handling of cash before they knew its real value', which 'prompts them to intoxication and riot before they have well digested their mother's milk'.[56] Under the strain created by this breakdown of the 'moral economy', in addition to extraneous political pressure exerted by national and international events, the 'Armagh Troubles' erupted four miles south of Markethill in 1784, after a faction fight between two Presbyterians on 4 July.[57]

When allegations circulated that Catholics had intervened on behalf of the victor, the loser rallied a gang of local Protestants to seek retribution. The defence of the Penal Laws appeared as the nominal motive for these Peep-o'-Day Boys – named for their dawn raids on Catholic homes. But the breakdown of established relations in land and religious solidarity operated as the material basis of these events. With Catholics increasingly prepared to outbid Protestants for sub-leases, landlords and middlemen appeared sanguine on the religious question amid a booming cash economy. This breakdown coincided with apprehension that some within the Protestant landed elite and emerging mercantilist class contemplated crossing the Rubicon and permitting Catholics entry into the political nation – an anxiety heightened by the Catholic Relief Acts of 1778 and 1782, which permitted papists to inherit and purchase land, to open schools, and to own a horse! Only the right to vote and bear arms remained elusive, and, as local Protestant landlords increasingly granted Catholics longer leases, the Peep-o'-Day Boys appeared intent on protecting their 'liberties'.

In response, the Catholic community and some radical Presbyterians formed groups of Defenders. By the following autumn, Protestant violence had expanded from raiding for arms to trying to drive Catholics from their homes. Initially, landlords, many flush with Catholic rents (including Richardson and Brownlow), attempted to calm the situation.[58] The Protestant magistracy's sympathy for Catholics was gradually eroded, however, as the violence spread after 1788, when overt political demonstrations began to replace communal faction fighting. Defenders armed themselves against attack and asserted territorial dominance in their strongholds. In short, 'many landlords believed that Catholics were entitled to the quiet enjoyment of their lives and possessions, but few could contemplate with equanimity a challenge to the proposition that all of Ireland was Protestant territory'.[59]

The popular ideology animating these Catholic Defenders requires attention. Even the best analysis, pledged to writing 'history from below', falls into a teleological trap. Jim Smyth's seminal work on radical politics in the period posits modernity and increased literacy as the chief engines of politicisation. As evidence, he points to a 'significant minority' of lower-class Catholics who signed the Catholic Committee's mobilisation of popular support in 1792, with 8,500 names from eighteen parishes in Tyrone and Armagh, concluding that 'the correlation between modernisation and English is confirmed by the linguistic map of Ireland in the late eighteenth century'. Likewise, in 1792, a pamphleteer observed that 'the inhabitants of Forkhill [south Armagh] and its adjacent neighbours are very illiterate, from their mountainous situation, that scarcely affords them potatoes and goats' milk, of course the English language in many families, is scarcely known'.[60] As Vincent Morley rightly argues, 'to believe that a pamphlet in English could have propagated a message as efficiently as a song in Irish at any time during the eighteenth century is to succumb to anachronism, to Anglocentrism, or to the combined effects of both maladies'.[61]

By that stage, Forkhill and its inhabitants had earned a gruesome reputation. After the death of the landlord, Richard Jackson, the local Anglican rector, Edward Hudson, set about 'improving' the area by making 'our savages happy against their will by establishing trade and industry amongst them'. The 'savages' duly shot Hudson's horse from under him. Undeterred, he sought to clear the native inbred 'squatters', and appointed a new schoolmaster who refused to teach 'anything but the Protestant prayers'. In January 1791, locals cut out the tongues of the teacher, his wife and her brother. Richard Musgrave, the propagandist of the Protestant Ascendancy, had little doubt that the papists 'hunted [the] new colonists . . . like wild beasts, and treated [them] with savage cruelty', and that such 'barbarous treatment of this colony by the Romanists' confirmed 'that the extirpation of Protestants of every denomination was the main design of the Defenders'.[62]

In fact, Kyla Madden has demonstrated that 'the opinion of Hudson, Musgrave' and other 'pillars of 18th century establishment', that 'the Protestant settlers in Forkhill were attacked on account of their religion' and that 'Protestantism was their only offence . . . is insufficient and, in a strict sense, untrue'. Rather, while 'the Defenders' campaign of intimidation and punishment against a handful of Protestants settlers was ruthless . . . it was not primarily sectarian'.[63] Madden paints a different picture, wherein sectarianism 'was not the only impulse regulating social behaviour. For most of the people most of the time, differences of religion between neighbours did not interfere with how one led one's life.'[64] What the testimony of Hudson and Musgrave points to, and what emerges consistently on every turn of the dreaded spiral in this area's history, is that, when their political and economic position appeared threatened, a landed elite whose tenure emerged from a colonial process would manipulate sectarianism to maintain its existing privilege and achieve its political objectives.

Elsewhere, D. W. Miller characterises the atrocity as the agency of 'an isolated local community, which no doubt had an elaborate set of social relationships little understood by outsiders, being threatened with "improvement" '.[65] In fact, Peadar Ó Doirnín had been the 'hedge' (or open-air illegal Gaelic) schoolmaster at Forkhill a generation earlier, his remains buried in the local graveyard in 1769. Thomas Crofton Croker described the reverence afforded to the Irish schoolmaster in the early nineteenth century:

> In an evening assembly of village statesmen, he holds the most distinguished place, from his historical information, pompous eloquence, and classical erudition. His principles verge very closely indeed on the broadest republicanism; he delivers warm descriptions of the Grecian and Roman commonwealths; the ardent spirit of freedom and general equality of rights in former days – and then comes down to his own country, which is always the ultimate political subject of discussion . . . [He] insists on Catholic emancipation; attacks the Peelers,

horse and foot; protests against tithes, and threatens a separation of the United Kingdom![66]

Ó Doirnín composed the famous *aisling* poem *Mná na hÉireann*, among many others and, as a mark of his renown, Art Mac Cumhaigh, a labourer and fellow poet, wrote his elegy.[67] Mac Cumhaigh himself penned perhaps the greatest *aisling* in Ulster Irish – Úirchill an Chreagáin – commonly referred to as the anthem of South Ulster.[68] An examination of vernacular sources in Irish challenges the 'enormous condescension of posterity' which typically writes indigenous people off as pre-modern, apolitical peasants. What emerges instead is a highly literate and culturally sophisticated community with a definite popular *mentalité*. Rather than any desire to get on by adopting English, Mac Cumhaigh lamented how Jane and 'Wully' were '*do mo chreathnú lena méiligh nua* (making me tremble with their new bleating)', and yearned for liberation lest '*saighde chlann Wully bheith 'tolladh fríd do chroí go deóidh*' ('Willy's offspring will forever pierce your heart').[69]

In a period of rapid economic and political change, George Rudé's 'sea change' took place, transforming protest by fusing a movement's inherent, local anger with the era's derived, political ideologies, forging a more powerful and nationally focused force.[70] Ó Buachalla has noted how, across the century, Jacobitism morphed into a rebellious rhetoric that challenged the status quo.[71] Around the 1770s, Mac Cumhaigh's poems testified to residual popular Jacobite sentiment in south Ulster, yet, under the force of circumstance, 'new themes gradually emerged: for the first time, vernacular song praised English-speaking Protestants and republicans, as Anglo-Irish patriots'.[72] The American Revolution meant that, for the first time, Irish poets 'applauded American victories – or, more accurately, British defeats'.[73]

Deep political divisions still separated those who rejected the post-1688 settlement from the British government. Yet a new idea now surfaced in Irish writing: that English-speaking Protestants might not remain eternal allies of Britain – a perception that would soon shift from page to reality. Morley wryly concludes that 'when James Napper Tandy', of the United Irishmen, 'set out to meet the Defenders, the path had already been prepared for him by George Washington'.[74]

Liberty

In 1688 Catholics still owned 22 per cent of Ireland's land. By 1703 the figure had fallen to 14 per cent, and it had collapsed to a mere 5 per cent by 1778. The Penal Laws excluded Catholics from all public offices and the legal profession. The chief philosopher of this 'Glorious Revolution', John Locke, described the Irish as a population of 'brigands' and counselled his readers to show no compassion for Irish papists, 'who are less apt to be pitied than others because they receive no other usage than what they [by the] cruelty of their own principles and practices are known to deserve'.[75]

Across the eighteenth century, the full enjoyment of a private sphere of liberty guaranteed by the law remained the privilege of a small propertied minority – even in merry old England. Irish Catholics, however, occupied a profane space, leading even the Unionist historian Lecky to judge later that the Penal Laws aimed to deprive them of their 'property' and 'industry' and 'to make them poor and to keep them poor, to crush in them every germ of enterprise, to degrade them into a servile caste who could never hope to rise to the level of their oppressors'.[76]

The American Revolution sparked political turmoil in Ireland. In response to fears of a French invasion, local landlords formed companies of Irish Volunteers after 1778. In County Armagh, Charlemont, Richardson and Brownlow led a Patriot tendency intent on taking advantage of Britain's American difficulty to exact legislative independence for the Dublin parliament. While most Patriots appeared content with the recent limited relief measures, divisions appeared concerning Catholics' capacity for liberty, particularly their inclusion within the constitution in terms of the franchise, as well as the rights to sit in parliament and bear arms. Indeed, the Williamite Revolution acted as the ideological basis for this movement. The Irish Volunteers' famous mobilisation outside the Irish parliament on College Green, which demanded free trade or else, took place around William of Orange's statue on 4 November 1779 – his birthday.[77]

In fact, the Armagh Volunteers summoned the famous Dungannon Convention on 15 February 1782. Stretched by conflict in America, the British granted 'legislative independence' to what came to be known as 'Grattan's Parliament', named after the accepted leader of the Patriot opposition. A further Dungannon Convention then demanded parliamentary reform, opening a debate on whether the Catholic 'underground gentry' and emerging mercantilist class could enjoy liberty. Indeed, one Gaelic poet eulogised the Volunteers of 'pórt Dún Geanainn – mórdha, macánta, cróga a ngníomh' ('The fort of Dungannon – noble, upright, brave their deeds').[78]

The Armagh Volunteers refused to send delegates to the fourth Dungannon Convention in 1793. In Armagh and Tyrone, the eruption and eventual elite manipulation of sectarian violence exposed the 'myth that the Volunteers were precursors of modern Irish nationalism'.[79] An alternative explanation comes to us from that great historian of the contemporaneous Haitian revolution, C. L. R. James. With the fall of the French monarchy and the papist barbarians at the gates demanding entrance to the sacred space of liberty, the northern septs of the Protestant Ascendancy lost their appetite for 'Patriot' radicalism:

> The first sign of a thoroughly ill-adjusted or bankrupt form of society is that the ruling classes cannot agree how to save the situation. It is this division which opens the breach, and the ruling classes will continue to fight with each other, just so long as they do not fear the mass seizure of power.[80]

Nevertheless, Belfast's Irish Volunteers took a markedly different turn. Like their Armagh neighbours, they initially mobilised within the Whig tradition. Four months after the first Dungannon Convention, in 1782, the Belfast Volunteers honoured the king's birthday by firing a twenty-one-gun salute on Cave Hill. The burgeoning town contained an expanding middle class linked to the textile trade, the famous Linen Hall (1785) standing as 'a monument to the handicraft stage of linen production'.[81]

Unlike north Armagh, however, Belfast's hinterland in counties Antrim and Down contained an 'overwhelming majority' Protestant (and mostly Presbyterian) population not in direct economic competition with the small number of Catholics. In 1783, the Belfast Volunteers 'defiantly' admitted Catholics to their ranks, and the following year attended mass in St Mary's Chapel – built with Presbyterian subscriptions.[82]

By Bastille Day 1792, they paraded the streets in military formation and sent a declaration of support to the French Republic. The Society of the United Irishmen had already been formed in the city amid the élan stimulated by events in Paris.[83] Nancy Curtin makes a compelling argument that the United Irish movement turned on a crucial alliance 'between the urban commercial and industrial middle class and the lower classes of both town and country'. Here, in a transitory moment, 'the interests of labour and the interests of capital could still be regarded as compatible under the general rubric of republicanism'.[84] In this rendering, the northern bourgeoisie, centred on Belfast and frustrated by the closure of parliamentary reform, took up the revolutionary gauntlet. In the process, Irish history had been utterly changed.

The French Revolution convinced many of these most radical Patriot reformers that Catholics no longer bore the mark of Cain. Theobold Wolfe Tone's *Argument on Behalf of the Catholics of Ireland* (1791) ridiculed anti-popery, arguing that events in France proved that Catholics could embrace liberty. In short, by 'directing so much of their propaganda toward the lower classes, the radicals included them in their imagined civic polity'.[85] Tone, therefore, proposed an Irish civic nationality founded on the unity of Catholic, Protestant and Dissenter.

A controversy surrounds the nature of this popular republicanism. Did it consist of a radical offshoot of earlier Anglo-Irish patriotism within the 'real Whig' ideology, or a novel revolutionary stimulus responding to events in America and France? Vincent Morley is surely correct that both positions reflect the 'experiences and perspectives of middle-class political activists in Dublin and Belfast' as recorded in English – the perspective, no matter how radical, of an 'articulate minority'.[86] By contrast, he has emphasised a series of important ideological continuities across the century within the popular Irish mind: a hatred of the English monarch, established church and the Anglo-Irish Ascendancy, and a hopeful anticipation of French invasion – 'irrespective of whether France was ruled by a Bourbon monarch, by republicans, or by the emperor of the French' – all funnelled into popular aspirations for the 'liberation of Ireland from England and Protestant rule'.[87]

The French Revolution provided the context in which inherent elements of this *mentalité* could fuse with derived republicanism. This process not only affected the alienated Catholic masses, but resonated with many of the inherent egalitarian and even levelling currents within Ulster Presbyterianism. Some flavour of the antipathy to the monarchy, for instance, can be gained from a republican toast of 1796, when a government informer claimed that Unitedmen and disloyal troops acclaimed in a Belfast tavern: 'May the hair of the Queen's c*** be manufactured into ropes to hang the King and all the royal family' and 'May the King be flead [*sic*] alive and his skin made into a drum head'.[88]

Freemasonry formed the reactor for this fusion of Presbyterian egalitarianism, Gaelic millenarianism and the radical Enlightenment. The United Irishmen deployed masonic lodges as an organisational conduit for their 'cell structure' – or, in Ascendancy minds, 'that most dangerous system grafted onto freemasonry'.[89] Interestingly, and despite papal bulls excommunicating masons, Catholics comprised most members in Ireland, and the Masonic complexion of Defenderism is undeniable.[90] In 1792, Freemasons in Tyrone proclaimed: 'Let every lodge in the land become a company of citizen soldiers – let every Volunteer company become a lodge of masons.'[91] Before their suppression, the Unitedmen had 100,000 members in Ulster alone, dominating rural society in many parts of the province. One Cavan magistrate moaned that 'every man and woman are now United. I almost doubt whether there is one in forty that is not'.[92]

In response, Orange lodges also spread using the same Masonic prototype; the order founded after local Peep-o'-Day Boys routed a combined force of Defenders at the 'Battle of the Diamond' near Loughall in 1795.[93] North Armagh would witness the expulsion of up to 10,000 Catholics after the event. This time the local magistracy backed the Orangemen to the hilt. The United Irishmen sought to capitalise on the discontent, and affect the merger of the Defenders into the revolutionary movement. Thus, on the contested terrain of the linen triangle, the radical emancipatory message heralded in France threatened to turn the world upside down. As one pamphleteer sardonically put it,

> If you Catholics will endeavour all that is in your power to rivet your own chains, and the chains of your posterity; if you be sensible of the great grace and favour of us your Orange lords and masters, in allowing you, as you and your forefathers have always done, to creep among our feet, and live upon the dust of our soles, why then we will graciously permit you to live; but if you presume to think of Liberty, of political consequence, of Irish independence, or of being friends with the Presbyterians, consider your awful doom, we have the means in our hands, and we will execute summary vengeance.[94]

The Unitedmen sent out a host of emissaries into the Ulster countryside to proselytise. Thomas Russell, the 'man from God knows where', epitomised this radical-populist ideology, insisting that property 'must be altered in some measure – he who knew the recesses of the heart loved not the rich'. A friend of the rural poor and opponent of slavery, Russell published his *Letter to the People of Ireland* in 1796 – a programme for political revolution and social emancipation.[95] Armed with this gospel, men like the Tyrone dancing instructor, Arthur 'Switcher' Donnelly, toured the local area, a man 'by nature form'd to be a most dangerous conspirator, very great address, good choice of words and fluency of speech and great agility of body. Amazingly muscular and with desperate intrepidy [*sic*]'. Donnelly's emancipatory message spread like 'quicksilver' through Donegal, Tyrone, Antrim and Derry, 'Switcher' being a notable member of 'a coherent, radical, middle-class Catholic leadership'.[96] The 'sea change' within the popular mind can be assessed in a song from Donegal in the 1790s:

> Thall ins an Fhrainc a chuala mé an chaint,
> Agus abraimse mo cheol le réasún,
> Go geal shoilsigh sí fríd dorchadas na hoích',
> Is bheir solas in iomadaí réagún.
> Nár thé an choinneal seo a choíche as
> Ach coinneáil i gcónaí i mbladhair' é,
> Nó go gcuirfidh sí críocha le clannaibh Gall
> Agus ar lorg Sheoirse.
>
> Over in France, I heard the speech,
> and let me sing my song with reason,
> brightly it shone through the darkness of night,
> and brought light to many regions.
> May this candle never go out
> but always be kept ablaze,
> till it puts an end to the English race
> and George's progeny.[97]

In response to the republican challenge, in 1796, the Protestant Ascendancy deployed the property-based and locally stationed yeomanry which, like the Orange Order, flourished in the Lough Neagh crescent under the guidance of Thomas Knox, the Dungannon MP and scion of the earldom of Ranfurly. Knox worked hand-in-glove with his brother, General John Knox. The elite secured their position through their unconditional backing of Protestant supremacy, with overwhelming violence as the instrument of its consolidation. In short, the Knox brothers flooded the yeomanry with Orangemen to 'prevent the United Irish tide from flooding down the Lagan valley into Armagh, and thence inundating west and south Ulster'.[98]

For many historians, 'what made Armagh [and East Tyrone] different from many parts of Ulster was a class of Protestants too humble to be considered fit material even for the Volunteers in the early 1780s'.[99] Peter Gibbon argued that 'proletarianisation' in north Armagh led to Orangeism, or the alliance of Protestant weavers and landlords, while in Antrim commercial farmers and independent weavers gravitated to the United Irishmen. These distinct class alliances emerged from the areas' relative degrees of modernisation in linen manufacture – the implication being that the republicans constituted the party of the anti-modern.[100]

But Ann McKernan's deep study of Richhill has undermined the notion of 'proletarian' weavers in the area, while Nancy Curtin argues that the material basis for republicanism actually mirrored the situation in revolutionary France, where an emergent bourgeoisie bridled under the *ancien régime*'s obstinate refusal to make their political position commensurate with their economic strength. Or, as Curtin has it: 'The divinely blessed industrious classes, those who worked and created the wealth of the nation, are thus pitted against the lilies of the landed elite, who neither toiled nor tilled, but yet commanded unmerited political power.'[101]

The bourgeoisie duly mobilised the *sans-culottes*, in response to which the *ancien régime* played the Orange card, turning the area into an Irish Vendée.[102] Curtin points to the concentration of 'proclaimed districts within the linen triangle, that area extending roughly from Belfast to Newry to Dungannon, characterised by the advanced development of the linen industry'.[103] In Dungannon, Knox proceeded to deploy the yeomanry in mass raids, 'to increase the animosity between the Orangemen and the United Irishmen', because, in his estimation, 'upon that animosity depends the safety of the centre counties of the North'. The judiciary duly followed suit, one observer at Loughgall noting that it became 'impossible for the Protestant gentry to keep up the farce of impartiality between the parties or to disavow the absolute necessity of giving a considerable degree of support to the Protestant party'. Such legalised lawlessness accelerated the Armagh expulsions of 1795 and 1796, thousands of Catholics being banished 'to hell or to Connacht'. By February 1796, the government's law officer claimed that 'a too scrupulous adherence to the tedious terms of law was not commendable policy when the constitution itself was in danger'. A year later, Dublin Castle advised General Lake, about to initiate a reign of terror in Ulster, 'not to suffer the course of justice to be frustrated by the delicacy which might possibly have actuated the magistracy'.[104]

In short, the imperialists used the Orange Order as a counter-revolutionary firewall, splitting the United Irishmen and Defender territories, and partially rupturing 'the nascent Presbyterian–Catholic alliance in mid-Ulster'. After the near miss of the French invasion at Bantry Bay in 1796, Dublin Castle acceded to incessant petitioning from Knox and Richardson by promoting the Orange Order across the Protestant Ascendancy 'until it reached the very pinnacle of Irish society'.[105]

Loyalism and Orangeism deployed the insignia of masonry, and spoke of 'civil and religious liberties', but remained unapologetically supremacist and anti-democratic. The rebellion itself descended into a bloodbath, and while Musgrave's propagandistic history would make much of the killing of loyalists, even his questionable figures pale into significance against the tens of thousands of rebels and ordinary Irish people butchered by a combined force of almost 100,000 regular and paramilitary British troops.[106] Faced with revolution, the local Protestant Ascendancy manipulated sectarianism and deployed enormous violence. As had recently been the case in Haiti, 'it was easier to find decency, gratitude, justice, and humanity in a cage of starving tigers than in the councils of imperialism'.[107]

This synthesis of land, linen and loyalty crystallised in Dungannon, at the western tip of the triangle. There, Thomas Knox, from Ranfurly in Renfrewshire, had in October 1692 purchased the manor and lands of Dungannon from the descendants of Arthur Chichester. His great-nephew, the local MP and Orangeman, became Viscount Northland in 1791, while his eldest son (also Thomas) was made earl of Ranfurly in 1831. There had been bleaching greens or yards at Moygashel, just outside Dungannon, since 1762. In 1795, a Quaker, Thomas Boardman, who had previously leased five acres from the Knox family, bought the mill or dye works site at Moygashel, just outside the town. That year,

Robert Stevenson and his brother opened their flax merchant's shop in Dungannon. His grandson, also Robert, bought the Moygashel site, and in 1874 installed a power loom fuelled by coal from nearby Coalisland. His eldest son, Robert (1866–1960) will appear again in later chapters. When the Ulster Volunteer Force emerged in Dungannon in 1913, the then earl's son, Lord Northland, commanded the force, with Stevenson, the leading local industrialist, acting as his second in command.[108]

Through the lens of Orange history, 'Ulster' embodied the precursor of subsequent expansion and the lynchpin of imperial survival. In 1914, at the height of the Home Rule Crisis, Uchter Knox, earl of Ranfurly and former governor of New Zealand, said that the British Empire was 'the greatest the world had ever seen', but that the 'present government were pulling it down through home rule, which would put Ulster Protestants under the heel of' their hereditary Catholic enemies. He continued that 'although it was but a small portion of the Empire, if Ulster had to go down it would be a prelude to the total disruption of the Empire and the destruction of the monarchy', since 'the increasing wave of socialism and republicanism in England, and even in the cabinet itself, might overwhelm the monarchy'. Elsewhere he asked 'what bravery' had Irish Catholics shown? 'They have fought not against men but against women and children and dumb beasts of the field.' Indeed, if they were truly Ireland's rightful rulers, 'where were their industries?' Ranfurly concluded by stating that his audience

> must not forget that there were two races in Ireland. The nationalists said the Unionists were only planted in Ireland. That was 300 years ago but 300 years is a good fixity of tenure so good that they did not mean to get out. The trouble was Rome. Rome had blasted every country that she had got the better of.[109]

Yet, this chapter has also charted the rise of a mass movement of thousands of Catholics, Protestants and Dissenters pledged to decolonisation. It outlined the basis of a 'history from below' hurtling on the dreaded spiral of capitalist development from colonisation through hand-weaving and ending on the cusp of a regional industrial revolution. While United Irishman and Defender clasped hands in fraternity, 'at the same time as the French, the half-savage slaves of San Domingo were showing themselves subject to the same historical laws as the advanced workers of revolutionary Paris'. Indeed, in October 1917, 'the Russian masses were to prove once more that this innate power will display itself in all populations when deeply stirred and given a clear perspective by a strong and trusted leadership'.[110] The remainder of this book will deal with another unsuccessful attempt at decolonisation shortly after the workers and soldiers of Petrograd stormed the Winter Palace. A movement among the descendants of the rhyming weavers, the Gaelic poets and the Methodist artisans who rallied to the banner of the Rights of Man and the clarion call of Tone, Russell and McCracken because it 'represented that complete emancipation from their former degradation which was their chief goal'.[111]

2

Belfast Beginnings

Belfast's a famous town,
Ships and linen its occupation.
And the workers have a riot on
The slightest provocation.

Belfast street ballad, c. 1900

At the end of 1911, James Connolly wrote from Belfast that his support for Irish Home Rule 'does not do me much good from the point of view of the [Irish Transport and General Workers'] Union in this Orange hole'. Still, he would 'take the chance'.[1] There appeared little prospect of much return on Connolly's gamble at the height of the Ulster Crisis in 1911–14. Yet, by the closing stages of the First World War, a group of Protestant socialists would proselytise across Ulster, helping to build an anti-sectarian labour constituency across some of the heartlands of Orangeism in North Armagh and East Tyrone. The spring of 1920 represented the high-water mark, as a militant wave swept across the whole island. In the next few chapters, I will trace its flow and tragic ebb across Ulster's famed linen triangle, running from the movement's epicentre in Belfast through the Bann Valley and orchards of north Armagh and westwards into the drumlins and bushes of east Tyrone. Before identifying the activist hub that nurtured this brief flowering of trade-union militancy, however, it is necessary to locate this cohort within Belfast's working-class and trade-union history.

Union: Linenopolis, Loyalism and Labour

The 1800 Act of Union heralded north-east Ulster's increasing economic and political integration into Britain. Across the proceeding century, Belfast would forge stronger economic ties with the industrial regions of west-central Scotland and north-west England than with the rest of Ireland.[2] By 1820, Protestants held nearly forty times as much industrial and merchant capital in Belfast as Catholics. Three east Ulster counties – Tyrone, Armagh and Antrim – dominated Ireland's linen market, accounting for over half of all sales, as the linen triangle's weavers hand-wove fine yarns from the wet spinning process introduced in the 1820s.

Belfast's shift from cotton to flax spinning, driven by the post-Napoleonic textile depression and the removal of Irish cotton tariffs, positioned it as a hub for wet flax spinning. O'Hearn describes linen as a semi-peripheral industry, reliant on adaptive strategies and 'prone to lower rates of profit, lower wages, lower capital-intensity, stagnation, and failure'.[3] Despite these challenges, linen fuelled Belfast's industrialisation, paving the way for textile machinery production and later expanding into iron, steel shipbuilding and marine engineering.

In 1800–31, Belfast's population surged from 20,000 to 50,000, as rural spinners and hand-weavers flocked to the town's repurposed cotton mills and surrounding areas for yarn. The *Belfast Newsletter* reported that some weavers lived off 'oatmeal unfit for cattle', with many 'reduced to skeletons from overwork and lack of sleep', while, by 1838, one contemporary described Belfast's working-class neighbourhoods as 'a mass of filth and misery'.[4] The province-wide domestic proto-industry collapsed, concentrating spinning production in Belfast and the industrial east. Despite profits for a new capitalist class, the industry's peripheral status fostered precarity and a race to the bottom, delaying mechanisation in weaving until the drastic reduction of the workforce resulting from the Famine's devastation made hand-weaving labour too costly.[5]

The dire conditions of the emerging proletariat and the upheaval caused by the decline of hand-spinning initially sparked revolt, with spinners and weavers resisting the new industrial order. In response, 'Belfast's and East Ulster's gentry, magistrates, merchants, and manufacturers – Anglicans and Presbyterians, Whigs and Tories – united as "gentlemen" and mobilised their considerable resources against the workers' threat to property and order.'[6] In 1816, shortly after the hanging of two weavers for bombing a wealthy merchant's home, the authorities acquitted a Lisburn manufacturer for murdering his employee, a trade-union leader. For neither the first nor the last time, local justice did not appear blind to matters of religion or class.

Despite widespread poverty, Belfast maintained an uneasy industrial peace. In 1838, manufacturer Alexander Moncrieffe offered a partial explanation of this to parliament, noting that sectarian divisions between Catholics and Orangemen undermined trade unionism and ensured a steady supply of cheap labour. By 1831, Catholics comprised 31 per cent of Belfast's population. Kerby Miller identifies this pre-Famine era, marked by industrialisation and the rise of a proletariat, as the seedbed of Ulster Unionist hegemony: 'The Protestant élite's successful imposition of capitalist relationships and mores on Ulster's Protestant poor necessitated the creation and continual reinforcement of a sectarian moral economy that combined "free labour" ideology with the selective reality, or at least the seductive rhetoric, of Protestant patronage and privilege.'[7]

During this period, Daniel O'Connell reshaped British utilitarianism to serve Ireland's rising Catholic middle class, famously declaring to Westminster that his followers stood 'ready to become a portion of the Empire, provided they be made so in reality and not in name alone; they are ready to become a kind of West Britons if made so in benefits and in justice; but if not, we are Irishmen again.'[8] However, even contemporary liberal observers relegated the Irish to a marginalised position. Irish Catholics faced relentless 'emergency measures', military tribunals and a hostile police force. Gustave de Beaumont likened their plight to that of blacks in the United States, calling them 'two phenomena of the same kind'. He condemned the 'unimaginable religious oppression' and the British 'tyranny' over what he termed a 'slave people', arguing that such institutional cruelty revealed 'a degree of egotism and madness beyond definition'.[9]

The Great Famine (1845–52) starkly exposed Ireland's colonised status, though a myth persists that Ulster escaped its horrors. Yet even the Lurgan Poor Law Union saw significant Protestant deaths, both inside and outside workhouses.[10] County Tyrone's population plummeted from 313,000 in 1841 to 151,000 by 1901, while County Armagh's fell from 232,000 to 125,000.[11] The British state facilitated the eviction of one million people during the Famine, prioritising economic liberalism over Irish lives.

In the half-century following the Act of Union, Ireland's landlord class drained the country of its wealth. As John Mitchel quipped during the Famine, 'How could the property of Ireland support the poverty of Ireland when it was already supporting the luxury of England?'[12] Home Rule emerged from the Land War (1879–82), a social revolution that dismantled landlordism and thrust the Irish Question into British politics. But Home Rule primarily served the interests of a rising Irish Catholic middle class. Theodore Allen argues that, while racial oppression in much of Ireland shifted to national oppression following the Famine to suit British control, it persisted in industrial east Ulster. By 1861, Catholics made up a third of Belfast's 120,000 residents. The abject poverty of linen workers suggested that class politics might well trump sectarianism, but 'just as it had been arranged in the case of the tenants three hundred years before, again it was arranged by the British ruling class, with all necessary deliberation, that the "pressure of exploitation" of Protestant and Catholic workers would not be a "common" one'.[13]

Twenty years after the first spinning mill opened, the linen industry consumed 150,000 tonnes of coal annually. In the wake of the Famine, power looms transformed weaving, and by the late nineteenth century, Ulster became the world's largest linen producer, importing over a million tonnes of coal. Across industrial Belfast, spindled mill and factory chimneys stood sentinel over sprawling, twisted arteries of red-bricked streets, like minarets calling on the malnourished inhabitants to sacrifice themselves each morning.

The structure of the mills stood as a living metaphor for the division of labour and working-class competition within Linenopolis itself. Inside the spinning mills, the ground floor housed the machines, flax store, roughing and hackling departments, where semi-skilled men and boys ate acrid dust and worked the flax. Above them, spinners produced coarse yarn, while women on the next floor spun finer material, all barefoot, their health wrecked by the 'insidious alliance of dust, heat, moisture and noise'.[14] The top floor, with cleaner air, handled dressing and winding. By 1920, Belfast contained seventeen of Ireland's fifty spinning companies, the rest scattered across Ulster. William Topping, a dresser for forty years, noted how Catholic women dominated spinning, while Protestants made up 75 per cent of factory weavers. This hierarchy placed mill workers below factory workers, who in turn ranked below the elite wareroom staff like Topping.[15]

From the mills, yarn then moved to weaving factories with their winding rooms, where women wound it onto bobbins for the shuttle or spools for the warping beam. From there, it went to the dressing shop, where workers prepared threads for the loom, and finally to the weaving shed on the ground floor, filled with heavy machinery. Like spinning, the dressing process occupied the top floor, closest to the gods.

By 1912, Ireland had 37,292 power looms – including 22,000 in Belfast and 13,000 across Ulster.[16] This division between mill and factory, rougher and dresser, Catholic and Protestant, even extended to language: factory workers called the lavatory 'parliament', while mill workers referred to it as the 'wee house'.[17] One weaver recalled: 'we were the "e-lite." We were the "swanks." They [spinners] were the "down" . . . we weren't really better than they were, but you thought you were above all that.'[18]

Belfast's Aristocracy of Labour

In Irish, *Béal Feirste* means 'mouth of the sandbank', and, through linen, Belfast's industrial rise appeared partially built on sand. The industry relied heavily on the hyper-exploitation of women and children. Between 1824 and 1890, Irish linen yarn output grew by just 0.27 per cent annually, while woven linen cloth declined by 0.21 per cent per year, lagging far behind England's cotton industry.[19] However, Belfast's proximity to Glasgow's Clyde allowed core industries to expand into the city. British capital played a key role, with parliament funding the Victoria Channel, ensuring dock access at low tide.

Shipbuilding emerged as a major industry, driven by firms like Harland & Wolff, the 'Big Yard', founded in 1858, and later Workman & Clark's 'Wee Yard' in 1879. Far from being peripheral, Belfast's shipyards constituted an extension of British core industry, leveraging innovative technologies and high-wage, largely migrant, skilled labour to compete with rivals in Clyde, Barrow, and north-east England.[20]

Belfast transformed dramatically over the nineteenth century, growing from a modest town into a major industrial city. Throughout this period of explosive growth, the Catholic minority saw its proportion of the population rise significantly around the time of the Great Famine before later settling at a lower, stable quarter share by the century's end. This decline was partly due to inward migration of skilled British workers and consequent increased sectarianism. Between 1881 and 1911, the British-born population grew from 11,000 (5 per cent) to 28,000 (7 per cent). From 1861 to 1911, Anglican and Methodist numbers steadily increased, while the Presbyterian share remained stagnant. The peak of shipbuilding and engineering between 1901 and 1911 saw the largest rise in English- and Welsh-born residents, which suggests that highly skilled British-born workers formed a large section of Belfast's 'labour aristocracy'.[21]

Many skilled workers arriving in Belfast brought not only craft trade-union membership, but also anti-Irish prejudice. In 1870, Marx observed that 'the ordinary English worker hates the Irish worker . . . seeing himself as part of the ruling nation', akin to the 'poor whites' in the US slave states.[22] Similarly, David Roediger argues that the US working class developed 'whiteness' in response to anxieties surrounding dependency and the imposition of capitalist discipline. In Belfast, anti-popery provided 'a touchstone against which to weigh their fears and a yardstick to measure their reassurance'.[23] These 'wages of whiteness' took hold in a city where, as Rev. Abraham Hume remarked in 1864, 'the natural position of the white, like that of the Protestant, is on the higher steps of the social pyramid'.[24]

While Hume tailored scientific racism to Belfast's sectarian cloth, craft unions like the Amalgamated Society of Engineers gained traction in the city's shipyards and foundries. Just as craft unions in the United States reinforced white supremacy, in Belfast, supremacism shaped what Du Bois termed 'craft and race unions', linking unskilled labour to degradation and making integrated work unthinkable.[25] As in America, craft apprentices often emerged as loyalist storm troopers, with young, male apprentice workers being especially prominent in riots.[26] As Bill Rolston notes, 'the two most volatile issues among the craft unions in the nineteenth century – apprentice ratios and the closed shop – were in part sectarian. Craft unionists who were also Protestants found themselves threatened by an influx of [Catholic] non-craft unionists.'[27] Accordingly, the apprentices' bravado masked their precarious position, and a fear of descent into the ranks of unskilled workers, dockers, and the Catholic underclass.

Belfast's socialists struggled to foster class consciousness and anti-sectarian solidarity against a backdrop of *Herrenvolk* democracy – rights for the 'master race', but tyranny for others – which reassured Protestants fearful of downward mobility.[28] This supremacism jarred, however, with the city's dual industrial economy: a peripheral linen sector reliant on exploited women and a core shipbuilding and engineering sector dominated by highly paid craftsmen. The divide between skilled (mostly Protestant) and unskilled (often Catholic) workers mirrored racial oppression systems, like those in the United States and South Africa, where oppressed groups occupied the lowest-paid jobs. Belfast's labour aristocracy thus took up 'the oppressive role of the Protestant yeoman' outlined in the previous chapter.[29] Supremacist riots erupted repeatedly – in 1857, 1864, 1872, 1886 and 1893. The 1886 unrest was sparked by Gladstone's First Home Rule Bill, following Parnell's Irish Party sweeping eighty-six seats, even in 'Protestant' Ulster, during the 1885 general election.

Lifelong socialist Robert 'Bob' McClung captured the febrile atmosphere during the 1885 North Belfast contest, when Alexander Bowman, a working-class Presbyterian from the Flax Dressers' Trade Union, stood as Independent Labour candidate against his former employer, William Ewart. 'The Pope and Home Rule for Ireland played a big part in the fight.' While 'Bowman had no intention of handing North Belfast over to the Pope . . . the Tories declared he would.'[30] McClung had little doubt that the 'Tory machine' had incited the mobs that wrecked Bowman's home in Berlin Street, as he fled with his young family out of the back yard:

> I can remember the stories being told . . . to the effect that the Home Rulers had already balloted for who would own the shipyards. I can remember being told that the man who came to our door and sold herring and Lough Neagh pollen was to own Ewart's Spinning Mills as soon as the Home Rule Bill became law. We were told that![31]

In 1907, Belfast and its hinterland produced £19.1 million of Ireland's £20.9 million in manufactured exports. The city's late industrial development also meant that working-class housing did not reach the squalid excesses of Dublin's decaying Georgian tenements, or the sprawling slums constructed in the shadows cast by Blake's dark satanic mills. The Liberal prime minister during the Ulster Crisis, Herbert Asquith, wrote to his wife that, 'to look at', Belfast appeared as 'a very superior Manchester'.[32] Indeed, in 1898, when the Irish Trade Union Congress (ITUC) met in Belfast, the Unionist lord mayor, James Henderson, eulogised the city as an 'Elysium for the working class'.[33]

In 1906, City Hall opened its doors – a symbol of civic and imperial pride for a privileged minority invested in Belfast's prosperity. For the impoverished majority, however, who would rock the establishment the following year during the Dockers' and Carters' strike, the imposing edifice of Portland stone, which cost £56 million in today's money, more closely resembled 'a wedding cake at a pauper's funeral'.[34] Born in 1888, the Presbyterian Connollyite socialist and future Irish Transport and General Workers' Union (ITGWU) president, William McMullen, vividly captured

> Great bumptious Belfast, with its slum schools, its rotten municipal system, its ludicrous pride, its bigotry and intolerance, and its hordes of little ragged starved workers. Belfast with its palatial town hall, its tinsel virtues, and its army of little white slaves, and its big poorhouses, and lunatic asylums and prisons.[35]

Trade unionism appeared relatively strong in Belfast, class consciousness less so. Sectarianism aside, the chasm separating skilled workers in shipbuilding and engineering from the unskilled majority constituted an equally significant factor. Bob Getgood, the future ITUC chair, later recollected: 'I must give [the skilled worker] credit for his craft pride. But he hadn't the broad human touch of the other fellow who carried the mud for him.'[36] Indeed, rates of skilled pay outstripped those in Britain, yet unskilled workers typically received a pittance in comparison, leaving a 'truly staggering' and 'yawning abyss' in relative rates of pay.[37] The Catholic quarter of the population disproportionately occupied the unskilled trades, though Protestant workers were also well represented among them.[38]

Belfast mirrored a British city in its growth of craft unionism. Craft-based New Model Unions like the Amalgamated Society of Engineers (ASE), which excluded unskilled labourers, spread to Belfast through its labour aristocracy. By 1907, Catholics comprised only 10 per cent of engineers and 7 per cent of shipwrights. A core group of shipyard workers and apprentices spearheaded the expulsion of Catholic workers in 1864, 1893, 1901 and 1912. They embraced social imperialism, celebrating the empire's material benefits. During the Home Rule Crisis, George Crothers of the ASE argued that 'Nationalists had never done anything to leave their mark on history as being capable of anything in the shape of a large industry: in fact, their only industry had been crime'.[39]

For most ordinary people, though politics took second place to 'getting by', discontent simmered.[40] Nellie Gordon, an ITGWU organiser, recalled: 'The only subject I knew was to ridicule the bosses . . . cursing came easy to me, as [it did to] all millworkers.' Working women, she noted, lived their lives 'dancing the night through and singing our songs, parodying the bosses with more curses'.[41] Getgood highlighted the courage required to join unions, as tuppence-a-week dues were a significant burden for ordinary workers who, unlike craftsmen, often survived on 'less than enough to live on'.[42]

Latent class consciousness pervaded the unskilled majority. In line with British events, the late nineteenth century, and particularly the early twentieth, saw the emergence of a relatively homogeneous working class.[43] In this period, socialist leaders promoted 'new unionism', which mobilised the unskilled in general unions. Nevertheless, the labourers' lot had improved little by the onset of the first eruption of class struggle in Ulster – the Belfast Dockers' and Carters' strike of 1907. In 1905, labourers in Antrim and Down earned 12s, while further west pay sat at a paltry 9s a week.[44] Irish syndicalism is still associated with Jim Larkin and James Connolly – the so-called 'tornado' and 'lighthouse' of the 1913 Dublin Lockout.[45] But both these icons of class struggle left their mark on Belfast's warren of red-bricked terraces before they roused the tenements of Strumpet City.

Larkin and the Dockers, 1907

Thomas Johnson retrospectively linked the 1907 Belfast dock strikes and the military intervention that followed with the eventual Irish revolution.[46] A member of the socialist Independent Labour Party since 1893, Johnson moved to Belfast in 1903, joining the Trades Council as a delegate for the National Union of Shop Assistants and Clerks. He secured Council support for fellow Liverpudlian Jim Larkin as Dock

Labourers' organiser in January 1907. A nonconformist, Johnson regretted how the strike's initial class unity gave way to sectarianism. After Larkin left, he helped bring James Connolly back from America to organise the ITGWU in Belfast. Together, they founded the Irish Labour Party in 1912, Johnson becoming its leader after 1916.[47]

In 1905 the Liberal government repealed the Trades Disputes Act, paving the way for increased union militancy. But the Liberals showed little interest in risking political capital on Home Rule.[48] This period also saw a split in Orangeism, the Tory establishment clashing with the more populist Independent Order. In 1905, Lindsay Crawford's *Magheramorne Manifesto* urged Orangemen to reconcile with nationalists.[49] By 1907 Crawford was using Seebohm Rowntree's methods from York to highlight Belfast's harsh realities: low wages, and the fact that 43 per cent of women and girls over ten worked, mostly in linen. Outside the aristocracy of labour, Belfast had a low-wage economy and, with the question of Home Rule on the back burner, an opportunity existed to mobilise the city's unskilled working class.

Larkin swept into the city like a storm, uniting non-unionised dockers and carters, and becoming the idol of Belfast's unskilled workers. Getgood remembered him as a 'superman' who stirred hearts, urging workers to stand firm and embrace militancy as the path to justice.[50] His Dock Labourers' Union drew members from all backgrounds – mostly Protestant carters and cross-channel dockers, as well as the overwhelmingly Catholic casual 'deep sea' men. In April 1907, members struck at Samuel Kelly's Coal Quay, refusing to work alongside non-union labour. (Ironically, this book ends with Kelly's failed attempt to spark an industrial revolution in Coalisland's collieries.) The Shipping Federation, led by Thomas Gallaher, escalated the conflict, however, locking out union workers and bringing in strike-breakers from Liverpool. As Larkin himself put it, the scene appeared set for Labour to shed 'its old humility and its respectful finger touching its cap'.[51]

On 21 June, Larkin called a general dockers' strike, joined in solidarity by 1,000 carters on 4 July. On the 12 July, Walter Savage claimed that one thousand Orangemen would sign a letter expressing 'our fervent prayer that James Larkin may long be spared to work for the emancipation of unskilled workers in his native land'.[52] On 26 July, Larkin led 100,000 people through the Shankill and Falls roads, joined by Independent Orange Order bands.[53] In an unprecedented move, the

Royal Irish Constabulary (RIC) then went on strike, prompting Dublin Castle to deploy 6,000 troops, who focused on the nationalist Falls Road, killing two rioters. Amid the turmoil, Dock Labourers' leader James Sexton met Asquith to negotiate a settlement – excluding Larkin. The deal secured higher wages and shorter hours for carters, but no closed shop. The dockers returned on 28 August, though many saw no raise, and employers blacklisted strikers. Sexton and the National Union of Dock Labourers officialdom had ultimately derailed growing working-class solidarity.

During the Dockers' strike, Protestant unskilled workers formed a 'formidable vanguard' in industrial agitation whose actions 'threatened other compelling supremacist imperatives'.[54] As the dispute wound up, employers like Samuel Kelly created 'bogus and sectarian employees' organisations' – a tactic that would reach its apogee with the Ulster Unionist Labour Association (UULA) in 1920. For Kelly or George Clarke of the 'Wee Yard', such methods helped break working-class solidarity, defeat the 1907 labour upsurge, and 'prepare the way for their own counter revolution'.[55] In December 1909, the Unionist Party sent spies to Independent Labour Party (ILP) meetings. Edward Bradshaw reported back, asking:

> whose fault was it that there were 2,000 socialists in north Belfast? I said it was the Protestant employers . . . and if the employers would start and weed them out and give employment to the Protestants and Orangemen who are walking the streets at present, you would have these men to work and vote for you on the day of election.[56]

Belfast Beginnings

In the early twentieth century, Belfast contained two labour movements whose viewpoints gradually diverged. The first focused on the Trades Council, founded in 1881, which later affiliated with the ITUC and generally attracted small, weak local unions in textiles and construction. The second, however, centred on the British-based amalgamated unions, which dominated the shipyards and the metal trades.[57] Under the influence of growing British socialism and the input of Larkin and then Connolly, the Trades Council gradually moved from a conservative and reformist standpoint, in line with Sexton's bureaucratic reformism, to a more class-conscious, socialist and eventually anti-partitionist outlook.

Nevertheless, for Trades Council pioneers like William Walker, labour issues mirrored those in Birmingham or Manchester. He championed gas and water reform over socialism, boasting that Belfast had advanced towards Municipal Socialism faster than any Irish city, and even led parts of Britain.[58] Walkerism rested on a naive faith in British social democracy – 'its trade union movement, its parliament, even its army'.[59] Indeed, John Gray argues that Walker exhibited an 'even narrower vision' and 'squalid opportunism' by essentially kowtowing to sectarianism during a series of electoral contests.[60] Walker arguably believed parliamentary reform would eventually render sectarianism obsolete – though this illusion weakened after 1907, as the Walkerites played an increasingly obstructive role in the ITUC, aligning with conservative nationalists to halt 'the progress of the new forces and the Irish trade union movement represented by Larkin and Connolly'.[61] Indeed, Walker later ran against labour in Belfast's municipal elections, before securing a government post under the 1912 National Insurance Act.

Walkerism ultimately ignored how Unionist employers like Kelly funded the Ulster Volunteer Force (UVF), exposing the business elite's willingness to operate outside the British democratic tradition 'in which Belfast labour leaders place such faith'.[62] Walker viewed Irish backwardness and British progress as commonsensical, affirming in 1911 'that it has now become impossible in Belfast to have a religious riot, and this is due to the good work done by that much despised body, the ILP'.[63] That illusion was shattered in July 1912, when loyalists expelled 3,000 workers, including 600 'rotten Prods', from the shipyards. Despite the best efforts of one such rotten Prod, or anti-sectarian socialist, David Robb Campbell, the Trades Council failed to offer its full support to victims, who only returned to work when Harland & Wolff's management threatened to close the yard.[64] Bob McClung later recalled how this crushed outdoor propaganda and left the ILP as a fading force, surviving due to the efforts of Sam Kyle and Dawson Gordon.[65]

Between 1910 and 1914, the Home Rule Crisis pushed Ireland towards civil war. After the 1910 elections, a Liberal government relying on Irish nationalist MPs revived plans for a Dublin parliament. Ulster's Unionists, led by Edward Carson and fearing Catholic-majority rule, mobilised massively, forming the 100,000-strong UVF and vowing armed resistance. Belfast became the epicentre of Carsonism – a paramilitarised version of traditional Protestant supremacism aligned to the most reactionary elements in British politics. The British Army's refusal to confront Carsonism in the 'Curragh Mutiny' shattered government authority. With both sides, the UVF and the Irish Volunteer Force, latterly the IRA, importing weapons, the First World War's outbreak in 1914 only delayed the looming conflict.

The Home Rule Crisis and Connolly's influence split the ILP into three factions: Walkerite Unionism in North Belfast, British Labourite acceptance of Home Rule's legitimacy in the Central Branch, and Connollyite socialist republicanism in East Belfast. The latter two ultimately aligned with the ITUC and the emerging Irish Labour Movement. By Easter 1912, four of Belfast's five ILP branches had joined Connolly in the Socialist Party of Ireland, part of the new Independent Labour Party (of Ireland).[66] Even Walkerites opposed partition, fearing separation from both British trade unions and Irish comrades.[67] Eventually, North Belfast ILPers like Dawson Gordon, McClung and Kyle became staunchly anti-partitionist. By the late 1920s, Kyle was still championing trade unionism, parliamentary labour representation and Irish unity, and condemning partition.[68] As Emmet O'Connor notes, Connolly's warning that partition would bring a 'carnival of reaction' appeared striking only in its eloquence.[69]

Through lectures at Danny McDevitt's shop, or the Bounders' College, on Rosemary Street, key Protestant ILPers like Thomas Johnson and D. R. Campbell shifted towards James Connolly's pro-Home Rule stance.[70] They steered the Belfast Trade Council towards the ITUC and Irish Labour Party (ILP&TUC), a bold move amid the Ulster Crisis and the mass expulsion of socialist and Catholic workers that summer. By 1914, both were prominent in the ITUC's anti-partition campaign.[71] Indeed, Peter Collins notes that even Unionist-leaning Trades Council delegates opposed partition by then.[72] Many delegates also opposed the war; socialist, suffragette and ILP member Margaret McCoubrey poignantly remarked that 'a woman looking down on a battlefield would not see dead Germans or dead Englishmen, but so many mothers' sons'.[73]

Campbell co-wrote the ITUC&LP's October 1916 manifesto opposing conscription and partition, warning that 'dismemberment' would shatter hopes of 'the unity of Ireland through the unity of the workers'.

Gordon even felt its stance on partition and conscription should have been 'made a little stronger'.[74] The manifesto's final call shaped northern socialist strategy over the following half-decade: 'Let every worker join a union, every union affiliate with the Trades Council, and every Trades Council unite through the ILP&TUC. Thus, the workers of Ireland will gain the power to rebuild the nation!'[75] At the 1916 ITUC Congress, Campbell stressed that organisation was not just about wages, but also educating workers, dispelling false doctrines and advancing class control.[76] His words underscored the divide between trade union and true class consciousness.

In February 1918, these socialists hosted Red Clydesider Willie Gallacher, whose syndicalism, anti-conscription stance and 'fairly strong language' resonated with the ILP but received a poor reception during public meetings at the Engineers' Hall.[77] Johnson and Campbell then organised Ireland's first anti-conscription rally, on 14 April at the Custom House steps. The *Voice of Labour* hailed Belfast's 'monster protest', where nearly 8,000 heard 'the true voice of Ulster – the voice of the working class'. Arthur Trew of the Ulster Protestant Association tried to disrupt the event, but needed police protection.[78] A second meeting, on 17 September at City Hall, met violent resistance, however. A 'number of men and boys from the shipyards' dragged a lorry through the crowd, overturned the platform, and sparked rioting on Castle Street, leading to the expulsion of five Catholic workers from Workman & Clark's.[79] Clearly, the Unionist leadership and loyalist shipyard workers closed ranks, driving the socialists from the city centre, Johnson being hit on the head by a 'chunk of concrete'.[80]

The small-scale expulsions in the 'Wee Yard' highlight key issues. While Protestant tradesmen like James Lawther and Jimmy Baird – both shipyard socialists – secured election as Belfast Labour Party councillors in 1920, their outlook commanded only marginal support among skilled workers. Baird, a staunch Home Ruler and socialist since 1883 – 'not in Cork, but in Belfast's Queen's Island' – attended his first council meeting in dungarees.[81] He later led expelled workers in 1920, before facing southern reaction as an ITGWU organiser during the 1923 Waterford farm strike.[82] Despite socialism having gained ground in Queen's Island and the foundries, loyalism remained dominant. As the post-war economic downturn, which first hit the linen industry, spread in 1920, labour's open hand met the clenched fist of reaction. Nevertheless, the

Belfast Labour Party's socialism reflected northern workers' realities, challenging the myth of Protestant prosperity, which masked deep social inequalities – exploited linen workers, marginalised Catholic labourers, and subsistence-wage farmworkers in the north's dominant agricultural sector.[83] Belfast socialists built their movement by organising workers excluded from the craft unions of the shipyards and foundries, particularly female mill-workers – the famous 'Millies'.

The Workers' Union and the Cost of Living

The mass casualties on the Western Front, including the Somme and Verdun, and the worsening working and living conditions in industrial centres set the stage for the resurgence of class struggle in 1917. The failure of the war effort, highlighted by mutinies and strikes across Europe, sparked revolution in Russia. In response, syndicalists sought to create general unions to fight capital and eventually govern industry. In Ulster, the Worker's Union had grown from nine branches in 1915 to 128 by the expulsions.[84] In the same period the Flax Roughers trade union went from thirty-three all-male branches with female spinners in seven mills, to representing men in fifty locations and female spinners in forty-four mills.[85] In short, Kyle, Gordon, McKeag and McClung organised female and male workers in almost the entire Irish linen sector and across large swathes of the unskilled in Counties Antrim, Down, Armagh and Tyrone. Despite these gains, this movement nevertheless lacked the organisational strength and political cohesion needed for full revolutionary agency.

By 1915 Sam Kyle, a former official in Mary Galway's Textile Operatives Society, had set his mind to the mass unionisation of Ulster's mill-hands. In 1916, he became secretary of Belfast's fifth Workers' Union branch, later serving as a full-time organiser and secretary of the Textile Federation. He ran in the 1918 general election for Shankill, and topped the poll there in the January 1920 municipal contest. Kyle himself outlined how he 'stood for the international working class and public ownership. Carson's candidates had the support of linen Lords, but real labour supported the textile workers' fight for proper wages'.[86] Despite booming profits from wartime contracts, Belfast's industrial elite forced men into the trenches through 'economic conscription', replacing them with underpaid women and youths. Harland & Wolff launched 400,000 tons of shipping, Workman & Clark's 260,000, both employing nearly 30,000 workers between them. War contracts (Ulster secured 160) pushed linen employment from 76,000 in 1912 to nearly 90,000.[87] Amid soaring inflation, trade-union militancy surged, and socialism took root particularly among previously unorganised workers hit hardest by the rising cost of living.

While the Federation of Engineering and Shipbuilding Trades dominated the politics of skilled labour, Belfast ILPers made significant inroads in the linen industry. Using strikes and wartime arbitration, they secured gains and built political loyalty among a segment of the working class. The Workers' Union played a key role, organising not just general labourers in foundries and shipyards, but also mill workers across Ulster's linen triangle and rural labourers demanding their share of wartime profits. In the countryside, the union absorbed two existing groups: Kyle left the Textile Operatives for the Workers' Union, which represented factory weavers, while Gordon remained secretary of the Flax Roughers' and Yarn Spinners' Union, serving semi-skilled men on the ground floor of spinning mills and female workers above. Officially, the workers appeared to register separately with these two unions; but propaganda and local organisation, outside Belfast at least, sheltered under the Workers' Union umbrella, which also covered other factory hands, unskilled workers and labourers not attached to the linen trade.

Founded in 1898 by radical socialist Tom Mann, the Workers' Union recruited casual and unskilled workers under the vision of a socialist society. Mann had built strong ties with Belfast ILP members.[88] After a slow start, the union thrived during the period of labour militancy leading up to the First World War, becoming Britain's fifth-largest trade union – a growth partly fuelled by a strong syndicalist undercurrent in the pre-war labour unrest.[89] The Workers' Union began organising in Ireland in 1915, early efforts being led by William Murdoch Adamson. By 1916, it had established twenty-one branches – five in Belfast, eight in Antrim, three in Tyrone, and one each in Derry and Down, Dundalk and Drogheda being the only branches outside Ulster. Adamson's 1916 report highlighted the creation of twelve new branches that year. James McKeag served as regional secretary, with Bob McClung as an organiser and Sam Kyle as secretary of Belfast No. 5 (branch 431).[90] By 1918,

Adamson returned to Staffordshire, leaving McKeag, McClung and Kyle to oversee growth as Ireland became a separate division. The union expanded rapidly across shipbuilding, engineering, textiles, chemicals and agriculture; in 'the North of Ireland particularly the Workers' Union [had] shown the way in organisation to thousands of hitherto unorganised workers'.[91] Indeed, by the time of the shipyard clearances in 1920, the Workers' Union had grown to 128 branches, including fifteen in Belfast, with most others spread across Ulster.[92]

In 1916, General Secretary Charles Duncan warned that many male union members had yet to grasp the impact of women flooding the workforce, stating that 'the whole position and standpoint of Unions like the Workers' Union is – and must be – beginning to change forever'. He concluded: 'Let us turn difficulties into advantages, and seeming dangers into glorious victories. That is the Workers' Union way'.[93] During the war, twenty female organisers helped grow women's membership in Britain from 5,000 to 80,000. Belfast's organisers often collaborated with their British counterparts; Lizzie Hayes served as secretary of Belfast's twelfth branch (1,189), representing Ormeau millhands.[94] In January 1917, Dawson Gordon, the Flax Roughers' delegate to the ITUC, joined A. J. Hanratty, the union's female organiser, in rallying mill-workers on Belfast's Crumlin Road. Hanratty stressed the need for unionisation among linen industry women, advocating for 'one big society' to secure fair wages. Gordon outlined how he had petitioned the Board of Trade to intervene in wage disputes as the cost of living had increased by over 80 per cent.[95] The Flax Roughers' minute book, penned by Gordon, recorded a membership surge due to Hanratty's efforts and successful arbitration. By April, the union's executive authorised expanded organising among women, reporting 1,200 new members across Belfast and rural areas.[96]

Although the Workers' Union's leadership, particularly Labour MP Charles Duncan, distanced itself from its militant socialist grassroots, many organisers clearly viewed it as One Big Union in embryo. Indeed, Bob McClung condemned 'win the war' Duncan for using government-backed scabs in a Down farm labourers' strike – though Duncan later defended Workers' Union members in a dispute with Lurgan Urban District Council.[97] By 1918, amid industrial militancy, the union's membership soared to nearly half a million, making it Britain's largest. Fuelled by favourable economic conditions, swelled by reservoirs of non-unionised workers, galvanised by successful strike action, and operating under wartime arbitration, thousands poured into the Workers' Union's flexible organisational structure. However, the post-war recession saw membership collapse to 100,000, leading to its 1929 merger with Ernest Bevin's Transport and General Workers' Union.[98]

Gordon's minute book provides some insight into the reasons for, and nature of, growing militancy. In September 1915, the Flax Roughers organised men in thirty-three mills and female spinners in seven – all but one in the greater Belfast area. In March 1916, the Flax Roughers' committee lamented the fact that 'practically all other classes of workers have received a substantial increase in their wages'. The Flax Spinners' Association refused any wage increase for 'roughers and spinners', however, blaming the cost of flax.[99] Joe Devlin raised several questions in parliament on behalf of the Flax Roughers in terms of the obvious growth in linen exports in relation to stagnant wages as a prelude to the linen industry's inclusion in the wartime arbitration process.[100] By May 1918, the trade union represented roughers, machinists and oilers in fifty locations, and counted female spinners, preparers, reelers and carders as members in forty-four mills. In short, it organised female and male workers across almost the entire Irish spinning sector.[101] The ITUC report stated that the Flax Roughers had 10,000 members by January 1920.[102] Therefore, amid a cost-of-living crisis, Gordon and Hanratty (likely Jane Hanratty, recorded in the 1911 census as a Catholic flax spinner from Lesley Street) transformed a largely male semi-skilled benefits union for roughers and hacklers into a mass movement of female unskilled workers.

Since the 1890s, the union had organised roughers and hacklers, including 'wonderful characters' like Jim Callaghan, an Ardoyne autodidact, who could quote 'whole poems by Burns and whole pages of Shakespeare' off the top of his head.[103] As living costs rose, it expanded in 1916 to include machine boys and oilers. But the influx of female spinners after 1917 transformed the landscape. For instance, women spinners joined from the Owen O'Cork mill in East Belfast. Nellie Gordon had previously organised 'the girls whom I had worked with' there, who 'gathered round me tears in their eyes with gladness at my success'. 'Millies', 'Shawlies' or 'Greasy Bellies' toiled barefoot from 6:30 a.m., surviving on cans of tea heated 'in the hot water trough belonging to the spinning frames'. Nellie recounted how the girls appeared 'happy until agitation opened our eyes', after James Connolly convinced her to become a full-time organiser, 'throwing off my shawl and wearing a hat and coat'.[104] After the ITGWU's collapse in Belfast following the Easter Rising, the Flax Roughers took up the fight for mill women, while the Workers' Union organised in the weaving factories.

The textile trade unions thrived by securing tangible results. Through the Board of Trade's arbitration, workers gained leverage for better pay and conditions. Before this, as Bob Getgood recalled, bosses often 'resented the idea of you coming in to tell them how to run their business', typically responding with 'gross offensiveness' and 'vulgarity'. They would 'open the door – [ask] what the hell you wanted and bang the door in your face after telling you to get away to hell as quick as you could'.[105] By 1917, however, employers like the Flax Spinners' and Power Loom Manufacturers' associations faced workers' demands before the Committee on Production.[106] In 1917, the Flax Roughers, citing an 87 per cent increase in the cost of living, rejected a minimal wage offer, pushing for arbitration with George Keith and arguing for greater militancy, as the 'position was splendid for us at the present in terms of public opinion and everything in our favour'.[107] Sam Kyle represented the weaving end on the Committee on Production, while Gordon looked after the interests of the spinners.[108] Kyle, secretary of the newly formed Textile Trade-Union Federation, highlighted how organisation allowed workers to secure 'war advances' amid the abnormal conditions of the time.[109]

Nevertheless, the influx of women did not meet with universal approval. Members of the Flax Roughers' committee objected to Gordon's decision to appoint a 'lady clerk' to deal with increasing bureaucracy at the headquarters in the Engineers' Hall. Gordon countered that mushrooming membership left it 'impossible for him to do all the work, however in future he promised to do all his own work and everybody else do the same!'[110] John O'Donnell, a Catholic hackler from Leeson Street on the Falls Road, consistently challenged Gordon, on one occasion describing the society's 'exorbitant' £4 per week printing account as 'veiled in mystery'.[111] O'Donnell later claimed that Gordon 'threw down on the table a big bundle' of paperwork, trying to 'confuse' him. When Gordon brought the accounts to the next meeting and 'challenged any member to examine' them, several members proposed that the committee drop the matter, as they were 'tired listening to Mr O'Donnell'.[112]

O'Donnell subsequently raised the 'serious problem' of 'females working at male labour in the different departments of the mill, especially when there is a surplus of male labour available'. For Gordon, the problem deserved 'the attention of all trade unionists', and he eloquently proposed that a 'woman received the same wages as a man'; but 'after some further discussion the matter [was] dropped'.[113] By May 1918, when the union ran a ballot for another full-time clerical position, several men 'raised the question of the organiser', a full-time official, A. J. Hanratty, 'canvassing for one of the candidates'. In the end, the female candidate, Sarah Ann Diamond, narrowly lost out to none other than John O'Donnell.[114] Clearly, then, the regular election of Diamond and Mary Murray to the five-person executive committee represented progress; but the idea that a woman might get a comfortable full-time position when a man could do the job appeared to be too much for some.[115]

Across the period, a pattern emerged whereby the Flax Roughers brought in female spinners across Belfast and then spread the trade union throughout country districts. Local organisers, with guidance from Gordon, then typically insisted that mill owners in the country pay workers the Belfast rate. Concerted strikes took place across the linen triangle to achieve this end. It then appears that the union gradually began a campaign to introduce closed shops.[116] Again, this began in Belfast, and, by September 1918 the committee had endorsed a series of strikes across spinning mills in the city to that effect.[117] Agitation then duly shifted to country districts, members at Gilford's six-storey spinning mill 'asking for instructions as how to act' to 'compel non-unionists to join up', as they wanted 'to see that all join the society'. The following month, female spinners had made Gilford a closed shop.[118] Interestingly, workers in the weaving end of the sprawling site formed a branch of the Workers' Union, with James Brownlee, a Presbyterian winder, acting as secretary.[119] The evidence suggests that a cohort of socialists, with a long record of involvement in the Belfast ILP, took advantage of wartime conditions and the government's arbitration process to unionise large swathes of Ulster's unskilled workers, especially women.

At the same time, they made moves to combine all linen workers, firstly by setting up a federation of textile trade unions and eventually moving to create One Big Union.[120] In February 1919, Dawson Gordon reported that the federation, through Sam Kyle, had applied to employers for a 'shorter working week [of] 44 hours' and 'for another advance in wages of 10s for men and 4s for women and boys and girls [and] that women doing man's work be paid men's wages'.[121] In June 1920, just prior to the shipyard expulsion, the Flax Roughers heard a proposal from Harry Midgley, of the Linen Lappers, for an amalgamated textile workers' trade union. Members including Thomas Dawson, a Protestant flax dresser at Ewart's from Hanover Street, in Belfast, and Daniel Burns, a Catholic machinist at Jennymount, off the York Road, proposed that the Flax Roughers join with the ITGWU – although Dawson admitted that the One Big Union, not allegiance to any specific organisation, constituted the objective. In the end, the committee proposed a vote of all members on both options. But fate intervened, in the form of the workplace expulsion.[122]

The Flax Roughers also showed a consistent political outlook, providing subscriptions and delegates to the ITUC.[123] In April 1918, the union agreed with the Belfast Trades Council's request to send representatives to the Belfast Labour Representation Committee.[124] The following month, the society affiliated one thousand members, and sent four delegates including Gordon and Hanratty.[125] The executive also gave financial assistance to the Belfast Labour Party, both before and after the general election.[126] The Flax Roughers then marched with other textile trades at the large 1919 May Day demonstration under the umbrella of the Textile Federation.[127] In anticipation of the January 1920 municipal elections, Gordon explained that the Belfast 'Labour Party should run candidates', due to its better chance of election under proportional representation, wherein 'each party would receive their quota'.[128] Despite some public reluctance, Gordon eventually accepted the Flax Roughers' nomination, as members felt only a full-time paid official could properly carry out their duties, if elected.[129]

Across a three-year time frame, Gordon, Kyle and other socialist activists helped to expand trade-union membership enormously among both female weavers and spinners and male roughers and labourers. They had also pushed the employers' associations hard at arbitration, and appeared intent on creating an amalgamated union for, at least, the linen trade. The downturn in linen production after the cancellation of war contracts damaged their position, but the propaganda produced by the Flax Roughers' detailing the enormous profits made by mills and factories indicated that these socialists envisaged a future where a united textile trade union would negotiate to regulate wages and conditions. Furthermore, organised workers would secure political representation through a democratic labour party. In response, employers and their political representatives promoted their own proto-fascist Orange labour association.

By March 1920, Dawson Gordon, now a city councillor, informed members that the Flax Roughers had refused to send delegates to the government's Linen Trades Board, because of the proposed inclusion of 'the Ulster Workers Union' (UWU). He continued that 'all the trade unions did not recognise this society as being in the interest of the workers or run for the benefit of the workers'. Gordon provided 'several instances' of employers using the UWU to smash strikes and divide workers. Likewise, Thomas Dawson proposed to exclude the UWU, 'as we believe that the said "union" is not run for or in the interests of the workers'.[130] Unsurprisingly, several committee members ended up on blacklists compiled in anticipation of the workplace expulsion that July. In September, the first meeting after the pogrom 'reported that during the past two months heavy liability had been cast up on the society [due to] the fact that a large number of members had been victimised from their work [during] the unfortunate disturbances'.[131]

While anti-sectarian socialism made definite progress, driven by an activist hub on the left, rivals for working-class support emerged from reactionary loyalists on the right. The eventual defeat of socialism in Belfast rested on this loyalist aristocracy of labour, for 'unlike their southern colleagues, northern craftsmen had no need of an alliance with labourers to secure their bargaining power'.[132] Skilled workers in the shipyards and engineering fused 'craft exclusiveness and sectarianism', wherein two-thirds of workers were highly skilled and affiliated to British-based craft unions, enjoying a major advantage in pay over non-skilled workers.[133] The UULA would exploit the developing southern IRA guerrilla campaign as the pretext for the mass expulsion of Catholic and socialist workers from the city's main employment centres. Furthermore, Unionist politicians, including Edward Carson, undoubtedly inspired and directed this pogrom – and reaped its reactionary dividends.

In early 1920, however, when faced with a free choice, thousands of Protestant workers ignored loyalist black propaganda. As a result,

Belfast Labour Party candidates consistently outpolled their opponents from the proto-fascist UULA.[134] The UULA, which had a mill-owner and future northern prime minister, J. M. Andrews, as its chair, effectively danced to the tune of the bigoted secretary of the Ulster Unionist Council, Richard Dawson Bates. The Unionist leadership and capitalist class employed this grouping and an ancillary yellow loyalist union, the Ulster Workers' Union (UWU), led by UULA committee member James Turkington, to crush socialism in Ulster. The ITGWU's *Watchword of Labour* claimed that, as UWU head, Turkington received £270 per annum from 'the blood money of the "profiteers of Ulster", made when the lads of the Ulster Division were shedding their blood in Flanders'.[135] The UWU balance sheet confirms it as a capitalist venture, which had not paid any strike pay, sick pay, lockout pay or funeral benefits.[136] Indeed, correspondence between the Ministry of Labour and the Linen Masters' Association revealed that the employers 'would take no part' on the proposed Linen Trade Board, unless the UWU gained representation.[137]

In the wake of the July 1920 shipyard expulsions, the *Watchword* excoriated 'the Turkington spawn': 'see vultures and you will find their bodies; see black legs or sectarian hate and you will find Turkington and his crew'.[138] But in January 1920 Turkington and his UULA running mate secured less than 500 votes, as against Sam Kyle's poll-topping 2,082, and 500 for Dawson Gordon in the overwhelmingly Protestant Shankill ward. A resilient working-class politics had demonstrated itself impervious to a year of black propaganda, thereby enabling Belfast labour's 'big stride', when official Unionist candidates (including the UULA) barely registered 50 per cent of the votes in the great Unionist citadel.[139] The spring of 1920 represented a high-water mark, as the movement's activist hub spread out across mid-Ulster.

The independent trade-union movement in Belfast directly challenged Unionist dominance among Protestant workers, many of its leaders playing key roles in the 1919 Belfast general strike. The Forty-Four-Hour Strike, explored in greater detail later, arose from wartime conditions when, 'it was said, money grew on the tops of the bushes. So too did prices, food shortages, and class consciousness.' However, while Red Clydeside's shop stewards earned a reputation for militancy, Belfast's shipyards remained a 'caste conscious and aggressively

Protestant environment'.[140] Emmet O'Connor notes that socialists like Jimmy Baird represented 'one of hundreds of union activists who veered away from the amalgamateds to Irish Labour in consequence of the '44 hours strike in 1919, victimisation in Belfast's workplace expulsions in 1920, and the willingness of British unions to accept wage cuts with the onset of the slump'.[141] Nevertheless, in 1919, the *Voice of Labour* speculated that many striking workers, as former Ulster Volunteers, might play a crucial role if tensions with English forces escalated. It optimistically suggested that dialogue between the UVF, Irish Volunteers, and the Citizens' Army 'might show that they now have more in common than was imagined. Much has happened since the Covenant was signed.'[142]

Editor Cathal O'Shannon's analysis in *Voice of Labour* echoed that of Dawson Bates, who discouraged direct Unionist intervention in the strike, to prevent workers from feeling 'let down' or becoming 'so embittered with the Authorities that they would join hands in a universal strike for the whole of Ireland . . . the consequences of which would be very far-reaching'. His proposal, an Orange manifesto, would therefore permit 'the decent men to secede from the Sinn Fein Bolshevik element'.[143] Rather than remaining passive observers, Unionist leaders coordinated a strike response based on their relative weakness in relation to the strike's popularity during the brief post-war boom. While the subsequent victory of an independent Unionist in the East Antrim by-election hardly constituted a fatal blow to their hegemony, local Unionists blamed 'a combination between the Roman Catholics and extreme members of the Labour Party together with a considerable number of relatively moderate Protestants' for the result.[144]

At the same time, Bates warned: 'the Labour question is becoming acute in Belfast and the North of Ireland . . . there is a general desire to kick against all authority and all discipline all over the three kingdoms, and this found vent in the East Antrim Election. We have got to face this sooner or later.'[145] Indeed, nominees of the Larne Trades Council would win five of the town's council seats in January 1920, the Antrim RIC county inspector bemoaning 'the return of men . . . who have very little standing in the community and little experience' of business, or any 'intelligence'.[146]

Ulster Unionists and their British imperial allies faced two major threats: republicanism and socialism. In response, the Unionist elite formulated a spurious conspiracy linking the efforts of Belfast's socialists to a global Sinn Féin–Bolshevik conspiracy bent on the destruction of the British Empire, all under the watchful eye of the Whore of Babylon in Rome. At the time of the Forty-Four-Hour Strike, Robert Lynn – Unionist MP, *Northen Whig* editor and future chair of the Northern Ireland education committee – believed 'the Church of Rome to be behind all of Ulster's troubles and saw the Labour left as its useful idiot'.[147] Likewise, before the 1920 Belfast shipyard expulsion, William J. McDowell told a loyalist audience at Portadown that the 'socialistic or independent Labour Party had circulated the slander that the UULA was out to smash the trade unions'. Rather, the Belfast Labour Party 'posed as a true friend of labour, but they were opposed to every Unionist principle, and they tried to woo the young men in the workshops so that they might use them as tools' to discard the Union Jack 'for the flag of Sinn Fein (Never!)'. In conclusion, McDowell 'begged them not to sell their principles as Protestants and Orangemen to men who were trying to get them into a trap'.[148]

The slaughter of the Western Front and grim conditions at home reignited class struggle in 1917. Inspired by revolution and syndicalist ideas, unions in Ulster swelled – organising thousands of linen workers across four counties. Yet, for all its reach, this militant movement still lacked the unity and force to seize power. The Forty-Four-Hour Strike, involving 40,000 workers, was a major challenge for Unionists. Many workers in core industries, such as shipyards, nonetheless acted later against their own class interests, helping to suppress the revolutionary momentum. While civil wars raged in Russia and Europe, the counter-revolutionary forces, supported by Entente armies and paramilitaries, ultimately triumphed. 'By the end of 1920 and early 1921', wrote Charles Maier, 'the left was in retreat everywhere' amid 'a world-wide Thermidor'.[149] In Ireland, the pogrom marked the beginning of a long period of conservative dominance, in which republicans, socialists and women activists retreated until the late 1960s, when local and global pressures cracked the conservative shell once again.

It is therefore essential to challenge the sectarian assumption that Protestant 'Unionist' identity is innate rather than socially constructed. Belfast's *Herrenvolk* democracy – sowed in the 1830s and nurtured during the First Home Rule Bill, and its results reaped in the bloody harvest of 1920 – served as a ruling-class mechanism of social control in response to potential and then actual working-class solidarity. Already, before the period discussed here, but especially within it, the ruling elite, in its own class interests, deliberately instituted a system of sectarian privileges to define and maintain its position. The consequences were not only ruinous to the Catholics of Ulster, but also disastrous for the great mass of Protestant workers themselves, whose class interests differed fundamentally from those of the Unionist elite.[150]

3

Women, Weavers and the Workers' Union

Men no more will be content under rulers of industry they do not elect themselves . . . Ireland must begin its imaginative reconstruction of a civilization by first considering that type which, in the earlier civilizations of the world, has been slave, serf, or servile, working either on land or at industry . . . These workers must be the central figures, and how their material, intellectual, and spiritual needs are met must be the test of value of the social order we evolve.

Æ (George William Russell), *The National Being*

Despite its admirable sentiment, the passage above from the Lurgan-born Protestant socialist and renowned poet George Russell (Æ) shares one weakness with my analysis up to this point: its narrowly male focus.[1] Clearly, the 'enormous condescension of posterity' afflicts questions of gender as much as those of class. Indeed, as the slaves of the slaves, in Connolly's memorable description, women stand doubly damned to judgement by the angel of history.

Nevertheless, across the Red Triangle women engaged in strikes and trade-union militancy on a scale equal to, if not greater than, that of their male comrades. Certainly, newly enfranchised female voters, especially mill-workers, swelled the ranks of northern Labour's new electorate. This made the period almost unique – and, with an extended post-war franchise, women exercised a degree of political influence that briefly matched their growing class consciousness. In one town in this study, Lurgan, spinners and embroiderers had historically asserted their rights and formed trade unions. Belfast's story remained more complicated, but women's struggle in both towns had important implications for understanding Ulster's burgeoning socialist politics in the immediate post-war period.

One thing remains beyond speculation: all the 'Millies', whether spinners or weavers, stared hunger and destitution in the face daily. The lifelong Shankill trade unionist Saidie Patterson, who entered the mill as a girl during the period, recollected working-class life under 'the beautiful cruel linen', starting at six in the morning, barefoot, 'covered in dust and moisture', in temperatures over 27°C. In 1911, Belfast had double the mortality rate of Manchester, with half the workers paid a penny a day. The women, some of whom had forced themselves to keep working even when they went into labour, were 'just a pair of hands, making profit for the industry. What happened to us really didn't matter.' Pathetically, Patterson recounted how sectarian divisions and segregated neighbourhoods helped mask the shame of their poverty, as 'Shankill people for reasons of privacy often used the Falls pawn and the Falls pledged on the Shankill'.[2]

In a 1913 manifesto to Belfast mill-workers, Winifred Carney, Nellie Gordon and James Connolly highlighted the dire conditions: 'Your hard work and low wages make you easy victims of disease,' they wrote, 'and your children are handicapped in life before they are born.' Condemning the mills as 'slaughterhouses for women and penitentiaries for children', the manifesto nonetheless criticised workers for their 'slavish submission' to such exploitation and their failure to unite for better conditions.[3]

Gordon joined Connolly in organising the Irish Textile Workers' Union – an offshoot of the Irish Transport and General Workers' Union (ITGWU), in 1912 – just as loyalist shock troops drove Fenians and rotten Prods from the shipyards.[4] The manifesto specifically appealed to spinners, who endured gruelling conditions – working in extreme heat, with water-soaked clothes and lacerated hands – for wages 'less than some mill owners spend weekly on a dog'. Collective action could transform workers from 'the helpless slaves of soulless employers' into controllers of the industry. In the short-term, the trade union urged recognition under the Sweated Industries Act, a minimum wage, and a female inspector for Belfast. It concluded that most demands could be won through direct action, including a general strike, with the rest 'conceded by Government as soon as you show yourselves in earnest in your demands for it'.[5]

Previous organising efforts among Belfast's linen workers failed due to divisions between spinners, weavers and finishers, exacerbated by sectarianism and the linen lords' hostility to unions. Mill owners exploited these rifts, enforced strict discipline and maintained austere paternalism, stifling collective action. Despite occasional militancy, such as the 1874 strike where 30,000 workers, led by women carrying black flags and Belfast baps, walked out for eight weeks, sustained organisation remained elusive.[6] The workforce nevertheless remained fragmented. While spinners laboured under precarious conditions, among the more skilled – mainly Protestants in the weaving and finishing stages – work often supplemented male wages, Catholics being more likely to stay on after marriage. As a result, only 5 per cent of Belfast's 35,000 Millies belonged to a trade union, in contrast to the levels of unionisation among most non-apprentice males.[7]

In 1893, Ben Tillet told the British TUC congress in Belfast that the city's Millies had to 'realise that they were to become the future mothers of the country and would have to see their own daughters growing up to fill their places in the factory'. They had to 'see that their children would have a better chance than they had that day'. They therefore needed not to 'depend on the Trades Council, on Lancashire, or on the philanthropists, or on the sister isle, but rely on themselves'. These appeals found expression in Mary Galway's leadership of the Textile Operatives' Union, which attracted a paltry thousand members. Bob McClung recounted how a twenty-two-year-old William Walker, with his long hair, Bohemian tie and soft black hat, chaired the meeting with Tillet, and briefly acted as the Textile Operatives' secretary after its formation in an Orange Hall in West Belfast.[8] Nonetheless, when, in 1897, 8,000 women struck because of new rules and higher fines for lateness and damages, Galway and the Trades Council reached a compromise with bosses – which the women promptly ignored, holding out until the abolition of the new regime.[9]

In May 1906, before Larkinism swept through Belfast, a major spinners' strike shook the city. For two weeks, predominantly Catholic female spinners halted work, parading 'the main thoroughfares of the city singing and shouting' until they obtained an increase of 1s a week.[10] While Galway's Textile Operatives focused on 'skilled' weavers, many women turned to the Flax Roughers and their secretary, Dawson Gordon. The Flax Roughers established a strong presence among women at the York Street Spinning Mill, particularly as the trade declined after 1908. Gordon and Hanratty would build on this foundation by 1917. Elsewhere, Larkin, and then Connolly, 'had obtained many benefits for the dockers, who, by this time, had been talking matters over with their women folk with a view to getting them organised in the Irish Women Workers' Union.'[11]

Nevertheless, Galway did advocate for unskilled hands and sweated labourers enduring harsh domestic piecework conditions. In 1906, the Irish Trade Union Congress (ITUC) demanded female factory inspectors be employed to debunk the myth that mill workers' poor health stemmed from 'the dirt of their houses', arguing that proper oversight would reduce the high mortality rate among young women.[12] In 1908, Galway pushed the ITUC to extend anti-sweating laws to protect pieceworkers. A staunch advocate of parliamentary reform, she asserted women's equal right to political representation.[13] By 1912, while Larkin worried that only middle-class women would gain suffrage, Connolly supported Galway, viewing women's voting rights as fundamental, even if it meant they might oppose him. Despite progressive voices, women's rights faced resistance, with 'much lip service' paid to organising women but little action, often due to many men's opposition to gender equality.[14] Nellie Gordon nevertheless recalled Connolly's deep respect for women, particularly mill-workers, who were often the primary breadwinners. Indeed, 'Connolly quickly exploded this notion of mine [that] the men knew everything.'[15]

Ironically, given their shared support for women's rights, Connolly's 1911 challenge to William Walker found organised expression in a clash with Galway's Textile Operatives' Society. Galway accused Connolly and the Irish Textile Workers' Union of 'poaching', though she focused primarily on skilled weavers and finishers, neglecting the unskilled majority. But Connolly gained traction by empowering women to resist oppressive workplace rules and increased machine speeds during reduced hours. Over a thousand spinners rallied behind him, seeking organisation. When employers threatened a lockout, Galway urged the women to return, but they instead cheered for Connolly, placing the struggle under his leadership. Connolly advised them to return

> and break systematically each and every one of the harsh rules. If a girl is checked for singing, let the whole room start singing at once; if you are checked for laughing, let the whole room start laughing at once; if anyone is dismissed all put on your shawls and come out in a body.[16]

The gradual shift of the Independent Labour Party (ILP) led figures like Sam Kyle, a former Textile Operatives official, to promote the mass unionisation of Ulster's mill-workers during the war. Through the Textile Trades' Federation, Kyle and Dawson Gordon organised thousands of female mill-hands, especially in areas new to unionism. By May 1919, Kyle represented the Textile Workers' Union at Belfast's May Day celebrations, and later in arbitration meetings, while Mary Galway continued to speak for the rump of Textile Operatives.[17] Between 1914 and 1919, the British Ministry of Labour recorded fifty-four strikes in Ulster's textile industry, involving 13,918 Belfast workers and 16,396 elsewhere, mostly women.[18] The war had reshaped women's lives, making socialism, in Rosa Luxemburg's famous dichotomy, a far more humane and attractive alternative than imperial barbarism. As Belfast ILPer Margaret McCoubrey powerfully declared, 'Only with women's help can true Internationalism and lasting peace be achieved.'[19] In terms of labour organisation among linen workers, then, Connolly appeared to have, posthumously and temporarily, won the debate; but, as we shall see, Galway would return after the collapse in trade during 1919 to frustrate Gordon and Kyle's new departure.[20]

Rather than primitive mobilisation based solely on wages, this new departure attempted to get 'every worker' organised, 'every branch' affiliated 'with the local Trades Council', and every Trades Council linked 'with their fellows through the' Irish Trade Union Congress. 'Thus, may the workers of Ireland become powerful for the re-building of the Irish Nation!'[21] In this manner, trade unionism swept down the Lagan Valley from Belfast and into North Armagh. Accordingly, Gordon and other Belfast ILPers, most notably Kyle, D. R. Campbell, James S. McKeag and the two Bobs, McClung and Getgood, promoted the British-based, syndicalist Workers' Union to rally Ulster's mill-workers, factory hands and agricultural labourers to the socialist banner.[22] But the demand for organisation came not only from outside agitators or union officials, but from local workers themselves. Rather, these socialists reaped a bountiful harvest, as thousands of workers sensed the opportunity for genuine advancement, rupturing the thin veneer of rural and small-town class harmony.

In January 1920, Kyle, Gordon, Campbell and McKeag won seats for the Belfast Labour Party, a group rooted in 120 delegates from the Labour Representation Committee, including the Trades Council and two ILP branches.[23] Anti-partitionist and staunchly socialist, the Belfast Labour Party criticised Irish Labour and Tom Johnson's decision to abstain from the 1918 general election, which they argued had handed victory to northern Conservatives. D. R. Campbell expressed disbelief that Irish Labour would 'lie down to Sinn Fein' so completely.[24] Known for their activism, prominence in Belfast's 1919 Forty-Four-Hour general strike, and relentless campaigning, the Belfast Labour Party gained some electoral traction. Ahead of the 1920 municipal elections, they reflected the British Labour Party's position at the time: social reconstruction and all-Ireland self-determination. (The British Labour Party leadership soon performed a volte-face, accepting partition.) Harry Midgley, a self-described 'constitutional revolutionist against the existing system', anticipated that 'they would be called Bolshevists. (Several Voices – "So we are," and applause)'.[25] The Belfast Labour Party's momentum reflected growing trade-union enthusiasm in and beyond Belfast, setting the stage for a wave of working-class militancy across Ulster's linen triangle.

Gordon's account highlights the fact that Catholics met in Orange Halls while Protestants met in Hibernian assembly rooms. Lisburn, like many towns near Belfast, saw Labour's progress accompanied by bands 'half Orange and half Hibernian', operating in 'perfect harmony'.[26] The Workers' Union had organised in Lisburn since 1915, led by William Goulding, an Anglican labourer.[27] William Gardner, steward of the male-only Flax Roughers at the Island Shop, raised early concerns about rising living costs.[28] By September 1915, the Island Shop branch urged the Belfast Trades Council to convene all textile workers for wage increases, spurred by ongoing disputes with employers who sought to cut wages by lowering rates for flax work.[29] In June 1916, roughers struck and secured local rates.[30] By 1919, the Flax Roughers were actively supporting the recently formed Lisburn Trades Council.[31] That June, Dawson Gordon 'got a tremendous welcome, the audience rising and applauding for several seconds', when he introduced Ellen Wilkinson, future chair of the British Labour Party, and Margaret McCoubrey, suffragist and Belfast ILP member who famously 'shouted herself hoarse on the question of equal pay for equal work' to a packed Orange Hall in Lisburn.[32] Gordon encouraged the town's workers, whom he had already organised, to support the strike by local shop workers for recognition of their union: 'Mill workers [should] be missionaries to that cause, a holy cause, and not spend one farthing in black leg shops until the principle of the union was conceded and the dispute settled.'[33]

By 1918, the Flax Roughers had organised spinners in Island, Hilden, Seapatrick (Banbridge), Gilford and Dunmurry. Gardner and Smith, Hilden's shop steward, demanded wages matching Ewart's in Belfast.[34] Hilden, part of the Linen Thread Company, which also owned mills near Banbridge and Gilford, consistently posted annual profits exceeding £250,000 between 1915 and 1918.[35] The Flax Roughers first sought a standard rate, then a closed shop, leading to a strike by 900 workers at Gilford in October 1918. This spurred the formation of the Gilford Trades and Labour Council, supported by the Belfast and joint Portadown-Lurgan Trades Councils.[36] Indeed, Belfast's ILPers had a history of spreading their socialist message in Gilford and Banbridge. Bob McClung, who organised farm labourers in County Down, recalled pre-war meetings when an overweight local policeman had asked, 'What brings you socialists to Gilford?' McClung's comrade replied: 'We want every man, woman and child in Gilford to be as well-clothed, as well-fed and as well-housed as the members of the [Royal Irish Constabulary].'[37] Henry Cairns, an Anglican bleacher, had been organising Banbridge linen workers since 1918. In June 1919, McClung established a Workers' Union branch in Banbridge, uniting labourers regardless of religion or politics, declaring they would 'demand a working wage and get it!' Sam Kyle pointed to the trade unions as the 'only way' to working-class emancipation, urging workers 'not to allow themselves to be sidetracked by old shibboleths as in the past'.[38] James Hayes, an Anglican labourer, served as secretary. By October, Campbell, Gordon and McClung helped form the West Down Trades Council in Banbridge, uniting textile workers and rural labourers under the Workers' Union.[39]

McClung cut a swath across rural Down, organising thousands of agricultural and general labourers. He reported in the *Voice of Labour* how, after addressing a meeting of 2,000 workers in August 1918, sixty female farmworkers joined the Downpatrick branch. Workers numbering 800 formed pickets to obstruct the flax crop, farmers alleging intimidation and the workers complaining that 'the farmers meet their arguments with guns, hatchets, and pitchforks'.[40] The Workers' Union registered forty-six branches across the period in County Down. Details exist for thirty all-male branch secretaries, which suggests that eight branches orbited weaving factories while the rest serviced agricultural, general, and domestic labourers. The religious breakdown sat at fourteen Presbyterians, ten Catholics and six Anglicans. Except for two publicans, all the secretaries were either mill-hands, labourers or servants. McClung's efforts resulted in County Down and East Down forming separate district committees; D. Mc Curdy from Newtownards and Henry Donnan, a general labourer from Killough, acted as secretaries.[41]

The downturn in the linen trade and the counterattack by employers also affected the linen mills and factories in these areas, however. By December 1919, roughers and spinners at Island Shop came out on strike against 'the action of the employers'.[42] At Dunmurry, management fired the shop steward 'because of his attitude and protecting the workers'.[43] Similarly, workers at Gilford came out in March 1920 against reduced pay, with the backing of the Flax Roughers; but the counter-revolutionary die was about to be cast.[44] Interestingly, in the January 1920 urban election, official Unionist candidates in Lisburn secured 1,035 votes against 773 for Labour, which returned three councillors.[45] That August, loyalist mobs tried to expel the town's entire Catholic population.[46] By the summer of 1920, in nearby Banbridge, John Crumlin, one of the chief instigators of the July shipyard expulsions in Belfast, told a meeting of the yellow Ulster Worker's Union that 'they had given socialism and Sinn Feinism its death blow in that city'.[47] Loyalist mobs had already tried to drive the Catholic population from Banbridge, in a prelude to Belfast's mass expulsions. This meeting may be the basis of Henry Patterson's observation that the Ulster Workers' Union (UWU) operated in 'linen centres like Banbridge and Lurgan, where it seemed to have aimed at stopping the recruitment of unorganised workers, not only to the ITGWU but to the British-based general unions like the Workers' Union'.[48]

The Workers' Union in Armagh

A clear correlation existed between an increase in unionisation in the linen industry after 1916 and a relative bridging of the chasm between prices and wages. Due to war contracts, employment in linen swelled from 76,000 in 1912 to 90,000 by the war's end.[49] As we have seen, the arbitration process and rising cost of living fuelled trade-union expansion, and socialism was strongest among the nominally unskilled, who also included agricultural and general labourers. Indeed, the Royal Irish Constabulary (RIC) inspector general reported in July 1918 that 'the demand for agricultural labour in some places appears to exceed the supply which is remarkable considering that emigration had practically ceased'.[50]

Interestingly, the Workers' Union's provincial organisers in Ulster also affiliated to the ITUC, and Cathal O'Shannon, a fellow member of the Socialist Party of Ireland, provided consistent sympathetic space and coverage in the *Voice*, and then in *Watchword of Labour*. As O'Connor has pointed out, 'By the time Dublin [ITGWU] was ready to push northwards, British unions like the National Amalgamated Union of Labour (NAUL) and the Workers' Union had already cornered the market.'[51] Yet these Workers' Union organisers belonged to an identifiable group shaped by 'Connolly's conversion of Belfast socialists from William Walker's pro-Union labourism to anti-partitionism'.[52] The newspaper archives abound with reports of labour meetings in rural Ulster, where Gordon, Campbell, Kyle, McKeag and McClung used the Workers' Union as a vehicle for rallying Ulster's unskilled mill-workers, factory hands and agricultural labourers to the socialist banner.[53]

Arguably, the Workers' Union eased cooperation between Protestant and Catholic workers in a way that the ITGWU, with its overt republicanism and identification with Sinn Féin, could not.[54] On the other hand, these Belfast socialists may also have felt that the southern labour leadership's proximity to Sinn Féin did not reflect the specific industrial economy, class relations and sectarian tensions that prevailed in east Ulster. For instance, before an audience of 200 workers at Armagh Town Hall on 23 September 1918, J. S. McKeag successfully formed a Workers' Union branch, which 'all sections of the labouring class joined'. However, the RIC described Cathal O'Shannon's 'attempt to form a branch of the ITGWU two nights later' as 'a complete failure'.[55] McKeag rightly introduced himself as 'a member of a fraternity of organisers who were out to secure better conditions' for the working class.[56] The following month, the crowd had swelled to one thousand, when local Catholic mill labourer and branch president George Carson introduced McKeag, who urged all textile workers and general labourers to enrol.[57]

In November the RIC noted: 'the relationship between employers and workmen is not so good', since 'strikes can be easily got up'.[58] Municipal labourers duly plunged the city into darkness, after the Armagh Urban District Council (UDC) refused to hear McKeag's demand for higher wages.[59] In December the town's carters struck for an increase, while bread servers for Ingles & Co (Belfast) merely had to threaten strike action to gain concessions.[60] The following March, Bob McClung reported how labourers resurfacing roads for Armagh County Council had gone on strike, securing an increase of 6s per week, bringing their wages up to the same level as agricultural workers.[61] In April 1919, Peter McKernan, a Catholic railway clerk, chaired a meeting in the Foresters' Hall, where Dawson Gordon and D. R. Campbell gave the inaugural addresses to the Armagh Trades Council.[62]

The Armagh Trades Council then held its first May Day rally, which saw 2,000 workers parading through the principal streets, before assembling in the Shambles Market Yard. The British suffragist and socialist, Kate Manicom of the Workers' Union, who addressed a similar meeting in Dungannon that week, demanded that the state establish industrial councils for every industry to regulate hours and wages, as 'workers demand those things essential to our existence' as well as 'more time to cultivate the higher things of life hitherto denied us'. In an ominous hint at the downturn in trade, Bob McClung and local man Owen Loughran called on the government to extend the unemployment scheme, or 'dole', to the textile industry.[63]

Nevertheless, Bob Getgood told a Workers' Union meeting that autumn that 'Labour was nearer victory than a great many people were aware of. There was going to be no peace in the industrial world until all the workers were united in one body, whereby they could control all the means by which they had to earn their living.' Felix Hughes of the Postal Clerks' Association then advocated a Co-operative Commonwealth, before McClung declared that 'those who engaged in the trade union movement were going to see about sharing the wealth of the country amongst the working classes who produced it until they took all the wealth they produced'.[64] Armagh town fitted the pattern of activism outlined above, in which central ideological agency fused with intense local demand fuelled by economic necessity, resulting in a familiar pattern of organisation and politicisation.

Across Armagh the Workers' Union formed twelve branches, starting in Armagh Town, where local Catholic mill labourer George Carson acted as secretary, and Lurgan, where Anglican labourer John Neeley filled the role. The trade union then spread to linen villages like Millford, Richhill and Keady, where Presbyterian Thomas John McClean acted as secretary, and where the union also organised a branch for scutchers. It also organised agricultural labourers at four centres, John Kelly from Tullydonnell acting as secretary for labourers across South Armagh. Of the seven identifiable secretaries, four were Catholics, two Anglican and one Presbyterian.[65]

Dawson Gordon had organised roughers and spinners in Tandragee before the red wave – though initially only male roughers at Wilson's Armagh Spinning Company joined. By 1920 the Flax Roughers had unionised both men and women in Armagh and Bessbrook, a model mill village near Newry, where flax workers later took industrial action. The unionisation of Bessbrook's famously 'loyal' workers raised some eyebrows locally. The *Frontier Sentinel* noted that, while James Connolly had failed to mobilise them years earlier, 'Dawson Gordon came some time ago and organised the workers', and 'the people are at last throwing off the fetters that once bound them to a yoke that was merciless in its severity'.[66] The Flax Roughers also recruited in Darkley, another 'model' village south of Keady with a spinning and weaving mill. By October 1917, Gordon's efforts secured workers the recognised rates, granting them an extra 8s per week.[67]

By March 1920, however, the trade union noted that employers had locked the workers out at Darkley and Armagh mills. Abraham Wilson 'refused to pay the Armagh workers their just wages'. Gordon urged all members to 'rally to the call of your fellow workers . . . who are fighting tyrannical employers, and whose efforts are to break up the workers organisation and place you in the same condition as existed in 1914. Do you desire this? If not, then organise and help.' Similarly, Gordon claimed that the Darkley employer 'had locked out all his workers for no apparent reason'. The Flax Roughers' committee voted unanimously to increase strike pay.[68] At Armagh, the local press claimed that 400 workers had gone on strike after roughers refused to do 'piecing out' work.

Wilson then brought in outside flax, and the entire workforce went on sympathetic strike. Interestingly, Wilson had already developed these tactics at his other mill in Newry.

At Darkley, the employer locked out workers after a strike provoked by the victimisation of four leading trade unionists. Management appeared determined to 'break up the union'. In addition, two workers received their notice 'because neither would do the work of the other. The employer's intention was to make **one** do the work of **two** in order to save the wages of one. As no person could be obtained to take up this work, the mill was closed down, and all the workers thrown out of employment.' The manager, T. S. McKinstry, who had previously worked in Bessbrook, claimed he was 'putting the workers out on grass to cool them'. In both cases, the Flax Roughers urged all members to pay the levy for strike pay: as 'the workers have shown their loyalty to one another, show them your loyalty by paying off the small contribution each week and demonstrate to these employers that you will stand by one another'.[69]

In May 1919, Newry Town Hall hosted a public meeting of textile operatives, which heard speeches from Gordon, the Textile Federation president, and Sam Kyle, 'organiser of the Workers' Union and secretary of the Textile Federation'.[70] Shortly after, at the Newry Spinning Mills, which Wilson also owned, the shop steward, Thomas Ward, pushed hard for a closed shop, as the employer had used machine boys to work flax brought in from outside and wrought by non-union labour. Ward 'declared that in a very short period of time' the firm 'would have sufficient non-union labour to keep the place going with the result that all society men would be thrown out of employment'. Gordon highlighted the dangerous precedent involved, and the trade union instructed the employer to cease the practice.[71] This led to a prolonged strike at Newry, beginning in July 1919. Under the dramatic title, 'Strike Epidemic', even London's *Pall Mall Gazette* noted how over 300 employees in Wilson's spinning mills 'struck work today owing to the employment of non-union men'.[72]

At an August meeting, headed by the Sinn Féin band and two other local bands, branch president Michael Kearney of Bessbrook told the crowd that the workers were 'struggling for a principle against the iron hand of tyranny, the same hand that had for years striven with might and main to keep the workers in the gutter'. Ward recounted how bosses had warned that a strike would lead to 'disease and starvation but the girls and machine boys, like the other strikers, had nobly refused to listen'. He asked local people and shopkeepers to boycott blacklegs, as 'they were not only up against a hard master, but they were up against the Spinners' Association', with Wilson paying £2 per week to scab labour if they abandoned the union. Gordon claimed that management had tried to get each man to do the work of two, continuing that Wilson thought that, as 'he owned the mill and the machinery . . . in effect he said he also owned the workers and that he could do what he liked, always forgetting that it was the worker who produced the wealth'. Gordon concluded, urging them not to 'allow the master to again trick them with their old catch cries of Orange and Green'.[73]

The strike ran into October and, once again, the Flax Roughers instituted a general levy – 'not a great sacrifice but the total means a lot to those workers on dispute'.[74] Wilson tried to split the workers through a policy of lockout and re-entry, but Dawson Gordon noted that 'the workers had [still] remained loyal' to trade unionism. Indeed, the Flax Spinners' Association used the Newry dispute as partial grounds for not implementing the agreed forty-eight-hour week in the linen trade, as 'they will not proceed any further until: first, Newry strike is settled and, second, until your society gives the employers an assurance that neither this society nor its members would interfere in any way with arrangements made by firms to work flax . . . anyway they think suitable'. The Flax Roughers resolved to 'give no such assurance as its object is to see that all employers pay their workers the recognised rates', declaring that such rights 'will only be obtained when the workers are determined to have it, therefore begin now and get your organisation into perfect condition, so that better conditions in the linen trade may be obtained from profits yet in the industry'.[75]

But by December some workers had returned to the mill, which Gordon felt 'was only natural . . . after a period of 18 weeks strike'. Nevertheless, eighty workers held out, relying on 'nothing only their strike pay'. The committee unanimously pledged £100 more in funds to aid the striking workers.[76]

The dispute also led to a rupture between the Flax Roughers and the Textile Operatives. Mary Galway intervened, accusing her members of 'very foolishly' striking at Dawson Gordon's urging, against her own executive's orders. Gordon denied this, stating that her members had followed instructions but that Wilson had locked them out regardless.

Gordon praised their solidarity, adding: 'If they did strike, it shows their loyalty to each other.' He then criticised Galway for cutting strike pay after six weeks, sarcastically remarking, 'we understood her society was a trade union, and not a benevolent society'. He then condemned her for negotiating a return to work with Wilson without consulting the strikers or the Flax Roughers: 'What business had Miss Galway to interfere in a dispute she knew nothing about, and without the sanction of the society concerned?' Gordon concluded by addressing rumours about their strike funds, challenging critics to review the Flax Roughers' publicly available quarterly balance sheets.[77]

Lurgan and the 'Victorious Eight'

North Armagh's key industrial towns – Portadown, and especially Lurgan – were central to the linen industry. Lurgan, located twenty-five miles west of Belfast, on Lough Neagh's shore, remained a hub for fine linen weaving, with forty-three factories in 1921 mostly producing cambric, handkerchiefs and hemstitched goods. Portadown, six miles west, was a thriving market town with nine weaving factories, a spinning mill, and several hemstitching facilities. Both towns faced rising living costs amid the 1918 Spanish flu pandemic, which caused sixty-two deaths in Lurgan and widespread workplace absences, including a hundred workers in Portadown. The crisis forced local schools to close in both towns.[78]

Due to specific local dynamics, the story of female trade unionism in Lurgan took a different turn from that of Belfast. The Brownlow family, dominant since 1629, spurred the growth of spinning and hand-weaving. By 1825, weekly linen sales reached £2,500 to £3,000, and the Friday market became a hub for the fine linen and cambric trades.[79] Hand-loom weavers later sold their goods in the Linen Hall. In 1855, James Malcolm introduced power looms, sparking a failed Luddite revolt by hand-loom weavers. The town council backed industrialisation, and by 1866 Malcolm expanded his factories. Unlike in Belfast, Lurgan's gender division saw men weaving while women handled hemstitching and embroidery, while children apprenticed and attended school on alternate days.[80]

By the First World War, Lurgan had four main companies: Johnston &

Allen, the Ulster Weaving Company, Messer's Malcolm Ltd, and the smaller W. J. Allen Company. The average wage for weavers had been stuck at 12s a week since 1886. Indeed, as early as 1885, the Lurgan Hemmers' and Veiners' Trade Union made the 'first successful attempt to organise women workers' after strikes in the handkerchief industry.[81] By 1889, the Hemmers and Veiners represented over 300 women, who paid a penny a week in union dues. Furthermore, the local town councillor and *Lurgan Times* editor, William White, supported the union. Despite these pioneering efforts, however, local trade unionism did not properly show itself until the twentieth century.

In 1901, during a strike at Matier & Sons, workers refused to handle outsourced work, supported by the reinvigorated Hemmers' and Veiners' Union, which contributed £100 from its old account. By 1902 the union had 900 members in a town with 1,500 manufacturing workers. In 1911 it represented 700 of Lurgan's 1,000 hemstitchers.[82] Minnie Rodgers, one of only three women delegates at the 1911 ITUC conference, alongside Mary Galway and Elizabeth McCaughey, highlighted women's growing role. Following the 1907 Belfast Dockers' Strike, the Ulster Weavers' & Winders' Trade Union organised Lurgan's women and men across the trade. Female making-up workers led the way, joined by male power-loom and general workers in 1907. By 1913, the Weavers and Winders had established a closed shop.[83] Lurgan's reliance on textiles, where a few capitalists employed much of the town, shaped its labour dynamics. The local petit bourgeoisie depended on workers' spending power and often backed reasonable demands, as higher wages boosted consumption. This led to stronger support for strikers from town councillors and small businesses. For example, White, a key figure, championed workers' rights and co-founded the Hemmers and Veiners union. This contrasted sharply with Belfast, where large capitalists heavily influenced Unionist politics and City Hall.

In January 1913, however, the Lurgan Weavers and Winders engaged in concerted strike action. Long-stagnant wages led the weavers to take their case for a living wage to the main employers, who rejected it out of hand. The weavers struck the following day (14 January), and the employers shut the factories for a week. The female hemstitchers did not pursue a sympathetic strike. When the men refused to return to work, the winders joined the weavers on strike. The RIC reported that, amid 'considerable friction', 1,400 were on strike, and four large mills closed for a fortnight. The police arranged 'with the strike leaders as to the wearing of badges [i.e. red ribbons] and limiting of pickets'. During the Home Rule Crisis, the report continued that, as 'political feeling is hot', pickets were 'of mixed religions, with the result that not a single instance of disorder has been reported'.[84] The employers refused to respond to arbitration efforts proposed by the town councillors, and the strike continued, buoyed by the arrival of £250 strike pay, which went to the 800 union members, while non-unionised workers held firm, partly due to public subscriptions.

On 5 February 1913, Charles Duncan of the Workers' Union told parliament that the strike involved 1,500 workers, who earned the paltry sum of between 10s and 12s per week. On 10 February the employers met in the Shankill Buildings to consider the weavers' demand for an increase of a farthing per yard on the output of woven cloth. They offered a half farthing and, although militants exhorted the men to 'Be brave, Be firm, a farthing a yard. Nothing less', a clear majority voted to accept, and the men returned to work – the winders receiving no increase. Nevertheless, the 1913 ITUC in Cork subscribed £3 to the strike fund, and congratulated the Lurgan workers on winning 'their magnificent fight'.[85] Edward Lunn, who would gain a seat as an Independent Labour councillor in January 1920, announced the result at a far from enthusiastic 'mass meeting of the Weavers held at 9 o'clock . . . in the Mall'.[86] At a workers' meeting in Portadown in November 1917, Lunn told his audience that he 'wore an Orange sash on the 12th of July but he did not care a straw if another fellow wore a green one. (Hear, hear.)' Neither did he care if opponents 'called [him] a Home Ruler because he advocated in the interests of labour'.[87]

In December 1917, the Belfast Trades Council sent a delegation to the newly formed joint Trades Council for Portadown and Lurgan, which included twelve societies, mostly local linen workers' unions with a history of striking.[88] The Workers' Union had already organised Lurgan UDC labourers; thirteen gas workers struck for higher wages after the council refused to recognise their representative.[89] The Trades and Labour Council ran between the two towns, which lay only six miles apart in the traditional heartland of the Orange Order. But, as Dawson Gordon noted, the price of living acted as a catalyst to solidarity. As the RIC county inspector reported gravely in the summer of 1919, workers were 'continually on the lookout for a rise of wages' – indeed, 'tea in Lurgan is approaching 5s in the pound!'[90]

Appointments to the Trade Council committee also divided between the two towns. Henry Cummins, the Presbyterian president, and William O'Neill, the Catholic secretary, of the Weavers and Winders, sat alongside William Vennard, an Anglican Orangeman and National Union of Railwaymen (NUR) official and P. J. Malone, the Catholic Post Office Workers' Union representative, both from Portadown. The first three would be successful Labour candidates in the two UDC elections in January 1920, while Malone narrowly lost out. Cummins and O'Neill lost little time in pushing the workers' demands. By February 1918, the Trades Council was threatening a general strike in Lurgan.[91] At a meeting in the Shankill Building, 2,500 veiners, hemmers and allied workers demanded a 50 per cent increase from the Lurgan Handkerchiefs and Fancy Linen Manufacturers Association.[92] By March, the RIC was lamenting how 'it is very easy to start a strike now', before reporting 'a threatened strike of Linen scutchers' – a notoriously underpaid sector in the preparation of flax. Most employers duly acceded to the workers' demands, although the report noted that matters were 'still unsettled with regard to four firms', which refused to grant the increase.[93]

In April, four hundred linen workers came out on strike for a pay increase at the four firms.[94] After the expiry of a fourteen-day notice, workers struck, and two of the factories had to shut. The dispute centred on the employers' refusal to agree to the arbitration award.[95] As the *Voice of Labour* reported, 'Lurgan is in the throes of labour unrest and strikes are spreading daily . . . all because the bosses have sworn to get their full pound of flesh.'[96] The workers of Glendinning's and McCaw, Allan & Co. then rejected a reduced offer at a 'crowded meeting' of workers, which lasted two hours. The *Newsletter* reported 150 hands still idle, while 'a considerable number of workers at some other concerns are also on strike'.[97] On May Day, the Flax Roughers' executive read an appeal from the Lurgan Hemmers and Veiners 'seeking assistance in their dispute with the employers of Lurgan who had refused to carry out agreement arrived at with the majority of the employers'. The committee voted to contribute the large sum of £20 in relief, as this matched the figure their Lurgan comrades had sent during an earlier dispute by the Flax Roughers at Roan Spinning Mill in Coalisland, County Tyrone.[98] By June, however, the RIC was complaining that 'wages are very high, and it is very easy to get up strikes' – an admonition partly spurred by Cummins and O'Neill's success in securing substantial increases for all workers after arbitration.[99]

Wage increases and the principle of union recognition and arbitration had been wrested from the employers; militancy continued in Lurgan into 1919. The joint Trades Council showed its political orientation by sending Cummins, Vennard and Malone as representatives to the Dublin United Trades Council's May Day celebrations. The situation in the linen sector was complicated by the Armistice, however. As the RIC county inspector reported in August 1919, 'all the mills and factories in the county are working under time but the wages of the hands continue as usual owing to the out-of-work donations'.[100] Nevertheless, in October he still recorded a strike of 250 linen 'folders' in Lurgan, which affected about 900 workers overall.[101] The following month, while again criticising the working classes' willingness to 'strike at any moment if they think they will gain by it', he noted that the folders' strike 'only lasted a short time and was settled by an advance in wages awarded by an arbitration board'.[102]

Lurgan Labour received its electoral reward in the January 1920 municipal elections, where 'the victorious eight . . . all nominated by the Lurgan Trades Council' won an outright majority of the council's fifteen seats.[103] An analysis of the background of Labour's councillors and the town's three wards shows that three of the eight were Protestants, with the Labour vote concentrated, but by no means confined, to the town's majority-Catholic North Ward – if one reads the invisible dividing line crossing Market Street at Castle Lane and Carnegie Street as a religious frontier.[104] Therefore, while the majority of the town's Protestants appeared to have voted Unionist, unambiguous evidence existed of a sizeable working-class Protestant socialist vote.

As elsewhere, however, the twin forces of economic depression and loyalist reaction effectively crushed working-class solidarity. As early as February 1919, Dawson Gordon had told the Belfast Trades Council that the end of government war contracts would lead to a reduction in time – a bitter pill sweetened by temporary unemployment benefit – or the dole.[105] In March, the RIC inspector general reported that the 'cessation of government orders and the accumulation of large stocks of war material have had a depressing effect on the linen manufacture', as had the 'cost and scarcity of flax'.[106] Gordon then reported that mills had closed in Dungannon and Newry, and that he was unsuccessfully struggling to make a special case for dole to be granted to the embroidery workers of Lurgan.[107] This ruptured the bargaining position of workers, and, when unemployment benefit ceased, the Labour-controlled council struggled in vain to alleviate 'the trade depression in Lurgan'.[108]

When clerks in the linen works subsequently struck, the *Watchword of Labour* reported that linen lords, 'in a state bordering on panic', turned to Turkington's yellow UWU, which held an Ulster Unionist Labour Association (UULA) meeting in Lurgan on 18 September 1920, addressed by Thompson Donald MP, James Lorimer of the ASE, and David Thompson, a UULA councillor from Belfast.[109] Lorimer claimed that Sinn Féin could be found on that day 'eating at the vitals of Empire and if the Imperial Parliament was ever so insane as to grant a Republic . . . none would feel the effects so severely as the artisan'. David Thompson urged his audience to 'beware of Lundys. There was one at Derry, and there were plenty around today, who would tell them that the UULA [opposed] trade unionism'.[110] Thompson Donald MP argued that 'blackguardly Bolshevists' were exploiting the honest discontent of the workers. As a result, one could find in Ireland 'trade union leaders with as many faces as [Belfast's Albert Clock], men associated with Dublin Sinn Feinism'.[111] This loyalist intervention appeared even more obvious in neighbouring Portadown, where the smaller Catholic share of the population removed some of the ballast enjoyed by Lurgan labour.

Portadown: The Hub of the North

As in Lurgan, a dispute with the Unionist-dominated Portadown UDC acted as a stimulus to Trades Council activism – although in this case the NAUL, under George Greig (a Belfast Walkerite), organised the thirty council employees. But the councillors' intransigence fuelled protests and agitation, in which William Vennard assailed aldermen in a pugnacious style that would later earn him verbal and physical reprimand.[112] The 1911 census recorded Vennard as a thirty-three-year-old Anglican railwayman living in Cavan town. In the intervening period, he had transferred to Portadown, or the 'Hub of the North' – so named due to its strategic location on the Great Northern Railway. An Orangeman and socialist, he successfully stood for the Portadown UDC in January 1920, at the head of a nexus of NUR men in junction towns who all collaborated with Campbell, Gordon and Kyle, and faced loyalist opposition from Turkington's UWU.[113]

Vennard also used his NUR connections consistently to attract socialist republican speakers to the town, and gained notoriety for proposing a resolution at an NUR conference in England against transporting military materials, inspiring the opprobrium of local loyalist railwaymen, some of whom ran against him as UULA candidates. Vennard nevertheless received public support from most of his branch in Portadown.[114] In July 1920 – the same month as his conviction for assault in relation to alleged intimidation by loyalists – he acted as a delegate to the ITUC.[115] He would later become an organiser for the ITGWU among railway workers in the Free State, spending a period in hospital after a fist fight with Larkinite opponents in 1925.[116]

In early 1918, labourers at the UDC went on strike for better pay. The Portadown Textile Operatives' Trade Union also pledged every help to the council workers in their struggle for a 'living wage', hinting at a sympathy strike from workers 'whose industry contributes so largely to the prosperity of the town'.[117] The Textile Operatives had already secured a war bonus in September 1917 and formed a satellite branch at Banbridge that October, and would win a pay raise for weavers in February 1918.[118] At the 'Portadown Citizens' Meeting', with D. R. Campbell on the platform, Vennard heaped vitriol on the 'Junkers of Portadown': 'Thirty shillings a week might seem to some people a big wage for a working man but let them take it to Councillor Topley's shop and see if he would give them as much food as would support a wife and five children for a week ("He would not.").' Vennard then warned the UDC that 'whether they liked it or not Trade Unionism was the coming power in this land'.[119]

At a mass meeting in the town square the following Saturday, Vennard proclaimed that 'everyone who reads the newspapers . . . could easily see . . . that things were coming to a climax in all the countries of the world. In the future Labour was going to rule in this and every other country.' He continued that workers did not receive 'a fair share of the wealth that they produced', before assailing Unionist councillor Charles Johnson for advising his colleagues 'not to take any notice' of the earlier meeting, claiming that the 'Tsar of Russia was wishing today that he had listened to the voice of the people'. Vennard continued that 'nothing could stop the present labour movement', as 'all the countries are on the move'. 'The employers said they could not afford to pay, but the country could now afford to blow away seven or eight million pounds a day on war' – money 'kept out of the stomachs of the people for generations past'.

At this stage R. L. Zigwell, the editor of the *New Way*, a Dublin socialist paper connected to the NUR, gave what the local press called 'a forcible address', promising £500 in strike funds. Zigwell challenged local Unionist councillors' criticism that 'it would have been far better for the men if they had not brought in strangers':

> He was taught at his mother's knee that all men were brethren, and he said that workers in Dublin, Belfast, Cork, Sligo, Waterford, and every other part of the country were comrades and brothers-in-arms. Because they happened to live in Portadown, were they going to put four walls up around the town . . . these barriers were being pulled asunder, the walls were being pulled down, in a short time these would be a thing of the past, and every man and woman would be a brother and sister working in harmony and peace for the benefit of all (Applause). He came there that day with a message from the workers of Dublin to . . . every man and woman in Portadown who was ready and willing to strike a blow for liberty . . . any injury to the workers of Portadown would be considered an injury to the workers of Dublin . . . If you are afraid to strike a blow for freedom, if you prefer your rags and your poverty to a free and healthy life, if you are not going to join in the great army that is marching towards the goal of democracy, then stop where you are . . . The great only appear great because we are on our knees – let us arise![120]

Johnson's Unionist colleagues duly rounded on the Trades Council and Vennard. Francis Crosbie asked if Vennard wanted the 8 million 'withdrawn', with 'those loyal and patriotic fellows . . . blown to atoms by the cruel Huns?' In response to Zigwell, Crosbie did not believe 'that the loyal men of Belfast were brothers in arms with the men in Sligo and Wicklow [*sic*]'. He concluded by asking why 'so much abuse was heaped on Mr Charles Johnson . . . one of the oldest and most respectable members of the council and the strongest Unionist there'.[121] Nonetheless, by March, the UDC gave the workers their pay rise.[122]

The Trades Council remained central to a cycle of wage demands and arbitration across the town, helping to win two small wage strikes by labourers against local coal merchants in October.[123] But October also saw what the RIC described as 'a novel strike on the part of insurance agents' in Portadown, which had spread from a regional dispute in Dublin led by John Doyle.[124] While introducing Doyle to a packed meeting in the Co-operative Hall, Vennard argued that three recent strikes proved 'the men of Portadown were beginning to realise that they needed a living wage'. He further claimed that 'the men who were not prepared to stand up for a living wage were not fit to collect premiums from trade unionists, and the teachers who did not go out on the one-day strike were not fit to teach the children of trade unionists (Applause)'. He also directly addressed Unionist black propaganda: 'they might be called Bolsheviks but . . . working men must stick together, and vote together'. Elsewhere, he declared that 'Sinn Feiner was the worst name they could call him, but Sinn Feinism would only mean being ruled by another form of capitalist. (Hear, hear.) His endeavour was to take the government from all forms of capitalist and give it to Labour (Applause)'. He concluded that it 'had been his ambition from a boy to assist the working class to rise', and

> there was no necessity for any thanks. He knew that the people who tried to exploit the working men did not like him, but even the capitalist Press could not but admit that it was the men who lived in these capitalists' houses who are not fit to serve in the army today.[125]

In a similar vein, Vennard led a succession of Trades Council delegations to the UDC to complain about the town's housing and living conditions, claiming that he was 'there to call a spade a spade, and not to rub them on the back like a pussycat (Laughter)'. In October 1919, he said that 'the opinion of the public was that the council was practically composed of landlords, who objected to building houses, and were trying to hoodwink the people'.[126] The following month, he lambasted councillors for their disregard, arguing that 'the reason why those men pay so little attention to the comfort of the workers is that they have never been criticised by the workers, who just took what was given with thanks'. Indeed, after defending Larkin's conduct during the 1913 Lockout, Vennard declared that the workers 'are now going to think for ourselves', before haranguing individual councillors: 'Would you ask your family to live under the same conditions as the majority of Portadown workpeople? Not Likely!'[127]

The Portadown Trades Council's manifesto for the January 1920 UDC elections declared that 'the crying needs of the workers, and the greed of private individuals compel us to fight the cause of Labour, and to assert the right of the working classes to live better and nobler lives'.[128] Unsurprisingly, Vennard won a seat on the UDC, along with two other Trades Council candidates.[129] In one memorable engagement concerning Unionist councillors' refusal to remove dry toilets from their properties, he told the UDC chair: 'I don't care that we are not finished till six o'clock in the morning before I sit down, I am going to state my opinion!'[130] Nevertheless, three UULA candidates, including fellow NUR man Richard Copeland, also secured election, along with another eight Unionist candidates.[131]

Partly in response to Vennard's propaganda, the UULA held a meeting in Portadown in October 1918. Thompson Donald MP told the assembled loyalist crowd he 'never yet knew a working man who benefitted from a strike'! He then criticised Vennard and his comrades, claiming he 'did not know whether the trades council represented the workers of Portadown or not (No!)'. Donald assured his audience that the Belfast UULA had secured good housing for workers in cooperation with landlords, councillors, and employers.[132]

Vennard's personality and rhetoric, combined with the town's heavily Protestant population and tradition of Orangeism, may have precipitated a quicker loyalist response than in neighbouring Lurgan. When the Great Northern Railway subsequently victimised Vennard, Richard Hennessy, from the NUR Branch in Inchicore, claimed: 'If Vennard had been employed on the Great Southwestern Railway instead of on the Great Northern they would not have sat down and seen him sacrificed as he was at present, but they would have put up a fight for him which would not have ended until they gained their object (Applause)'. In a futile echo of earlier optimism, Hennessy hoped that soon 'the little suspicions and divisions which prevented them cooperating on questions like this would disappear, and that they would work together as a solid body of railwaymen when any effort was made to victimise a comrade'.[133] Meanwhile, the Portadown UULA consistently condemned industrial action, called for the dismissal of striking postal workers, opposed the NUR, and condemned the munition strike, urging their bosses to 'organise and be prepared to take their stand against the forces of disorder'.[134] The UULA and its trade-union adjunct, the UWU, played a similar role in subverting socialism in Tyrone.

Our attention now turns to matters across the River Blackwater. We have seen how trade-union militancy and labour politics grew in County Armagh from the beginning of 1917 up until the local government elections and sectarian counterattack of 1920. We have also seen how what Bob McClung called a 'fellowship of good comrades, men and women' organised thousands of unskilled northern workers, according to a plan partly developed by D. R. Campbell with comrades in the ITUC.[135] These socialists mobilised workers, formed federations and trades councils, and founded labour representation committees, achieving promising results in local government elections in 1920. Harry Midgley's 'constitutional revolutionists against the existing system' clearly caused significant disquiet among employers faced with demands for advances in wages, the closed shop, and a future where trade unions and a local Labour Party looked to unite Catholics and Protestants and challenge Unionist political hegemony. Their response can be characterised as that of unconstitutional counter-revolutionists.

A more detailed treatment of the vicious loyalist reaction forms the subject of upcoming chapters – one in Caledon, near the Tyrone-Armagh border in 1919, which will lead into a detailed examination of the far more significant workplace expulsions of July 1920. The defeat of socialism in Belfast and Ulster rested on direct loyalist action amid an economic depression. The UULA exploited the developing southern IRA guerrilla campaign as the pretext for the mass expulsion of Catholic and socialist workers from the city's main employment centres. In both Caledon and Belfast, political Unionism, whether John Fulton of the Caledon Woollen Mill or Edward Carson and Richard Dawson Bates, at Westminster and Belfast respectively, undoubtedly inspired and directed these developents, and reaped the reactionary dividends from premeditated sectarian violence.

At a rally in Portadown in August 1920, the leading pogromist and future Unionist MP, William Grant, admitted that the UULA had carried out the expulsions, which were 'bound to occur', since 'they had to take the law into their own hands'. He continued that the loyalists 'had been asleep for too long. Even in the city of Belfast . . . they had allowed the enemy to practically overcome them, but now he was glad to say they were aroused with a vengeance, and those who were opposed to them would have to look out (Cheers).' Likewise, John Holness erroneously claimed that, when 'their fellows went to the war to defend their country, Sinn Feiners came in to fill their places'. He then said that 'before Christmas they were boasting that it was the Protestants who would go now', before luridly recounting how loyalists 'could see the pistols sticking out of their hip pockets, and they said they were going to change the tune of the Protestant workers on the island'. Holness triumphantly concluded that 'they had bitten off more than they could chew, and they were going to get something to swallow, and they may take it from him, but it would require a good drink to wash it down'.[136]

While most Ulster Protestants supported the Union during the revolutionary period, thousands embraced an anti-sectarian socialist alternative, challenging the case for partition. As we have seen, the growing role of women in this socialist movement was ultimately crushed by a reactionary alliance of Unionist elites and labour aristocrats. As early as May 1917, Dawson Gordon and D. R. Campbell faced criticism from the *Northern Whig* for attending a Dublin Labour demonstration, which declared 'our determination as trade unionists to resist by every means in our power any and every attempt to divide us from our fellow workers in other parts of Ireland', and sought to 'bring into the ranks of trade unionism every man and woman working for wages in Ireland', so that 'our position as wealth-producers can be strengthened, and our class secure the full product of its labour'.[137] Robert Lynn, the *Whig*'s editor, gave some flavour of the Unionist position, claiming in 1921 that there were 'two peoples in Ireland, one industrious, law-abiding and God-fearing, and the other slothful, murderous and disloyal'.[138] When a proper historical account is taken, it becomes clear that the forces of reaction, racism and chauvinism overwhelmingly aligned with the Empire and the Union.

Indeed, D. R. Campbell told the ITUC Conference in June 1917 that most northern workers opposed partition, while Gordon argued that linen workers in Belfast had been 'chained down as slaves, worse than slaves', and he 'assured them that the people of the North would stand with those in the South'.[139] Bob Getgood gave retrospective confirmation of this anti-partitionist outlook when he recounted how 'the one thing that mattered was the human needs of the people and not where they belonged or where they professed to belong'. The point was to 'bring about a kind of unity amongst Protestant and Catholic . . . it was the common poverty of the common people that brought them . . . together and they should work for the creation of a condition of things in which this poverty and want would have no longer a place in our lives'.[140] Writing to a comrade in Soviet Russia in 1927, Margaret McCoubrey lamented how, 'in this old world of ours at the present time, with chaos and disorder and misery around us, and many disappointments in our own working-class organisations, comradeship is a very precious thing'.[141]

As the following chapters will show, the pogrom meant that Orange allegiance rapidly came to define the difference between employment, on one hand, and poverty and want, on the other. Having valiantly stormed heaven, socialists across Ulster ate the bitter dust of defeat and betrayal. Memories soon faded of Labour's victorious eight on Lurgan UDC, or of William Vennard's lampooning of Portadown's house lords. For a brief, tantalising moment, the poorest of the poor, Ulster's wretched of the earth, summoned the courage to challenge their status as the bottom dogs. After the pogrom, their solidarity lay smashed, the better and nobler lives they had aspired to now merely a cruel dream or bitter memory that lingered as many boarded the boat for Britain's industrial north-west or the cold streets of the City of Brotherly Love. At least now, however, their story has been told – a partial, if inadequate, recompense for the poor hemstitcher, the 'obsolete' weaver, the Utopian artisan, and the followers of the Red Flag.[142]

4

Tyrone: Revolution Among the Bushes

Girls, women, came in groups,
In confused swift procession,
Head-shawled, gliding without talk,
Towards the light of the mills.
Alice Milligan, 'An Idyll of the Red City'

In his seminal analysis, Fergus Campbell rightly points out that 'the revolution in Ireland resulted in the creation of a conservative state, but not all Irish revolutionaries were conservative'.[1] Campbell cites Kevin O'Shiel, moderate Tyrone Sinn Féiner and land court arbitrator, who claimed that County Galway had experienced 'a revolution within a revolution'.[2] O'Shiel might have looked closer to home. Revolutions within revolutions appeared typical across Ireland, whether in western demands for land redistribution or the explosion of trade-union militancy in his native county.[3] O'Shiel reflected the snobbery of much of the provincial Catholic bourgeoisie when he described the working-class area of Brook Street in Omagh as

> a vile squalid lane reeking with foul smells and inhabited largely by slatterns and down and outs and good for naughts [*sic*], all mainly in rags. Respectable people would not venture down that ill-lit street at night because of the drunken orgies of its disorderly inhabitants . . . It was mainly, but not wholly, Catholic, I regret to say.[4]

O'Shiel's self-serving memoir exposes, quite unconsciously, the petty prejudice of Tyrone's small Catholic professional class. Indeed, he would go on to become a legal advisor to the Free State government, sharing many of the deep class hatreds typical of the new state's founders.

Yet, for two years in Tyrone, the 'slatterns and down and outs and good for naughts' numbered among the thousands of Irish workers who sought a fairer and better future for themselves through trade unionism. The archival evidence suggests that, in the two years leading up to the Armistice and just before the delayed onset of the post-war slump, an abortive social revolution swept the Ulster countryside, spurred by 'defiance of authority' in 'movements of social protest, in which the underlying conflict of poor against rich is clearly visible'.[5] This forgotten history offers a powerful alternative to the two-warring-tribes version of Ulster's past and, in the spirit of Connolly, let us hope that, as Irish people 'progress to a truer appreciation of correct social and political principles', these 'stones rejected by the builders of the past' might 'become the corner stones' of our future.[6]

Under the Red Hand: The Fractured Heart of Tyrone

Tyrone straddles a contested space between nationalist and Unionist – and indeed agricultural and industrial – Ireland. Of a total population of 143,000 in 1911, Catholics formed a slender majority of 55 per cent, or just over 10,000.[7] By 1911, most of Tyrone's Presbyterians (19 per cent of the population) lived in the Cookstown and Strabane Rural Districts, while the county's Anglicans (23 per cent) mostly inhabited the expansive plane from the south-west tip of Lough Neagh across the Clogher Valley, marking Tyrone out as 'a contact zone between the two major units of British settlement': Ulster-Scots and Ulster Anglo-Irish.[8]

While the Irish Transport and General Workers' Union (ITGWU) adopted the red hand as its crest in the wake of the 1913 Dublin Lockout, the red hand county itself saw little activity from Ireland's One Big Union. Indeed, the contested nature of the symbol spoke to deep divisions within the county itself – whether the loyalists' Red Hand of Ulster or the ancient Gaelic emblem of the O'Neill. Even popular images reflected the apparently immutable gulf between Planter and Gael. The great Tyrone poet, Alice Milligan, Connolly's friend, fellow socialist and feminist, described the depths of this division within her own community, and how her nursemaid frightened her siblings with cautionary tales of Fenians lurking in the shadows, ready to pounce. Milligan famously responded:

> But one little rebel there
> Watching all with laughter
> Thought When the Fenians come
> I'll rise and go after.

Nevertheless, Milligan acknowledged: 'This feeling of apprehension had been, doubtless, engendered, and increased by heredity; generation after generation of northern landowners and land-tillers must have gone to bed nightly with an uneasy feeling that the rightful occupiers of the soil were prowling around in the dark outside'.[9]

But Milligan never reconciled herself to the permanence of such divisions. Indeed, for over two years, partly emulating Alice herself, Catholic and Protestant female workers in the local mills and factories across Tyrone marched village streets, formed pickets, raised the red flag, and showed solidarity in the face of 'the modern machinery used in the crushing of human beings who had dared to seek their rights'.[10]

In this respect they followed in the footsteps of their esteemed county woman. Milligan had published James Connolly's first forays into Irish politics in her journal *Shan Van Vocht*, writing: 'Whilst in full sympathy with Mr Connolly's views on the labour and social questions, we are absolutely opposed to the scheme he puts forward for the formation of an Irish Republican party in the British Parliament.'[11] Furthermore, in terms of the irreconcilable antagonism between Planter and Gael, Catherine Morris has powerfully shown how Milligan objected to 'this type of dichotomous politics being imposed on Irish identity by colonial assumptions' – particularly to 'simplistic labels' forced on the Irish by the English.[12]

Nellie Gordon vividly recounted how James Connolly once took her to a lecture in an old loft on Connswater Street in Belfast, delivered by none other than Alice Milligan, a figure renowned for her remarkable writings and poetry. Milligan left a profound impression on Nellie, far surpassing that of Constance Markievicz. Unlike Milligan, the countess, along with Maud Gonne, had advised the women of the Falls

Road to focus their efforts on cultural activities. But, as Gordon noted, these were difficult times, and such pursuits were hard for impoverished, half-starved girls to take seriously. In contrast, when Gordon addressed the crowd, speaking directly to their lived experiences in terms they understood, the women responded with fervour, stamping their feet and cheering so loudly it seemed they might bring the house down. The countess later confessed to Connolly that she envied Gordon's ability to connect so deeply with her audience, saying 'she would have liked to be in my shoes as I had the power to make my audiences laugh or cry with me'.[13]

Milligan, too, recognised the limitations of cultural revivalism. She acknowledged that, while poetry and literature remained vital, there would come a day which would 'require more than the poet's thoughts'. This marked a response to Connolly's synthesis of republicanism and socialism in *Shan Van Vocht*, and particularly his argument that the Irish Republic 'might be made a word to conjure with – a rallying point for the disaffected, a haven for the oppressed, a point of departure for the socialist, enthusiastic in the cause of human freedom'.[14] Milligan's reply, alongside Gordon's grassroots appeal, underscored the growing recognition that cultural revival, while important, must be coupled with tangible political and social action to address the pressing realities of the time.

As Milligan demonstrated, while colonial history left an indelible mark on the collective Tyrone psyche, notable exceptions survived. As late as July 1913, the local Royal Irish Constabulary (RIC) estimated that around 5 per cent of the Protestant population, primarily among the Presbyterian tenantry, supported Home Rule.[15] James Baird, the son of a Clogher Valley tenant farmer, obviously carried this tradition of radical dissent to Belfast's Queen's Island. In a tradition with deep roots in the 1790s, local Defenders allied with the United Irishmen, forging a coalition between Dissenters and Catholics. Joseph Cassells, a Methodist watchmaker from Aughnacloy – a village twelve miles south of Dungannon on the Monaghan border – captured the spirit of this unity, describing it as based on 'Liberty and Equality'.[16] Nevertheless, the colonial cleavage, whether expressed through religion, nationality or race, still dominated local politics. O'Shiel described how, growing up, a 'kind of involuntary or unconscious "apartheid" existed . . . sanctioned by the custom of circumstances and accepted as inevitable'.[17]

In terms of the leadership of Ulster Unionism, the landed interest still predominated, and local manufacturers occupied secondary positions. By a neat historical accident, five generations after Thomas Knox had fused the interests of the Big House and plebeian Orangemen, Uchter Knox, the fifth earl of Ranfurly, played Orange tribune in the resistance to the Third Home Rule Bill. Indeed, 'Tyrone was probably the most densely organised county, where over a third of adult [Protestant] males were Orangemen in 1912'.[18] The Order formed the centrifugal element in a cross-class Unionist identity, and the seedbed of loyalist militancy. In general, two opposing social pyramids – one orange, one green – occupied the same geographical territory. The privileged position occupied by local Unionists, whether granted by plantation, providence or preferment, also explained their pre-eminence in the two major aspects of the local economy: land and linen.

In 1911, 64 per cent of Tyrone's adult males engaged in some form of agriculture, with labourers and farm servants on the bottom rung of the social ladder, accounting for a quarter of the farming community.[19] Just over three-quarters of the population therefore lived on agricultural holdings, which marked Tyrone out as something of a transition zone between the more urban east – Antrim (excluding Belfast), Armagh, Down and Derry, which all had figures close to 60 per cent – and the rural west – Cavan, Donegal, Fermanagh and Monaghan, which registered figures of over 80 per cent. Tyrone's farmers and labourers were also relatively poor, 58 per cent living on land valued at £15 or less, a percentage point lower than the national average. In Ulster, only Monaghan, Cavan and impoverished Donegal surpassed this figure.[20]

By 1911, 20 per cent of adult males worked in industry, primarily along the western shores of Lough Neagh around the three mill towns of Dungannon, Coalisland and Cookstown. William Coote's woollen mill, near Ballygawley, thirteen miles south-west of Dungannon, and John Fulton's at Caledon on the Tyrone–Armagh Border, represented exceptions, as they lay in isolated rural villages. Fulton and Coote would play central roles in the loyalist campaign against trade unionism in Tyrone. Indeed, Hugh de Fellenberg Montgomery, the leading landlord and Ulster Unionist Council delegate, wrote that, even though Coote was 'not altogether an admirable person', he 'represents the Unionist and Orange democracy here'.[21] North-west Tyrone had four manufacturing concerns, particularly Herdman's in Sion Mills and two sizeable garment factories in Strabane, satellites of Derry city's established shirt trade. The county town, Omagh, had some small factories, but served mostly as a market town, fair, and administrative and trading centre for the county's Catholic central mass in the Sperrin Mountains.

Class Consciousness and the Unskilled

This chapter deals mainly with the initially successful efforts of Belfast socialists to deploy the Workers' Union to organise the unskilled across East Tyrone between 1917 and 1919. Yet, although the most notable, this was not the first such attempt. Early in the period of the 'new unionism', Richard McGhee, the first president of the National Union of Dock Labourers and future Home Rule MP for Mid-Tyrone, formed the Ulster Labourers' Union to organise unskilled agricultural workers in his native province, as well as potentially stemming the flow of migration to northern Britain. McGhee organised a strike at the waterworks scheme in his native Lurgan, noting the 'miserable wages paid to the working men in the North of Ireland'.[22] New unionism differed from the old in both tactics and organisation, as it catered for unskilled and poorly paid workers without distinction of employment.[23]

Class consciousness in Ulster owed a debt to seasonal and permanent migration to Britain, particularly Scotland. Indeed, McGhee had himself migrated from Lurgan to Glasgow, where as a Protestant Home Ruler he entered the orbit of fellow Ulster-Protestant exile Baile John Ferguson and Tyrone-born trade unionist Edward McHugh, who gravitated towards the democratic left of the Home Rule Party. These radicals faced marginalisation in the wake of Parnell's hegemony after the Kilmainham Treaty in 1882, especially as the uncrowned king's elitist strategy partly challenged Ferguson and Michael Davitt's 'great principle of Irish Democracy'. By May 1888, Ferguson was helping to form the Scottish Labour Party, although both McGhee and he inclined more to a Lib-Lab tendency, which looked to pursue democratic progress, including the elevation of the working class through the existing constitutional movement.[24]

Interestingly, the Dungannon Ulster Labourers' Union invited Ferguson as guest speaker for their first significant demonstration.[25] McGhee himself organised the Lough Neagh fishermen after hearing their 'tale of petty tyranny which only required exposure to bring to an end'. The fishermen grated under an annual three-pound taxation and the alleged intransigence of local Unionist magistrates. McGhee promised that 'if the men around the lough shore engaged in fishing will join the Ulster Labourers' Union, the power of that organisation would be used to test the question in the higher law courts, where local magistrates have no jurisdiction'. McGhee then pointed to future state investment in 'harbours and piers for the landing of their boats and fish'.[26]

Another former Scottish trade unionist, John D. Crockett, played a significant role in the Labourers' Union's local progress. The proprietor of the *Tyrone Courier* and a Protestant Home Ruler and Poor Law Guardian, Crockett gained notoriety for highlighting the failure to build labourers' cottages. He had come to Dungannon as manager of the Congo coalmine, before buying the *Courier* in 1893 and adopting a radical editorial line. But he was forced to sell the paper to Tory rivals due to bankruptcy at the end of 1895, when his successor lambasted Crockett's 'wobbling' principles and attacks on the Unionist elite.[27] Crockett had also previously acted as an official in Alexander Macdonald's Miners' National Union in his homeland, and shared the pro-Home Rule Lib-Lab perspective of Macdonald, McGhee and Ferguson.

At a mass meeting in Dungannon Foresters' Hall, Crockett implored his audience to lift themselves from the 'degraded state of slavery and abject poverty to which you have been, and are at present, wallowing and floundering'. He forcefully argued 'that the great majority of those who are poor and affected with poverty are poor, not by their own fault, nor by their own choice, but because of the conditions imposed by society at large . . . poverty is not an individual or personal crime, but a social crime'. He then encouraged his audience 'to devise some means of regulating your supply of labour to the demand made for it in Dungannon'. Crockett went on to pinpoint local sectarianism as an obstacle to progress:

> But it is a sad and remarkable fact that no matter what the movement is, some men, for sinister motives doubtless, always give it a religious or political colour. I desire to say that this is a movement devoid of all religious, political, or party bias. It is a movement for the improvement of labouring men, be they Protestant, Catholic or Pagan . . . The first duty of a church is to minister to the poor . . . But so far as we can

> gather from the demeanour of most churchgoers and office-bearers in Dungannon, the first duty, according to their view, is to the rich.

Crockett then lambasted his own church, as, 'since the inception of this new-fangled [Ulster] Unionism', Presbyterians had combined with the Church of Ireland 'in favour of upholding the demands of the rich against the rights and liberties of the poor'.[28]

This led to the formation of Ulster Labourers' Union branches in Dungannon, Coalisland, Stewartstown and Ardboe. At Coalisland, several hundred labourers crowded the market square to promote 'combination among workers of all classes, but more especially the country and farm servants, who were being driven into the large cities and towns to seek employment, and consequently keep down the wages of the workers in town'.[29] A local supporter, Bernard Campbell, complained in a public letter that there was not a 'single labourer's cottage in the whole district covered by the Dungannon [Poor Law] union'. Campbell highlighted 'actual starvation' among the labouring classes, quoting Robert Burns regarding 'man's inhumanity to man'. He then described the town labourer's average wage of 9s a week as a scandal, since 'the capital invested in local industries, and especially Coalisland, is producing as large returns percent as any in the three kingdoms'.[30]

By 1897 workers in Coalisland's Ulster Fireclay Works went on strike for one month, securing a 3s increase on their weekly wage of 12s.[31] On 4 December, seventy local miners came out at the Congo mine between Dungannon and Coalisland, objecting to preferential rates gained by English miners over their own lower rate of pay. The mine employed several members of the Irish Republican Brotherhood cell located at Old Engine. On 16 December, the strikers accompanied by the Irish National Foresters' band and 'a mob numbering three or four hundred imported for the purpose from long distances, came to the colliery and remained drumming, shouting and firing pistol shots until after eight o'clock the following morning'. The police baton-charged the strikers and, on the testimony of the pit manager, arrested six ring leaders, including local Fenian John McMahon. Two of his seven children having been born in Lanarkshire, McMahon may have resented the manager's claim that Irish workers earned less due to inferior skills in comparison with English miners.[32]

After an initial hearing charging the men with unlawful assembly while armed, they were released on bail, escorted by supporters and the Foresters' flute band. The Tory *Mid-Ulster Mail* mocked the workers, scoffing that 'parading streets and beating drums' would not convince the public of their cause.[33] Strikers picketed English workers and local scabs, and on 16 January three men received a month's hard labour for threatening a blackleg.[34] Two of the accused were relatives of the six men arrested before Christmas.[35] The strike ended in early February after arbitration by a local landlord, Colonel Burges, following a newspaper exchange between the manager and strike leaders Patrick Slean, an officer in the Dungannon Foresters, and William Hazleton, an Anglican from nearby Killyman. Workers returned with higher wages and promises to seek commutations for imprisoned men.[36] Though economic hardship and division led to the Ulster Labourers' Union's decline in the late 1890s, local labour militancy endured, the same families again taking up the cause of labour two decades later at the end of the First World War.

The Red Wave in Tyrone

Analysing trade-union militancy in Tyrone requires an understanding of the county's east–west divide in organisation and affiliation. Early industrial action appeared strongest in East Tyrone, particularly in Dungannon and Coalisland, the focus of this chapter. Notably, mill owners emerged as key figures in the earlier Unionist campaign against Home Rule; some, like Major Robert Stevenson, the owner of Dungannon's largest mill in Moygashel, held leadership roles in the Ulster Volunteer Force (UVF).

In 1917, workers at Roan Spinning Mill in Coalisland went on strike twice within a year, demanding wages equal to the district's Flax and Spinners' Association rate – a demand met only in November.[37] Located near Newmills, a small Protestant village by Roughan Lough, the mill was founded in 1842 by John Stevenson, later convicted of overworking employees. John Wilson acquired it in 1854, and in 1874 his family merged with another John Stevenson, a Coalisland weaving factory manager. Originally from Lurgan, Stevenson partnered with Ledlie Clark of Manchester to establish the area's first power-loom factory, shifting production in Coalisland from hand-looming to mechanised weaving.[38] By the period we are concerned with, Henry Wilson ran Roan Spinning Mill, while Christopher Beatty managed Clark's weaving factory. Both were prominent Unionists and Orangemen.

By late 1915, the Flax Roughers had organised workers at Roan and Herdman's in Sion Mills. Dawson Gordon negotiated with Henry Wilson in Coalisland for 'the recognised country rates', but Wilson refused, leading the union to blacklist his mill, some workers leaving for Belfast to find work.[39] By 1917, and despite increasing profits, Wilson continued to deny workers the rate. Indeed, rather than cash-in-hand, he partly paid staff in redeemable tokens, which workers could only spend at the mill shop. Meanwhile, War Office contracts contained a Fair Wage Clause, prompting arbitration in linen mills. In September 1916, the Flax Roughers unionised Adair's Greenvale works in Cookstown. Gordon pointed out that, as Adair's were 'doing government contracts they should be compelled to pay the recognised rate of wages', to the tune of an extra 7s per week in this case. Adair's refused, and the men went on strike, receiving 16s per week in strike pay, and eventually achieving the rate after arbitration. Gordon then noted further correspondence with Wilson, who had refused to pay the rate agreed by the Flax Spinners' Association.[40]

Wilson argued that he did not have to pay the rate, as he held no government contracts, though his mill's yarn went across town and fed the looms at Clark's in Coalisland, which produced cloth, canvas, and eventually shells for the war effort. At the beginning of May 1917, he offered 3s per week for men and 2s for women, which the workers refused. Wilson then locked out twenty-one men, refusing them re-entry unless they agreed to his terms. Then, on 17 May, Wilson laid off some of the women from the reeling room. Their comrades walked out in solidarity, demanding reinstatement. Rather than compromise, Wilson locked out all 300 employees. Wilson and his managers believed they could starve the workers into submission, and directly refused any government arbitration on the grounds that the firm did not receive war contracts.

On 30 May, 400 people attended a public meeting in Coalisland, while the women workers marched from the mill through Brackaville and into the town centre. The meeting resolved that 'the workers and inhabitants of Coalisland hereby pledge the moral and material support of the people of this district to the application of the Roan Spinning Mill's workers for a living wage'. Joe Devlin, the constitutional nationalist MP for West Belfast, argued in parliament that Wilson paid workers 'at a rate considerably lower than the standard paid by the firms in the Ulster Spinning Association', even though 'the work of this firm has increased considerably as a result of the War'. Devlin argued that, even it was not directly engaged on war contracts, Wilson's was 'largely supplying other firms in Ulster who are engaged on Government work and are thus indirectly doing Government work'. Devlin elaborated on how Wilson had thrown '300 workers out of employment . . . causing them and their families privations and suffering'. Pointing to the military service record of employees and their families, Devlin demanded that the case go to arbitration.[41]

In early July, the Flax Roughers unanimously accepted a strike levy – 2d per week for men, 1d for women. Dawson Gordon remained hopeful for a resolution, as the Board of Trade had appointed a special investigator to mediate the dispute, but Wilson seemed willing to let the business fail rather than pay a living wage, offering women a mere 3d raise and nothing for men.[42] The lockout dragged on until October. Meanwhile, Neal O'Donnell, a Scottish-born Catholic organiser for the Workers' Union, ran a ballot to support locked-out workers. Having already unionised Clark's 400 millhands into a closed shop, O'Donnell would play a key role in local labour activism. Interestingly, by June 1920, Christopher Beatty triggered an unsuccessful strike at Clark's Weaving Factory by refusing to dismiss non-union workers.[43]

In October 1917, however, the Flax Roughers still needed £38 per week in strike pay. They 'appealed to the members to show the true spirit of trade unionism', as 'these workers have made a stand in your interest, and it is not too much to ask that you will see they are supported by giving a small extra contribution weekly'. Gordon reported that the Flax Roughers 'had held their own with the aid of subscriptions' from other trade unions, including £200 from the Lurgan Hemmers' and Veiners. James Boyle, secretary of the Flax Dressers' and Linen Workers' trade union, also located at Engineers' Hall, sent £35, expressing the hope 'that the day is coming when the workers in every sphere will be allowed a fair share of what they produce in the form of a fair wage'.[44] Like the Flax Roughers, the Flax Dressers affiliated to the Irish Trade Union Congress (ITUC) and the Belfast Trades Council, and by the end of 1920 it had merged into the Workers' Union.

Courtesy of Ciarán Ó Brolcháin, private collection

Belfast Labour Party Candidates for the Shankill ward in the January 1920 Belfast Municipal Elections, including Dawson Gordon and Sam Kyle

The necessity for long-term strike funds clearly created pressure, but in the context of a burgeoning trade-union movement this looked like a conflict that the workers could not afford to lose. During an interview with Gordon, Wilson retorted that 'he may open the mill in course of time but not on our terms'. As a result, the Flax Roughers took steps to authorise 'the trustees to either mortgage or sell the trade union's bonds in case of necessity'. Gordon pointed out that this would keep the trade union on a fighting foot, 'as ready cash may be required to the advantage and the support of the members' in Coalisland, and so the union would not be hampered in future disputes through lack of strike pay.[45] The Roan Spinning Mill strike, therefore, constituted a vital test case in the resolve of the trade unions and the belligerence of employers. Throughout, the shortage of labour, booming trade and the process of arbitration strengthened the hand of the worker.

Two local arbitrators – the Catholic curate, Fr Quinn, and Robert Patterson, an Anglican publican and grocer at Patterson's Corner who had provided relief and food parcels for workers – then contacted the Flax Roughers 'asking for lowest terms', as both intended to 'wait upon Mr Wilson as a deputation and try to obtain a settlement'. Dawson Gordon proposed 3s per week for all women and 5s for men as the bottom line, if Wilson promised to make up the difference in three months.[46] The following month, the Flax Roughers thanked Quinn and Patterson for 'their kindly interest in the matter'. They then went on to note that 'this district which also comprises Cookstown and Dungannon is the lowest paid in the whole North of Ireland, and it is hoped, within a short time, to have the wages brought to the level'. Indeed, 'Dungannon workers have only received an advance of 2s per week since the outbreak of war as against 7s received by the women workers in all other firms, [and] this is entirely due to the want of organisation among these workers'. Gordon concluded that, 'as the workers have now become organised, we hope in the near future to be able to do something for them in this direction'.[47]

In August, a Workers' Union meeting in Dungannon heard that a Coalisland victory would act as a precedent for future disputes, and 'this battle is waged on behalf of all the workers of this district'.[48] In October 1917, Gordon argued that 'Dungannon workers could fight as well as those in Coalisland who had now been fighting for five months and were going to continue fighting until they would get what they were out for and it was believed, from the support they were getting all over the country, that they would get their demands'.[49]

In the end, Wilson agreed to pay more than the workers initially demanded. Roan Spinning Mills never recovered, however, suffering falling profits and then debts, partly due to the loss of valuable international markets during the lockout.

A month later, speaking at St George's Hall in Dungannon's working-class Protestant district, Gordon claimed that they now lived in 'a period in history . . . when nothing else could be done except try their strength with the other side and the strongest side won'. In Coalisland 'the society was the strongest side', and that 'dispute had done a great deal of good, because the employers in Dungannon and Cookstown would realise that the society was fairly strong and had been able to fight a strong battle and at the end win.'[50]

In December 1917, the RIC commented on the impact of strike activity in Belfast, ominously predicting its rapid spread.[51] By 1918, Tyrone saw escalating labour unrest, with major disputes in every town. In January, Cookstown witnessed two strikes: one at Adair's spinning mill, where sixty boys walked out, sparking a sympathy strike at McCann's in Killymoon.[52] The Workers' Union organised 500 weavers at John Gunning & Son at Millburn Works, while both the Flax Roughers and the Workers' Union represented workers at Adair's Greenvale factory. There were several other mills and factories around the town, which runs along one long street. Cookstown would become notorious locally for the partisan character and sectarian violence of its police under George Hall and its Special Constabulary under John Knox McClintock between 1920 and 1922.[53] Yet, for a brief period, workers felt capable of challenging the bosses, and Protestants and Catholics came together under the banner of trade unionism. Not all employers matched Wilson in their belligerence or McClintock in their brutality, however. Major Robert Stevenson (Dungannon) and General Ambrose Ricardo (Sion Mills), both Ulster Unionists and 'B' Special commanders, accepted union wage demands and opposed sectarianism; but, to paraphrase C. L. R. James, there were good and bad governors, good and bad managers, as there were good and bad mill-owners. 'But this was a matter of pure chance. It was the system that was bad.'[54]

By April 1918, the Flax Roughers had obtained 'for Dungannon workers the last advance in wages. This makes a total advanced of 8s per week since January for these workers.' The key point appeared to be that the unions had 'established in different firms the full advances as given by the Committee on Production'.[55] As had been the case in its spread down the Lagan Valley and into Armagh, trade unionism thrived where organisers could improve the workers' material conditions, filling the ranks and using arbitration to hold employers to account. While roughers and spinners registered with Gordon, the weavers and finishers joined Kyle's Workers' Union, which provided a banner of convenience for the entire movement. By September 1918, Maggie Fee, a Catholic weaver from Sloan Street in Dungannon replaced the elderly Anglican, Sarah Ferguson, from Milltown as shop stewardess at Dickson's weaving factory.[56] By this stage, Gordon had organised roughers at Sion Mills, Cookstown and Coalisland, as well as female spinners, preparers and reelers at both of these sites and at Dickson's in Dungannon, which did not rough its own flax.[57] The Workers' Union had organised rural labourers and linen scutchers across the district as well.[58]

The Workers' Union formed eleven branches in East Tyrone. Cookstown had two; a Presbyterian machinist, James Mayne, represented linen workers, while local Catholic Thomas McCann acted as secretary to a branch of agricultural and general labourers. In Coalisland, Neal O'Donnell represented local mill and factory workers, while Patrick Crawford, who would go on to lead the local IRA Company, acted as secretary to the scutchers' union. The branch in Dungannon listed local Catholic Gerard Murray as its first secretary, succeeded by John Buchanan, a local Anglican – both were local mill-workers. Charles McKeown acted as secretary to the soap workers in Donaghmore, but agricultural branches also popped up in Ballygawley, Ardboe, Stewartstown, Pomeroy, Benburb, and as far west as Fivemiletown in the Clogher Valley, where local Anglican branch secretary Annie McClintock worked as a cook in the village hotel. In terms of the religious breakdown, Mayne was the only Presbyterian, with six Catholics and four Anglicans acting as secretaries.[59]

This wave of militancy culminated and then broke in the Caledon Lockout of March 1919, which followed a year of successful local industrial struggle. Caledon differed, however, as the ITGWU, rather than the Workers' Union, organised the strike.[60] While the Transport Union would later be accused of poaching from British skilled amalgamated unions, a quite different relationship existed with these non-skilled unions. It is possible to identify three converging streams of trade unionism in Tyrone. The Workers' Union thrived in the industrial area concentrated on the mills of Dungannon, Cookstown and Coalisland. This activism operated within the gravitational pull of Belfast, and the overtly political and anti-partitionist tendency around the Belfast Labour Party.

Omagh and Strabane, the other two main urban centres, fell within the orbit of the less overtly political Derry Trades Council and its leading exponent, James McCarron, 'which diverged from the trajectory taken by southern labour after 1907'. Union leaders set up trades councils in Omagh and Strabane and, like the Maiden City, remained 'committed to the strategy of the amalgamated unions', and kept 'politics and trade unionism separate to the great extent'. Because of the sizeable Catholic majorities in Omagh and Strabane, their trades councils tended to be more explicitly nationalist in their politics, unlike Derry, where 'positions on the constitutional question are firmly held and defended beyond the shop floor'. The third tendency again reflected the late arrival of Peadar O'Donnell's socialist republican agency as an ITGWU organiser, which cut a northward swathe through existing trade unionism from the winter of 1918 and led to the confrontation between anti-sectarian labour and Orange capital at Caledon in 1919.[61]

Tyrone also saw activism by agricultural labourers, the National Amalgamated Union of Labour (NAUL) organising in the western and northern parts of the county joining the trade councils in Omagh and Strabane, while the Workers' Union organised a network of labourers in East Tyrone. As for the NAUL, 'the ITGWU saw it as having the same spirit and goals and frequently gave it friendly reports in the *Voice of Labour*', while the provincial leaders of the Workers' Union were all strongly associated with the ITUC.[62] Across rural Ulster, the Workers' Union and NAUL had 'chalked up victories in 1918 . . . but they encountered stiffer resistance in the spring of 1919'.[63] The ITGWU's foray into Tyrone took place in the context of the growing challenge by employers to the demands of unskilled workers.

Dawson Gordon, Bob McClung and Sam Kyle played a prominent role in this concerted campaign of union militancy, initially among textile workers in 1918, but then spreading to most local manufacturing, and eventually encompassing East Tyrone's agricultural labourers in 1919.[64] That these men helped organise regional activism with the heavy demands on their time in Belfast speaks to their determination to build a broad anti-sectarian movement, primarily among the province's unskilled workers. Gordon had consistently articulated an anti-sectarian and anti-partitionist politics – a point his loyalist opponents appeared at pains to emphasise; yet Gordon himself also pointed to the war's crucial impact on the progress of local trade unionism, all based on the ability to extract concessions from employers.

In this climate, poorly paid and unskilled Catholic and Protestant workers seized the opportunity to demand better wages and gain union recognition in an unprecedented fashion. The evidence demonstrates this was a consciously anti-sectarian movement, which also showed significant militancy. In line with grassroots initiatives across Ireland, 'the emergence of sabotage and violence preceded the independence struggle by two years', its form 'determined primarily by the "pioneering" and localised character of trade unionism'.[65] In March 1918, sixty workers struck at the Coalisland spoke factory. In the same month, the police reported the threatened strike at Brown's soap works in Donaghmore. This involved 140 workers, and the court cases surrounding the disturbances during the strike provide interesting details concerning the nature of the trade-union movement and employers' response to it.[66]

Brown initially refused to recognise the Workers' Union or the demand for a 10s-a-week increase. 'Considerable friction' therefore developed, 'and consequently the local police force [was] augmented from the surrounding stations.'[67] The *Voice of Labour* urged the Irish working class to 'adopt an attitude of strict neutrality' and buy other 'equally good' Irish-made soaps.[68] Police arrested the Workers' Union secretary Charles McKeown and fellow striker Joseph O'Neill for stone-throwing and assault, as part of a crowd that attacked two Ulster Workers' Union (UWU) blacklegs (McIvor and Potter). The police also baton-charged the picketers, while the Tory *Mid-Ulster Mail* ruefully prophesied the closing down of the concern because of the actions of outside agitators, claiming that David Brown only kept the factory going out of 'goodwill' and 'sentimental feelings', and might forthwith sell the copyright to an English firm.[69]

Every day during the week-long strike, workers attacked blacklegs, female strikers such as Annie McCluskey being prominent in the violence. McKeown and Robert Stewart hijacked the company lorry and drove it through the front gates. Protestant employees who remained at work taunted the strikers with Union Jacks, while the strikers paraded the village with a red flag bearing the words 'Up the Workers' Union'.[70] The Donaghmore strike went to the local arbitration court, which produced a result favouring the workers.[71] The Workers' Union organised a dance in Dungannon in support of strikers, preceded by an impressive torch-lit procession from Donaghmore.[72] Several Protestant workers struck, but the manipulation of sectarian animosity by the factory owner (who had supplied the Union Jacks) foreshadowed more concerted later efforts to fracture local working-class unity.

Contemporary with the first Donaghmore strike, the conscription crisis proved that a marked divergence existed between lower- and upper-class Protestant attitudes to compulsory military service.[73] The ITGWU's chief provincial organiser Cathal O'Shannon stressed the depth of popular feeling at a meeting in nearby Armagh, claiming that '250,000 members of the Transport Union would resist it'.[74] Nicholas Smyth claimed that several former Ulster Volunteers had joined the IRA in Dromore in opposition to conscription.[75] Indeed, O'Shiel recorded how Protestants in Clanabogan – a small, largely Anglican village outside Omagh – vehemently opposed the measure. Interestingly, the ITGWU organised a successful strike of farm labourers in the village that August.[76] Elsewhere, the Ballygawley Branch of the Workers' Union pledged to 'join with our fellow Irishmen in resisting it by every means necessary', while, in Coalisland, the 'entire town . . . shut down' during the general strike called by the ITUC and Irish Labour Party (ILP&TUC).[77]

The summer of 1918 saw militant trade unionism across the county among factory workers and agricultural labourers. In July, workers struck again at the Roan Spinning Mill, when 'three non-union workers were taken on and the other workers went out on strike', with the result that the non-union workers joined the union.[78] By August, the local police reported that 'relations between employers and workmen [were] not so good'. The ITGWU had organised 'a strike in the County Council's quarry at Carrickmore'.[79] There were also several scutcher's strikes locally, with the general wage set by arbitration.[80] The same month, striking textile workers at Omagh destroyed produce and wounded an RIC man during a riot. James McGillion, a labour member of the local Urban Council, railed against the lockout at Chapel Factory in Irishtown, and local activists showed their close connections to Derry by addressing meetings in the city and calling for a sympathy strike.[81]

The use of scab labour triggered similar disturbances in Strabane.[82] Previously, female textile workers had paraded through the town behind a red banner in solidarity with striking comrades in Derry, before police drew batons.[83] By August, female workers in Doherty's factory in Strabane were out on a three-week strike, after the owner apparently 'put the girls out' and 'told them to take their union with them'. Con Doherty, the Derry councillor and Strabane strike organiser, who spoke for 4,000 women factory workers in Derry city, addressed the resultant meeting. The speeches suggested the development of definite class consciousness and the demand for control of production.[84] Led by

Minnie Duddy, the local union president, female workers paraded behind a white flag bearing the motto 'Unity is Strength', before police drew their batons to protect scabs returning home across the bridge to Lifford. The women relentlessly picketed nine non-union workers, subjecting them to serious ostracisation and intimidation, to the extent that Duddy 'announced amid loud cheers' that one of them, 'struck with the umbrella had become a convert to trade unionism and decided to join her fellow workers'.[85]

Local employers tended at this stage to shrink before the challenge of labour. For instance, workers only called off a strike at Omagh Asylum when the Tory-dominated board agreed to their demands.[86] In 1918, the RIC county inspector reported that a half-dozen serious strikes 'all ended favourably to the workmen'.[87] Where employers appeared intent on suppression, as at Monaghan Asylum, the workers' strength and militant tactics overcame opposition.[88] Prior to the 1918 general election, the Omagh Trades Council advised working men to 'act independently'. John Farnan of the ILP&TUC claimed that 'as an organised body of labour they could not link themselves up with one side or the other, no matter how many there were' on each side. James McGillion UDC claimed 'that no party of any shape or form . . . had ever come to their assistance, so that they had to organise themselves under the banner of trades unionism to obtain some redress of the grievances that existed'. Quite legitimately, he claimed that 'the working man was hardly known except on the day of the poll and on the next day they were not known at all'.

The meeting eventually voted in favour of 'agreement with the decision of the Irish Trades Congress', and the council resolved that 'any person associating himself with either political party is not authorised to speak in the name of Labour'.[89] The delegates at Omagh also recognised the conservatism of many Sinn Féiners. Elsewhere, Pat McHugh of the Trades Council argued that the local working class 'had too long been tied to the tails of political parties, and even at the present time these parties were doing their best to prevent labour being organised'. He urged members to 'keep out of the election and prepare for the day, which was coming soon, when Labour would show its strength'.[90] In March 1919, the Strabane Trades Council organised 'a big labour meeting' in the town hall to celebrate the settling of a strike by the town's labourers.[91] During the strike, workers erected roadblocks, intimidated 'scabs' and overturned Bannigan's potato cart before disabling Devine's tea van.[92] By September, upholsterers and cabinet makers joined with the carpenters in the town, successfully demanding a forty-seven-hour week and 1s 8d per hour.[93]

By May 1919, the Workers' Union organisers led a parade in Dungannon, just days after their involvement in the monster May Day celebration in Belfast. Contingents converged on the market town from Workers' Union and Roughers' and Spinners' Trade Union groups in Donaghmore, Benburb, Cookstown, Pomeroy and Coalisland. Several pipe-and-flute bands led the procession, while the platform included local Catholic and Protestant trade-union organisers and the English socialist suffragette, Kate Manicom, speaking for the Workers' Union. Robert McClung promised that socialism could 'win for the workers an ever-increasing share of the profits accruing from their combined labour until the present system which gives control of industry to those who live upon rent, interest and profits was abolished'. McClung 'hoped the day was not distant in Ireland that labour would come into its own':

> In the past labour was paid with mere pittance, gathering up the crumbs from the rich man's table, but he hoped that in the future they would get up off their knees as working people, and live the life that God intended that they should live . . . they intended to show to the country that if they stood shoulder to shoulder together that ultimately they would take over this whole wealth that they produced.

Dawson Gordon commented on how 'the mill workers of that district were the lowest paid of any mill workers he knew'. Responding to Unionist taunts about the green-and-gold banner of the Flax Roughers' Union, Gordon told them the banner had 'floated at demonstrations in Belfast long before the Sinn Fein movement was started'.[94] This referred to efforts by the Ulster Unionist Labour Association (UULA) to frustrate the celebrations, and alluded to heckling among sections of the crowd. Similarly, in Derry, the UULA issued a public statement urging Protestant workers, male and female, not to take part, as the demonstration was 'of a revolutionary and Bolshevik nature and supported by Sinn Fein propagandists'.[95]

Gordon nevertheless continued that 'the object of that demonstration was to break down the barriers separating Protestants and Catholics, so that they would all realise that they were workers and that they must organise, if they were to improve their state of life'. He concluded by asking: 'Why should they as workers live in the hovels they had lived in in the past? It was up to them to sweep these things away, and make Ireland a place worth living in, and they had the matter in their own hands.' Sam Kyle claimed that those present were neither 'Bolshevists [nor] Sinn Féiners. They were there as workers and labourers first and last. Some people said that the demonstration was organised as a Sinn Féin demonstration, but he denied that was so as they stood as workers and workers alone'. Kyle then claimed that they

> wanted to make this world a place fit for heroes, and safe for democracy. What had the governing classes offered those of them who offered their services in the late war? An unemployment dole (Laughter). They of the working class never brought on war, as they were always against it. The war was brought on by twenty men in Europe, and the actions of these twenty men brought misery into twenty million homes. If the working class could get control of industry, they would be able to live to develop their faculties and bring up their children in the proper way . . . there was no other movement that could emancipate the workers.[96]

Peak and Retreat

When women soap-wrappers at Brown's walked out in May 1919 to protest non-unionised workers, the entire Workers' Union in the village went out on sympathetic strike. Again, several Protestant workers struck, but Brown called in Turkington's UWU to act as blacklegs, and a bitter conflict ensued between the Workers' Union strikers and loyalist scabs.[97] The factory manager told the local union organiser, Neal O'Donnell, that, this time, he was 'prepared for any trouble which may arise', and that he refused to 'discuss the question with an official of the [Workers'] Union or any outsider', subsequently telling the workers themselves to 'go to the devil!' O'Donnell claimed that several Protestants including Stewart, whom the company refused to reinstate, had gone on strike, the employer merely playing 'the old game to get the workers divided', but that 'fortunately the last trump card is played in that game and the workers will not allow themselves to be deceived by such tactics'.[98] In fact, the employment of UWU scabs and the decision to move sections of the concern to Belfast and England eventually broke the strike.[99]

In May 1919 the RIC Tyrone county inspector noted continued serious 'unrest' among the labouring class, and 'rumours of a strike of agricultural labourers'. The Trades Councils then looked to flex their muscle in Strabane and Omagh. Across the trades, and even among the towns' labourers, sustained strike action took place for a living wage. By May there were strikes at the council quarry at Carrickmore and among builders in Omagh. James McGinn of the Omagh Bricklayers and Masons' Union stood trial on a charge of intimidating a blackleg.[100] John Welsh Leebody, the county surveyor, dismissed the five union leaders from the County Council–run Carrickmore Quarry, forcing the remaining twenty men out. Nationalist district councillors alleged that Leebody 'victimised four or five men on the strength of some private information he had received' that 'they were leaders of the union'. Leebody retorted that he 'did not know about a labour organisation having interfered until the output per man had reduced', and he dismissed the men for underperformance.[101] Arthur McNally, the branch secretary of the Labourers' Union at the quarry, wrote to the local pro-Sinn Féin, *Ulster Herald*, asking 'how Mr Leebody will do the whole work himself and fight trade unionism at the same time'.[102] While several strikers emigrated to England, others remained on strike until 3 November, when they returned to work.

After the strikers' return, Leebody provoked another dispute, causing workers to walk out again without warning.[103] The Sinn Féin-led Omagh RDC backed the strikers, though nationalist councillor John Donnelly admitted fearing the Labour Union as much as any of his fellow farmers. Unionist MP William Coote could not believe that nationalist councillors 'really came there to support this sort of Bolshevism which was going on all over the country'.[104] In 1924, the gerrymandered Unionist county council rewarded Leebody with a £1,000 salary as surveyor, plus a £140 car allowance.[105] Coote, meanwhile, expressed outrage when Omagh Asylum workers won a pay raise in April 1919. When they sought another the next year, he warned, 'We don't like a pistol put to our heads.'[106] Having already played a key role in the Caledon Lockout, Coote later urged the council to 'put down their foot and say that . . . they did not want to be trampled on and if there was a strike, they should say that not one of these people would come back'.[107]

Antipathy to labour did not remain the preserve of Unionists, however, although they provided the most consistent and formidable opposition. By the end of 1919, early working-class solidarity had dissipated, partly due to a general post-war slump, especially in linen, which fuelled competition for scarce employment. In addition, the demands of labour stirred opposition within the nationalist middle class. Indeed, as Michael Laffan argues, 'While Sinn Féin would not tolerate injustice or oppression, neither would it associate itself with class war.'[108] However, in June 1919 Sinn Féin commissioned a report from William Forbes Patterson to investigate new avenues for republicanism in Ulster. Patterson suggested the party emphasise the Dáil's 'progressive' and 'radical' Democratic Programme, 'to weld labour interests and Irish nationalism together'.[109] The underground government in Dublin and its local acolytes ignored his recommendations.

This position had been clear since 1919. In October, Omagh painters received a substantial increase, but workers' audacity fuelled resentment among the pro-Sinn Féin press and their commercial allies.[110] When workers at Donnelly's in Omagh struck for better pay and a closed shop, the owners called in receivers to 'collect all accounts due to us', in a bid to break sympathy for the strike in the town. The *Ulster Herald* printed the firm's response, which claimed that 'the organisers of the strike evidently thought that as none of the proprietors of the business were in a position to give their time to it, it would be an easy victim to the Larkinite methods which they adopted, but in this case, they were mistaken'. The resulting editorial appeared 'confident that the people of Omagh and district have no sympathy with Larkinism, they will not tolerate it, and those who are unfortunate enough to find themselves out of employment as a result of the adoption of such tactics have only themselves to blame'. The paper criticised the union for breaking a 'written or even oral agreement with employers', which it 'condemned as immoral and inimical to the public welfare'.[111]

In short, Tyrone's Sinn Féin leadership reflected the same petit bourgeois antipathy to socialism as the party's national elite, epitomised by Arthur Griffith, who had sided with big business during the Dublin Lockout. When nationalists temporarily gained control of Tyrone County Council in June 1920, support for strikes evaporated. For example, in July, Omagh bin men, or 'scavengers', failed to secure better conditions.[112] The nationalist council also defeated the strike at Omagh asylum in December 1920, despite previously having poured invective on Coote for opposing the workers' demands.[113] The leading Sinn Féin politician and lifelong associate of Kevin O'Shiel, George Murnaghan, 'took an active part in resisting demands for increased wages by the Asylum Attendants Union'. Interestingly, after the failed strike, 'Murnaghan's son was appointed inspector of machinery at the asylum displacing a [union] man named Rafferty'.[114]

When the conservative elements within Sinn Féin eventually established the Free State, after the Anglo-Irish Treaty and the prosecution of a brutal civil war, Kevin O'Shiel acted as the provisional government's legal secretary. Indeed, in December 1921 Michael Collins and Arthur Griffith invited seven men to join the Constitutional Committee to craft the 1922 Constitution, including Murnaghan and O'Shiel. The group excluded republicans, women and trade unionists. During the civil war, O'Shiel infamously told the prime minister, W. T. Cosgrave, to avoid legal niceties, because 'if we are to function as a Government, if the foundations of the State are to endure, we will have to clear up Irregularism [the IRA] at all costs within a very short time'. At the same time, he identified the trade-union movement and Labour Party as 'our most formidable opponent', arguing that 'one day of parliament may be more damaging to us than months of warfare', and that '[t]he advantages of the censorship would be largely undone, as all kinds of questions got out to our prejudice'. As Claire Fitzpatrick rightly concludes, the O'Shiel memorandum underlines 'the unease such "unenthusiastic democrats"' had about parliamentary democracy.[115] It also confirmed their deeply ingrained contempt for working people.

In *On the Condition of the Working Class in England*, Engels recorded the diverse ways in which workers face their situation. Some succumb to it, allowing themselves to be demoralised. Others passively give in to their fate and conform as best they can as respectable, law-abiding citizens, taking no interest in public affairs, and thus helping to tighten their chains. But real humanity and dignity are to be found only in the struggle which the workers' conditions inevitably produce. Rather than meekly resign themselves to their fate or supinely genuflect before their social superiors, be they landlord, grazier, factory manager, parson or priest, many working people have deeply resented and consciously challenged their subordinate social position.

Courtesy of the deputy keeper of the records, Public Record Office of Northern Ireland (D1295/22/101)

Northern Ireland's first cabinet. Front row: Lord Londonderry, Lord Craigavon, J. Milne Barbour, J. M. Andrews. Back row (left): E. M. Archdale. Associated with them (back row, left to right): Col. Spender, M. T. Moles, and Capt. Charles Craig.

When the opportunity arose in Ireland, as across Europe, in the latter stages and immediate aftermath of the First World War, this resentment found full expression in a cathartic cacophony. As O'Connor rightly suggests, 'one cannot understand the illegality and violence that obtained during these years without appreciating the depth of hostility to property and capital that grew up in the later war years'. A hostility manifested in 'an irrational will for justice [that] defied economic rationale'.[116] Under these conditions, the labour movement offered 'an alternative to the bourgeois state, in terms of the Co-operative Commonwealth or the Workers' Republic'; but, rather than being a leadership initiative, this militancy was 'due primarily to the upsurge of social revolutionary impulses that paralleled the rise of republicanism'.[117]

The immediate post-war period produced particularly favourable conditions for labour insurgency in Tyrone. The Caledon Lockout took place after a year of successful local working-class struggle (see Chapter 5).[118] The previous social peace marking local labour relations masked deep resentment among workers. While the motive for militancy appeared constant, the economic boom and a revolutionary atmosphere, both at home and abroad, presented workers with the crucial means and opportunity. Peadar O'Donnell's ability to attract workers in Caledon rested on successful ITGWU activism. Likewise, Minnie Duddy and Dawson Gordon's similarly successful efforts to gain union recognition and pay increases for female workers at opposite ends of the county showed that, under favourable circumstances and growing confidence, militancy could develop. Across Tyrone, central organisers – whether Belfast Labour Party socialists through the Workers' Union, republican socialists like O'Donnell in the ITGWU or union officials linked to Derry – harnessed genuine popular militancy, in which thousands of workers sensed the opportunity for advancement, rupturing the thin veneer of rural class harmony.

Nonetheless, all this energy and hope for a better future produced few if any positive results. Peter Hart has argued that 'there was no socially revolutionary situation in Ireland even in prospect'.[119] Fergus Campbell counters that 'the revolution in Ireland resulted in the creation of a conservative state, but not all Irish revolutionaries were conservative', and that 'there were radical impulses' which 'demonstrate that the revolution was neither innately or inevitably conservative'.[120] The Sinn Féin leadership's social conservatism was not universal. While its separatist demand captured the Catholic, working-class imagination, the Central Executive, and then the Dáil Ministry, dealt exclusively, throughout the revolutionary period, with its middle-class counterparts in Omagh. Nonetheless, many within the working class, who held a long-term republican commitment, entertained a vastly different conception of the revolution. A clear left-wing republican constituency existed and survived in East Tyrone. In Coalisland, local republicans had supported trade unionism since the 1890s, particularly at the Roan Linen spinning mill and Congo colliery. The town experienced militant strikes in 1918. When other northern workers ignored the Trade Union Congress's anti-conscription 'workless day' in 1918, Coalisland 'shut down'.[121] As late as February 1920, a strike at Stevenson's yard proved that workers still demanded fairer wages.[122] The IRB cell in Old Engine contained mostly former miners and workers at the local brickyard, all of whom joined the ITGWU, and will appear in the final chapter.

Clearly, Labour's ultimate failure rested partly on the movement's heterogeneous character. While O'Donnell, through the ITGWU and the Belfast Labour Party, preached socialism, the western trade councils appeared content with the moderation of the general labour leadership

Belfast Spinners. In a crowded factory, mostly female 'Millies' face the camera at Blackstaff Mill, Belfast, ca. 1918

– as O'Connor points out, 'for many union leaders, the dream of industrial unionism had already come true'.[123] Less generously, the Irish Labour Party leadership acquiesced in the Sinn Féin demand of freedom first, socialism second, which left them easy prey to a counter-revolutionary assault after the Anglo-Irish Treaty.[124] Nonetheless, despite labour's internal divisions, or indeed Sinn Féin's reluctance to fulfil the promise of the Democratic Programme, the defeat of the working-class movement in Tyrone relied primarily on the agency of Ulster Unionism under deteriorating economic conditions.

Like a Roman candle, this intense period of activism and solidarity briefly electrified local politics before quickly burning out, leaving only the faintest trace. The 1920 shipyard expulsions effectively meant that 'a new loyalist industrial order was created after 21 July, premised on a purging of the trade-union leadership'.[125] The Unionist business and political class had already adopted this policy in microcosm at Brown's in Donaghmore, and most notably at Fulton's in Caledon (see Chapter 5). Furthermore, in a depressed labour market, the later Unionist seizure of local government patronage and the prospect of employment in the

Ulster Special Constabulary shattered the political and economic basis of working-class solidarity. The 'slatterns and down and outs and good for naughts' were once again consigned to a precarious existence in squalid lanes reeking with foul smells, whether among the dreary steeples of Tyrone, the looming tenements of industrial Britain or the sprawling human masses of North America's eastern seaboard.

5
The Caledon Lockout

Gradually the Union Jacks gave way,
and the red flags took their place.

Peadar O'Donnell

For those of a certain generation, Caledon will forever be associated with the Irish Civil Rights movement. The scene of the famous 1968 squat that led to the first Northern Ireland Civil Rights Association march, from Coalisland to Dungannon, for some the village's very topography physically expressed the gulf between Planter and Gael. An anthropological study conducted during the Troubles described how the neat terraces and clean streets aroused local Unionist pride in Ulster's industrial past and the virtues of an open bible, particularly in contrast to Catholic sloth and backwardness. Indeed, local nationalists advised the American author to avoid the village, warning that it was a 'black hole' full of 'bitter' people, where 'No Catholic would ever be allowed to live.'[1] *Sic semper erat, et sic semper erit* among Churchill's notoriously 'dreary steeples of Fermanagh and Tyrone'.[2] Indeed, over a century ago, the nationalist *Freeman's Journal* dismissively reported that, in Caledon, 'no dog barks unless to the tune of Dolly's Brae'.[3]

Yet, for ten weeks in 1919, Catholic and Protestant workers in the local woollen mill marched the village's well-kept streets to a very different tune. Peadar O'Donnell vividly described how, 'In South Tyrone, in a town where the majority of workers are Protestant, we have a mighty

Red Flag procession – "No Surrender" emblazoned on one side of the flag, "Up the Irish Transport" on the other. The flag that thus can unite our Irish workers is the flag we want'.[4]

The 1919 Caledon Lockout ended in the workers' defeat, but the incident sheds new light on three critical aspects of the Irish revolution. Most fundamentally, it challenges the deeply entrenched consensus on the immutability of sectarian antagonism in Ulster. Secondly, it calls into question the accuracy of the widely held interpretation that 'there was no socially revolutionary situation in Ireland even in prospect'.[5] And, thirdly, it directly contradicts the argument, regarding the defeat of anti-sectarian labour, that while 'the local bourgeoisie were happy to see trade unions weakened and the left attacked . . . [this] occurred because of developments over which they had little or no influence'.[6]

A Quiet Village Ignites: The Caledon Lockout

Caledon nestles on the edge of the Blackwater Valley, Armagh, Dungannon and Monaghan towns lying around ten miles to its east, north and south, respectively. Glasslough and the border sit only five miles to the south. The second earl of Caledon, Du Pre Alexander, commissioned most of the town's neat limestone terraces during the third decade of the nineteenth century. The six-storey flourmill operated from 1823 to 1879, before Sherrand Smith & Co. recommissioned it for wool in 1882. John Fulton owned the mill from 1902 until its liquidation in 1930.[7] In 1910, 614 people lived in Caledon.[8] A year later, the census recorded 164 residents in the Caledon District Electoral Division as working in some branch of woollen manufacture, the majority residing in two terraced rows adjacent to the mill itself. By the time of the lockout, in early 1919, and as result of significant orders for army blankets, the mill employed 220.[9] While the Big House also loomed large, with many working on the demesne, Fulton's dominated the local economy. This sleepy village hardly appeared a likely setting for violent confrontation between capital and labour.

Nevertheless, in 1919 this normally quiet part of rural Tyrone witnessed significant labour militancy. Firstly, the year of impressive and mostly successful working-class struggles had culminated in this confrontation (see Chapter 4). The social peace that marked local labour relations during wartime apparently masked deep and gathering resentment among workers. The pent-up frustration seems to have exploded in the context of an economic upturn by the war's end, while grievances both fed into and drew strength from a revolutionary mood that swept not only Ireland and Britain, but much of post-war Europe. With equal measures of self-pity, envy and class condescension, the Royal Irish Constabulary (RIC) county inspector for Tyrone lamented that the labouring class had an 'abundance of money. The people who are really suffering are the respectable middle class who have small, fixed incomes derived from investments or who are in government employ.'[10] Caledon constituted the peak of a wave of local trade-union militancy – though the leading role played by the Irish Transport and General Workers' Union (ITGWU) marked it as distinctive.

I have already noted how the Workers' Union had effectively 'cornered the market' in neighbouring Armagh and Dungannon.[11] Indeed, this activist hub emerged from '[James] Connolly's conversion of Belfast socialists from William Walker's pro-Union labourism to anti-partitionism.'[12] For example, John Hanna, the leading Belfast Labour Party member and future leader of expelled workers in Belfast, appeared on the ITGWU platform at Caledon.[13] The ITGWU's foray into Tyrone also emerged in the context of growing resistance from employers to the demands of unskilled workers. In short, while Peadar O'Donnell and ITGWU involvement marked Caledon out somewhat, it still fitted into a pattern of anti-sectarian, and ultimately anti-partitionist, mobilisation in the area. Indeed, the mill initially formed a branch of the Workers' Union, before 'Monaghan Pete' convinced local workers to switch to the ITGWU and the Flax Roughers' sent strike funds to the striking workers at the height of the dispute.[14]

The Caledon strike also took place at a crucial juncture in Ulster politics – in the immediate aftermath of a general strike in Belfast, which involved 'about 60,000 hands and [was] seriously affecting the citizens.'[15] The Orange grand master and local landlord, James Stronge, who helped facilitate the defeat of the workers at Caledon, admitted in early February: 'no one has time to consider the Irish question being fully occupied with labour questions.'[16] Events in Belfast over the next two years significantly influenced labour relations in Caledon; but, equally, the reactionary means by which the employer and the local Unionist establishment defeated the workers at Fulton's mill acted as a premonition of violence on a much larger scale in Belfast itself.

In response to the threat from independent labour, official Unionism promoted the Ulster Unionist Labour Association (UULA), which would contribute to the defeat of the Caledon strike and spearhead the reactionary clampdown on labour that followed in Belfast. As early as October 1918, Richard Dawson Bates warned Carson of the threat from independent labour.[17] Ulster Unionism's promotion of the UULA partly represented a response to the Representation of the People Act, which the South Tyrone Unionist MP William Coote described privately as 'a most dangerous franchise bill'.[18] Carson, the UULA's first president, told members that 'revolutions go on whether you like it or not. It is idle for anyone to suggest that the war has not brought about a great revolution'. Accordingly, the UULA acted as a bulwark against those 'trying to set labour against capital and capital against labour'.[19]

Bates represented the spider at the centre of the Unionist web, the 'master mechanic' of the political 'machine' located in Belfast's Old Town Hall, who 'had all the threads of a complex network of organisation in his hands [and] always knew what was going on in out-of-the-way corners, and where to turn for the right man for any particular piece of work'.[20] James A. Turkington, vice-chairman of the UULA and secretary of the Ulster Workers' Union (UWU) represented the 'right man' in the Caledon case. When the employer, Fulton, sought assistance through the Orange Order and Bates, Turkington, the Unionist cat's paw within the UULA, duly sent the UWU, a yellow union employed to break working-class solidarity and provide scabs for Orange employers across rural Ulster, to break the Caledon strike, in which it was successful.[21] The *Freeman's Journal* neatly captured the relationship between the Unionist leadership and UULA in a hostile piece that autumn:

> The Covenanters are at best a tiny minority amongst Irish workers, and the men who pull the Carsonite strings are much more anxious to keep Labour the underdog in Ulster than they are to give even the shadow of political authority to Orange workers unless they can be trusted to pull the capitalist chestnuts out of the fire regardless of their own interest as trade unionists.[22]

The Lockout

In his annual report for 1918, the county inspector in Tyrone labelled the Caledon dispute a 'Sinn Fein' strike.[23] The following year, he reported that the employer had defeated the six-week dispute after a 'strenuous fight'.[24] However, the Sinn Féin label 'tended to reveal almost as much about the writer as about the subject'.[25] The strike actually emerged from advice given to the workers by the prominent socialist republican, Peadar O'Donnell, who had recently led the successful campaign of the Monaghan Asylum 'soviet'. Indeed, success there represented 'the deciding factor in [the local community] opting for the ITGWU' over the more established Worker's Union.[26]

By the time O'Donnell left Liberty Hall as the provincial ITGWU organiser, in October 1918, the National Amalgamated Union of Labour (NAUL) and Workers' Unions had already organised thousands of rural unskilled workers. Undaunted, O'Donnell 'blazed a trail of glory clean across Ulster' and, by February 1919, had been involved in forty-eight wage movements and three strikes.[27] In Monaghan, the strikers constituted the 'first of many groups of workers to self-consciously adopt the name of "soviet" during their strike'. O'Donnell intervened there after employers reneged on a pay rise won in March 1918. Having seized the asylum, barricaded all entrances and elected O'Donnell governor, a hundred workers hoisted the red flag in defiance of the police force surrounding the asylum.[28]

The strike succeeded in reducing the working week from ninety-three to fifty-six hours, permitting married workers to reside at home and securing pay parity for women. The ITGWU – with O'Donnell at its head – supplanted the Workers' Union in Monaghan Town, both the secretary and membership switching unions. Impressed with these results, local Orangeman Willie Hare encouraged O'Donnell to intervene in a wage dispute at Caledon Mill.[29] The 1911 census records Hare's father, Robert (a woollen cloth finisher), living on the main street.[30] O'Donnell's ability to attract workers therefore rested on successful activism. The demand for organisation did not emerge from outside agitators or union officials, but from local workers themselves. Central organisers – whether Belfast Labour Party socialists through the Workers' Union or republican socialists like O'Donnell in the ITGWU – made hay when thousands of workers sensed the opportunity for genuine advancement.

Many years later, O'Donnell remembered the strike as a great mistake. His introduction to the village did not augur well: in the enthusiasm at his arrival, a throng of workers knocked O'Donnell unconscious as he disembarked at the Clogher Valley Railway platform. When he came to his senses in the Charlemont Arms Hotel, Armagh, O'Donnell reluctantly agreed to return to Caledon. Under the same tree where Wesley had preached on three occasions in the eighteenth century, O'Donnell proselytised in the cause of socialism. The class divisions in the village provided grounds for initial optimism:

> There was a tree with a big veranda of cement around it. (They couldn't take a hall) . . . There were men in that town that sold tea and bread and butter and sugar and tobacco, flour and whiskey, and men who sold cloth, who all lived on a fairly decent level. There were other fellows who only had their sweat to sell, and they did not seem to sell it as well as the others. They were the ones that I wanted to organise and make demands on. When I felt I had a good grip of my audience, I said 'I'm going to tell you a good one. I'm the man you knocked the devil out of last night!' . . . Then I stepped down from the tree, somebody produced a table and a couple of chairs, and we began taking down names[.] We formed a big branch of the Transport Union.[31]

O'Donnell addressed the meeting on 14 January at the big tree, the proceedings illuminated only by bicycle lamps.[32] The RIC reported that 200 members joined the ITGWU in the days following O'Donnell's meeting, adding that the 'workmen believe and apparently on good grounds that they can get any terms they demand by going on strike and naturally they do so'.[33] The local ITGWU secretary, James McMenemy, described the low pay 'until the Union was being felt', with workers gaining an increase of 14s. The winders then also got an increase of 6d in every shilling earned, and the weavers received about 3s increase, the former's average wage prior to that being about 16s to 18s and the latter's, including war bonuses, about 25s a week.[34] Similarly, management moved the starting time from half-past six to eight o'clock in the morning 'without demand'. 'The organiser's work of showing the benefits of the union . . . thus made easy', the workers 'did not thank the employers for the better terms then, they thanked the union', which the workers 'looked upon as deliverers of the people'.[35] To this point, the workers had nearly doubled their pay without strike action, but the employer appeared intent on breaking the union.

Management then dismissed two Catholic brothers – prominent union men – the Goans, allegedly 'to make room for two discharged soldiers who had fought in the war'.[36] The *Voice of Labour* claimed that Fulton had 'scrapped union live wires and . . . dared the organiser to make the other men follow him'.[37] On 20 February, O'Donnell held 'an open air meeting' in which he 'put the matter before them from the workers' point of view'.[38] Since foremen had used 'threats of dismissal' to persuade workers to desert the ITGWU, O'Donnell urged them to 'demand that all . . . in the mill be compelled to join the union [or] refuse to work with non-union members'.[39]

The following day, workers struck and picketed the mill, which generated 'frequent clashes with the police and scabs', O'Donnell twice becoming 'the victim of beatings'.[40] The RIC did not discriminate with their batons, the *Voice of Labour* reported: 'whether its owners be orange, green or tricolour, a skull must be cracked if it impede the capitalists' progress'. Despite the repression, 'prospects [appeared] bright for a clean win through by the strikers'.[41] The Unionist *Belfast Newsletter* recorded how extra police billeted the town to guard non-striking workers:

> During the past few weeks several open-air meetings have been addressed by officials of the union, and feelings have been much embittered amongst the employees. Matters reached a climax at breakfast hour on Friday, when about one hundred and fifty of the hands ceased work. The mills continued to work with about fifty hands, and on Friday evening the attitude . . . towards these became so hostile that a number of police, under District-Inspector Bain, Aughnacloy, were drafted into the town to preserve order and protect the employees who remained at work. The strikers paraded the town on Friday and Saturday nights, headed by a band and torchlights.[42]

After the RIC openly sided with the employer, 'O'Donnell enrolled a citizen police force to protect his pickets, and then astonished the mill owner by hiring the Orange band for his demonstration'.[43] The RIC inaccurately reported that, by the first week of March, 'about 220 workers in the Woollen Mill there went out while about 60 remained', while District Inspector Bain 'and 60 additional men [were] there on duty and their presence is still required'. Fulton then shut the mill – the Caledon Lockout had commenced.[44]

The following week, 'the local band greeted Peadar O'Donnell with a red flag emblazoned, "Up the Transport!" Besides leading the strike of 156 textile operatives, O'Donnell figures in incidental roles such as fire-fighting captain, chief of police etc. Workers of all political hues stand solidly together. Orange and Green will carry the day.'[45] O'Donnell recounted how he 'paraded the streets of that town, Caledon, for six weeks'. Authorities soon learned, to their consternation,

> that we had the Lambeg drum on our side. We had a man called Willy Harlock [i.e., Hurlock], and I remember him making a speech. He said, 'I am an Orangeman, and I'm a Black Man' (We cheered him like a parish priest), 'and an Apprentice Boy from Derry!' (and that was almost as good as a vision). I [O'Donnell] paraded behind the Union Jack to the tune of 'The Boyne Water' and 'Derry's Walls'. Gradually the Union Jacks gave way, and the red flags took their place.[46]

The contemporary record suggests that O'Donnell mobilised genuine enthusiasm for the strike, and that working-class Orangemen clearly identified with the cause emblazoning the ITGWU's banner with 'No Surrender' on one side and 'Up the Irish Transport' on the other. O'Donnell proclaimed that 'the flag that thus can unite our Irish workers is the flag we want', admonishing his comrades in Dublin somewhat by concluding: 'Don't let the hoisting of it in strikes be left so much to me!'[47] The torchlight processions of Caledon made the Dublin press.[48] Nevertheless, news of the strike would also soon echo in the Palace of Westminster, signalling an Orange counterattack. O'Donnell retrospectively recounted that, after 'the Ulster Unionist [Labour] Association got the big drums and the full forces of reaction out against me . . . quite a number of the workers seceded from the union'.[49]

The Caledon Counterattack

In Westminster on St Patrick's Day, William Coote portrayed the strike as an attempt to oust Protestant workers. Ironically, Coote employed an exclusively Protestant workforce at his own woollen mill at Lisdoart, twelve miles west of Caledon.[50] He asked Ian Macpherson (chief secretary of Ireland, January 1919 – April 1920) about how the ITGWU, 'a Sinn Fein organisation', had recruited 'the majority of workers . . . of the same political faith', who then commenced 'to beat with hurleys and sticks and otherwise abuse the fifty-three workers who remained'. Shockingly, Coote asserted that the police refused to intervene when 'women workers were beaten' and 'local shopkeepers [were] threatened if they should supply food to these fifty-three workers'. The chief secretary replied that strikers did not have 'hurleys', the strike resulted from the dismissal of union members, and the approach to shopkeepers had involved no intimidation.[51]

Coincidently, the following day, after four weeks and with 130 workers still on strike, Fulton introduced UWU 'blacklegs', and began readmitting strikers on a sectarian basis.[52] This initiative was directed by UULA vice-chairman, James Turkington, who in 1920 would be denounced as the 'emancipator of the Caledon blacklegs' when he had the 'audacity' to stand as a 'Labour' candidate in the municipal elections.[53] Denis Houston told the Belfast Trades Council that the UULA under Turkington had organised scabs, and that 'the names of men desiring employment at the mill must first be submitted to the local Orange Lodge' before they would be given work.[54] The UULA repudiated Houston's allegation, concluding that they had 'no connection, either direct or indirect, with any trade union or labour organisation'; but the symbiotic relationship between the UWU and UULA rendered the claim unsustainable. The Caledon pattern repeated itself across Ulster, *mutatis mutandis*, at Ballymena, Banbridge, Portadown, Lurgan and Donaghmore, where a brief flowering of anti-sectarian, working-class politics lay smashed between the hammer of loyalist violence and the anvil of economic depression.[55]

O'Donnell detailed UWU tactics in the *Voice of Labour*: 'fibs for the Ministry of Labour, free beer for the scabs, and five pounds for each striker who reneges on the union, are amongst the dope handed out by the mill management, but with as little success as previously had the bobbie's batons'.[56] Nevertheless, by early April, the county inspector reported that, while 'the strike at Caledon Mills continue[d]' there were 'signs that it [was] approaching an end'.[57] Indeed, by the month's end, the ITGWU had issued 'an urgent appeal . . . to weigh in with red gold . . . for Caledon's strikers dependants', ominously concluding: '*The need is urgent* – that should be enough!'[58] In the first week of May, the ITGWU called off the strike and attempted to paint a more positive version of events than the reality suggested:

> The strike at the woollen mills has come to an end after ten weeks of heroic struggle. The spirit of the workers is beyond all praise. The employers' utmost efforts to employ prejudice and religious bigotry against the union were unsuccessful. Proprietor Fulton would not even discuss the issue with the 'Papish' organisers, so the workers have sought and secured work elsewhere, leaving Fulton with his damaged trade and an incomplete staff to re-build it. The best of his operatives have refused to work for Fulton at any price.[59]

Coote, after having consistently alleged Catholic mistreatment of Protestants in the local press, gloated at the strikers' defeat. When O'Donnell challenged his allegations, pointing out that 'the local secretary of this union was an Orangeman', the South Tyrone MP provided an enlightening explanation immediately after the strike's collapse:

> This fact does not disprove my statement, but quite the contrary. I said, 'Sinn Fein was attempting through Ulster, by rear-guard subtle action, to do what it could not do by frontal attack *viz*, destroy Protestant industries and drive out Protestant workers from Ulster'. If in this enterprise they can detach a Protestant, or, better still, an Orangemen to their side, they are delighted. They use him for the time as a decoy, and they at once make him an official, to do their dirty work and then leave him as they left our Orange friend at Caledon, and as they left, after an eight weeks fight in which all the most abominable and savage practices were performed, their own Roman Catholic co-religionists, to starve in the streets or clear out, having withdrawn all funds for their support . . . May I also put right a sentence in my speech which, as reported, seemed to imply that the management of Caledon mills did not keep the places for returned soldiers which they held prior to enlistment for them on return. This is somewhat misleading – they not only kept these places but are offering positions to other demobilised men.[60]

At the same time the Orange Order, under Grand Master Sir James Stronge of Tynan, ostracised striking members. A meeting of the three local lodges 'stoutly repudiate[d] having any connection with the said Irish Transport Union . . . nor have we at any time or in any way, supported, either by our sympathy, or by subscriptions from our funds, those amongst the strikers who are, or have been, members of the Loyal Institution'.[61] From the perspective of the ITGWU, the imposition of yellow unionism and the Orange drum loomed large:

> The mill still continues to work. Those who refused to go on strike, those who left the strikers and returned to work, and those who went in as 'scab' workers, have formed a 'union' among themselves – a branch of the Ulster Workers' Union – and taken into their hands the power of employing workers in the mill. It is said that a vote is taken on each applicant in the Orange Lodge. Some Protestant families have applied for re-admission to work and been admitted; others who remained on strike all through the trouble prefer to leave the town and the country rather than abandon their Catholic fellow strikers. Some Catholics have applied, but have not been admitted, so that the only Catholic remaining in the mill is one who clung to the firm all through the strike.[62]

That summer Fulton organised a social gathering in the village for returning ex-servicemen: 'Caledon's double celebration: Overthrow of the Hun and Irish Bolshevists.' He thanked 'the local people who had come forward to take the place of the strikers [and] the outside sympathisers who gave their moral support'.[63] Fulton acknowledged the key role played by the local Ulster Unionist MP, the Orange Order and the UWU.

The Caledon controversy continued throughout May, when the ITGWU took both the Devlinite *Irish News* and the Unionist *Belfast Telegraph* to task for claiming they had 'betrayed the Caledon workers'.[64] It also challenged Coote for his manipulation of the strike in the East Antrim by-election on 28 May 1919, in which he repeated that the ITGWU 'drove Protestant non-union workers out of Caledon mills and displaced them by Papishes from Dublin and Donegal'. After calling Coote out as a 'liar', the *Voice of Labour* pointed to exemplary class consciousness and solidarity among Protestant workers in particular: the 'best and most militant trade unionists in Caledon were amongst the Orangemen', the *Voice* observed, and 'a master of an Orange Lodge presided' at ITGWU meetings.[65] Coote attacked the independent Unionist candidate in East Antrim, George Boyle Hanna, asking:

> Who were the fellows behind the Hannanites? (A Voice: Sinn Feiners!) Well, they would not see any Sinn Feiners about him if they came to South Tyrone. The Sinn Feiners were coming down to Ulster in ones and twos and threes and burrowing in among the Protestants [to] cause discontent and strikes . . . [H]aving done that they would soon see that every man who wore an Orange sash had to leave the country as part of the English garrison.[66]

While the victory of an independent Unionist in the East Antrim by-election hardly constituted a fatal blow to Carsonite hegemony, the East Antrim Unionist Association claimed that defeat had resulted from 'a combination between the Roman Catholics and extreme members of the Labour Party together with a considerable number of relatively moderate Protestants'.[67]

Ruth Russell had little doubt that 'this is the way labour killed Carsonism. I saw it done. I was in at the death. There was a parliamentary seat vacant in East Antrim. Carson, whose choice had hitherto been law, backed a Canadian named Major Moore.' From Russell's US perspective, 'Labour put up a sort of Bull Moose candidate named Hanna. The Carsonists realised the issue. During the campaign they reiterated that Carsonism was to live or die by that vote.' Russell then painted a vivid picture of how social issues impinged on tired Ulster Unionist catch-cries:

> One evening near a stuccoed golf club at a crossroads in Upper Green Isle, with the view of the Belfast Lough shining in the distance, I waited to hear Major Moore address a crowd of workers. As the buzzing little audience gathered, boys climbed up telegraph poles with the stickers 'We Want Hanna', and a small, pale-faced man with a protruding jaw was the centre of a political argument for Hanna. At last, the brake arrived. The major, a tall, personable man, stood up in the cart. But all the good old Ulster rallying cries he used, seemed to miss fire. 'Sir Edward Carson's for me' – 'Stand on your own feet, Major Muir', interrupted a worker . . . he went on: 'The Unionist party stands for improved social legislation' – 'What aboot [*sic*] old

age pensions?' and 'Why didn't the Unionist party vote for workingmen's compensation, Major Muir?' As he was preparing to drive away from the booing crowd, one of his supporters began to distribute dodgers. I had two in my hand when the small, pale-faced man with the jaw applied a match to them and cried out as they flared in my hand: 'That's what we do with trash.'[68]

Nevertheless, Caledon served as an early precedent for a sectarian and reactionary tendency that found full expression in the Belfast mass expulsions of 1920. That September, Fred Crawford, Ulster Volunteer Force (UVF) gunrunner and James Craig's paramilitary linkman, wrote in his diary that

> Jack Fulton showed me a letter . . . addressed to his mill manager, threatening him with death. The manager is going to take it to the R.C. Curate and tell him that if he is shot every R.C. in the village of Caledon . . . will be shot, and that the first man will be the Curate himself, who is the leader of the Sinn Feiners in the district. About two years ago when the war was on and most of the Protestant workmen were out fighting their places were filled by R.C. workmen. They tried to boycott the Protestant foremen and struck against them. The war by this time was nearing the end and the Fulton's closed the mill for a time. As soon as there was enough Protestants to run any department of it, they opened that department, but none of the strikers were taken back. When the Parish Priest saw that the game was up, he came whining for lenient treatment. He was told that he had come too late. So long as he thought there was a fair chance of persecuting a Protestant out of the village, he said nothing, but now when he saw his parishioners leaving and going to Scotland or elsewhere (naturally it was hitting him very hard) he came to ask for these men to be taken back again. If he had come when the strike began and told his people that their claims were unjust and unreasonable and had insisted on them going back to their work, then at some lenient treatment or concession, but he did not do so. This was put plainly to him, and when asked why he did not take that course, which he could have done – his people would have taken his advice, or, to put it more correctly, his commands – and pressed on the point he had nothing to say.[69]

The priest in question, Fr Booth of Aughnacloy, unsuccessfully petitioned the management for the return of Catholic workers after the strike's defeat, but played no part in the earlier proceedings.[70] In his own private account, Crawford conflated trade unionists and Sinn Féiners. Similarly, the claim that Catholics stole ex-servicemen's jobs and then intended to expel Unionists from the village mirrored Coote's base attempts to sow division at the time of the strike. Interestingly, these very same ingredients – Labour as Sinn Féin subterfuge; Catholics coveting the jobs of returning servicemen; apocalyptic warnings about the expulsion of Protestants – all featured prominently in the counter-revolution in Belfast the following year.

The claim that Catholics stole Protestant servicemen's jobs deserves further attention, because it justified subsequent loyalist actions across Ulster, and loomed large in the subsequent Belfast expulsions. Indeed, the wholly sectarian Ulster Ex-servicemen's Association played a vital role in loyalist direct action. Nowadays, great store is placed on the commemoration of Irish Catholics' and Protestants' shared sacrifice in the First World War. The reality of the post-war experience indicates that only loyalist enlistment counted. The Ulster example mirrored the experience of the European far right, particularly in fascist Italy, where 'these Rambos of their time' represented 'natural recruits for the radical Right'.[71] In the context of opposition to an emergent working-class consciousness, these war veterans were 'irretrievably lost to organised socialism and ill-disposed towards the commonplaces of the traditional parties'.[72] A similar outlook prevailed among Belfast's loyalist pogromists, who would join the Ulster Special Constabulary (USC) en masse in the autumn and winter of 1920.

The fact is that at Caledon – as in much of industrial Belfast – the size of the workforce had increased significantly during wartime to meet insatiable demand for war materiel.[73] After the strike's defeat, the ITGWU papers described how the 'Fulton-Stronge clique' dominated 'this sacred spot of injustice and sweating' for those who profited from 'miles of cloth and thousands of blankets'.[74] An analysis of the 1911 census identified 164 woollen mill workers in the Caledon District Electoral Division: seventy-two Catholics, twenty Presbyterians, three Methodists from the same family, and sixty-seven Anglicans. Although comprising a minority of the workforce, Catholics constituted the largest individual denomination in the mill. Within the village proper, 136 people worked in the mill, including fifty Catholics. Catholics did not steal Protestant jobs; they had always worked in the mill, which hired additional hands having 'obtained khaki orders'.[75]

Coote's attempt to correct his earlier comments from May indicates that the issue of ex-servicemen's jobs operated as camouflage for sectarian expulsion. Indeed, the Catholic Goan brothers – expelled for supporting the ITGWU – had both served in the military, while a third brother, James, died in September 1918 of wounds received while serving with the 2nd Battalion, Inniskilling Fusiliers.[76] While economic necessity dictated that many Protestant workers return to the new regime in Fulton's, there were others, 'Orangemen also, who because of their loyalty to their class and the Transport Union were forced to leave the country'.[77] One aged Protestant worker reportedly claimed that she would 'rather lick limewash off the walls and live on it than go back to work for Fulton'.[78] O'Donnell claimed that forty-seven Protestant workers took the train and went across to England. Later, while being held as an anti-Treaty IRA prisoner in Curragh Camp, he received 'greeting[s] from a group that met in a public house in Yorkshire of these people that went off'.[79]

At the beginning of June 1919, the RIC clearly identified a rump of around sixty strikers, allegedly 'loafing about Caledon in idleness'. Their 'temper towards the mill' was reported to be 'most dangerous', with the result that 'a police guard has had to be maintained on it, night and day'.[80] At this point, Fulton again intervened and expelled strikers and their families from houses rented from the company. The *Watchword of Labour* detailed the 'dirty game' in which Fulton evicted 'some of his strongest opponents'. 'Failing to drive them out of the country as the others were driven has led to even dirtier tricks' – all part of 'the modern machinery used in the crushing of human beings who had dared to seek their rights'.[81]

These included seventy-year-old Catholic Margaret Downey, whose son and son-in-law had fought in the war, and who lived five doors up Mill Street from her sixty-year-old Protestant neighbour Ellen McMenemy, the mother of James, the ITGWU secretary. Bernard Harvey, a Catholic member of the ITGWU, lived on the same street, and all are recorded in the 1911 census.[82] They took and won a case against Fulton for unfair eviction.[83] Nevertheless, three families that had lived and worked in the mill before the war suffered eviction in retaliation for their links to trade unionism. Indeed, the land valuation books for Mill Street indicate new tenants occupying most homes there in the years after the strike.[84] The case of the McMenemys made nonsense of Unionist accounts of the strike: James's brother, Thomas, who described conditions in the mill as 'scandalous', was a decorated soldier who had served two-and-half-years in France and suffered a gas attack:

> Here was a Protestant who served in the war with such distinction that he won the Military Medal and because he objected to work for 6s a week he is evicted, together with his mother. One does not wonder that McMenamy [*sic*] should tell the court he was sorry he threw himself in the way of some of the Germans getting over.[85]

The Caledon example suggests that the bourgeoisie, in concert with political Unionism (South Tyrone MP William Coote owned his own woollen mill), employed the UWU as a weapon to fracture working-class solidarity. This rested on economic coercion and blatant lies. The issue of servicemen's jobs furnished the loyalist backlash with ideological camouflage, but had little or no basis in fact. Indeed, the ex-servicemen who operated as scabs displaced their former comrades from employment at the behest of a local employer and a Unionist establishment bent on smashing trade-union and pan-sectarian unity in one fell swoop.

Having successfully subverted trade unionism at Caledon and elsewhere, Unionist employers pushed hard to have the UWU included in government arbitration boards to undermine the negotiating power of bona fide trade unions. In January 1920, the Flax Roughers, Power-loom Tenters, Portadown Textile Operatives, Flax Dressers, Yarn Dressers, Lurgan Winders' and Weavers' Union, Workers' Union, Textile Operatives, ITGWU and Women Workers' Union all objected to the inclusion of Turkington's yellow union on the proposed Trade Board for the preparing, spinning and weaving side of the linen trade. But Unionist bosses refused to participate unless the UWU sat on the opposite side of the table. The 'trade unions objected to the employers nominating any workers or alleged workers' representatives on the board', and contended, with good grounds, that Turkington's union 'was being used by the employers against the interests of the other trade unions'.[86] Rather than lions led by donkeys, donkeys led by liars might stand as a better description. Furthermore, loyalist direct action in Belfast the following year aped this very modus operandi. Ironically, this counter-revolution would then further pollute the social atmosphere in Caledon, leading to the sectarian expulsion of Catholics from the village.

Counter-revolution in Caledon

By 1922, the implications of the expulsion of 10,000 Catholics and rotten Prods from Belfast's industries and the pogromists' formation into the USC spilled onto Caledon's well-kept streets, where only three years earlier Catholic and Protestant workers had marched in solidarity under a red flag. In the period between the signing of the Anglo-Irish Treaty and the outbreak of the southern civil war, loyalist violence laid the foundations of the discriminatory Orange State.

While Michael Collins negotiated his first pact with James Craig at the end of January 1922, he simultaneously acquiesced to a joint IRA northern offensive if it failed. On 8 February 1922, less than a week after the pact broke down, the pro-Treaty IRA, crossing from the south, kidnapped over forty Unionists in Tyrone and Fermanagh to act as hostages against the campaign of sectarian assassination directed against Belfast's Catholics.[87] On 30 January, Eoin O'Duffy, now Free State chief of staff, told Collins that he had 'arranged the kidnapping of one hundred prominent Orangemen'. Alluding to local pressure over partition, he explained: 'there are 54 affiliated [Sinn Féin] clubs in Co Monaghan', which, if the necessary action were taken, should translate into '108 votes . . . for the Treaty'.[88] Events took a further twist after the fatal shooting of four 'A' Specials in Clones on 11 February, which provoked an 'inevitable sequel' in Belfast, where 'twenty-four persons, including six children' were killed and seventy wounded.[89] Two days later, two Special Constables from Caledon encountered heavy machine-gun fire near the Monaghan border.[90] The Monaghan IRA continued to snipe into Tyrone until June 1922. These incidents caused the death of Robert Scott, a Protestant civilian, and provoked the clearance of nationalist families from Caledon.[91]

On the day of the kidnappings, John Fulton wrote to Dawson Bates that 'possibly there will be serious reprisals in [Caledon and] district tonight, as, naturally, our people cannot, and will not, put up with actions of this kind from the other side . . . Have extra police drafted into this town without further delay, as those in responsible positions here cannot guarantee that the peace will be kept'.[92] The setting-up of the border commission (a three-way liaison between British, Free State and Unionist forces) appeared temporarily to dampen loyalist ardour. Nevertheless, by March, continued sniping at a border bridge and incidents in the loyalist village of Glasslough, Co. Monaghan, provoked a severe reaction.

On 10 March 1922, the *Irish Independent* reported that even 'Col. Bates of the Northern Commission [admitted] that the Unionist population were not being interfered with in the Free State and that the Irish Army had actually protected them'.[93] Nevertheless, James McKenna of the Free State Army remembered 'the pleasure it gave me to take over the police station' and Orange Hall in 'a Protestant stronghold' like Glasslough, which now housed a barracks of twenty Free State soldiers.[94] McKenna's men also allegedly harassed local UVF members and sniped at USC attempting to dismantle Ballagh Bridge. On 12 March, two 'northern sympathisers' from Glasslough fired into the house of Henry Maguire of Tynan, 'probably [in] reprisal for certain treatment by IRA Police'.[95] Two days later, in Caledon village, a bomb seriously injured three young Catholic men 'standing at a street corner after leaving Chapel'.[96] The next day, 'B' Specials shot a prominent local IRA volunteer John Garvey and his friend Patrick McPhillips as they returned home to Benburb.[97]

Events escalated further on 18 March, when armed 'B' Specials forcibly evicted five Catholic families from their homes in Caledon: 'At 5 p.m. lorries filled with armed men arrived, placed pickets outside, and proceeded to load the furniture onto the lorries. All five families are identified with Sinn Fein in some way and their eviction is thought to be a reprisal for the eviction of five Protestant families from their houses in Glasslough.' Without a hint of irony, the RUC claimed that 'if proceedings were instituted at present it would have the effect of increasing party bitterness'.[98] The border commission's British representative reported that 'in order to provide accommodation in Caledon for these refugees' from Glasslough, 'the civilian population there have compulsorily evicted . . . southern sympathisers'.[99] The RUC Inspector General, Charles Wickham, identified Johnston and Elliott from Glasslough as two prominent southern 'refugees', who used Free State soldiers' attendance at mass on 19 March as cover for their 'escape'. Wickham claimed that Caledon Unionists were

> prepared to be reasonable and to do nothing to embarrass the Government but they point out that the firing has been from the Free State side until it became intolerable and that the evictions of Unionists and the seizure of the Orange Hall at Glasslough, which practically is a Unionist village, are direct acts of provocation on the part of Sinn Feiners. They demand that action be taken to protect their co-religionists in Co. Monaghan or else that such treatment as is given to them should be given to the S.F. sympathisers on their side of the border.[100]

In fact, on 27 March the British border commissioner revealed that 'Elliot and Johnston who originally stated that they were evicted from Glasslough . . . now state they left Glasslough voluntarily through fear of remaining there.'[101] These men attacked Maguire's on 12 March. In May, Free State troops arrested Elliot at his job in Glasslough, the northern border commission noting that they 'appear[ed] to have good cause', as Elliot was 'the leader of a gang which caused considerable trouble in Caledon about two months ago, in connection with the attempted eviction of Roman Catholic families'.[102] Their arrival in Caledon, combined with the circulation of false rumours, sparked the clearance of numerous Catholic families. Some clearly represented Sinn Féin sympathisers, and in one a case an IRA volunteer, James Doran.[103] On 29 March, loyalists forcibly evicted James McGrann, 'a Sinn Fein sympathiser'.[104] However, Patrick Campbell also received a letter to 'get out, signed Red Hand of Ulster' – although the RUC admitted: 'he is not an IRA man'. On the same date, an armed gang visited Joseph Kerr's in Benburb, inquired for his sons, and left, firing several shots.[105]

On 27 March, the Unionist representative to the border commission reported that 'B' men had fired into the south, noting that 'some of them are hot headed and determined to take the law into their own hands. In the opinion of the commission the leadership of the "B" Class Special Constabulary in Caledon has got into the wrong hands.'[106] On 22 March, John Fulton again wrote to Bates: 'a great number of [Caledon's residents] have approached me, with a view to requesting the Northern Parliament to take immediate steps to put an end to the state of terrorism prevailing at present'. Loyalist farmers remained, 'unable to get on with the putting in of their crop, and attending to their daily duties, owing to the intense fire, which is kept up on them as soon as they appear anywhere in the open'. Fulton then provided the normal proviso:

> unless something is done without further delay, a very serious state of affairs may arise, as the people cannot stand this long, and will not be responsible for their actions to local Sinn Feiners or Roman Catholics. I assure you we, who are responsible, are using our best endeavour to have the peace kept, but things have got now to almost breaking point . . . they may blaze up at any moment.[107]

In fact, intense loyalist violence had gripped Caledon for the previous fortnight, while even the USC Commandant John Knox McClintock admitted: the 'only place where Unionists can't work is Ballagh Bridge'.[108] Dr Con Ward of the southern border commission confirmed that the sniping would cease 'provided the Northern Authorities would guarantee not to demolish the bridge'.[109]

At the beginning of April, 'a "B" Special in Caledon whose name cannot be obtained' expelled the Catholic station master at Tynan. On 4 April, loyalists set fire to several 'nationalist houses', as well as the home of Henry Sherry, who was 'forced to leave for the Free State some time ago'.[110] On 18 April, 'B' Specials killed Frank Riley of Rahoney, 'when returning with others from cockfight at Glasslough Co Monaghan'. Although the driver, Patrick Maguire, had links to Sinn Féin, the other two passengers, William Moore and William Irvine, were Protestant labourers.[111] Wickham told Bates that it was 'most important that Mr Fulton and other leading residents in the Clogher Valley should use their influence to restrain the B men from premature or inadvised [*sic*] action'.[112] As a result, the earl of Caledon held a conciliation meeting in the village to encourage restraint.[113] This apparently fits Bew's thesis that a liberal unionist leadership became prisoners to grassroots extremism.[114] Nevertheless, the example of Caledon's most 'responsible' citizen, John Fulton, presents a somewhat different picture; rather than being prisoner of recalcitrant loyalists, he unleashed animosity to secure his own interests. Indeed, his authority and position relied on sectarianism.

The story of revolution and counter-revolution in Caledon sheds light on events in Ulster as a whole. For a brief period, the majority of working people in a small Tyrone village, many of them Orangemen, embraced an egalitarian ideology, and many maintained solidarity with their class despite economic and physical coercion. The counter-revolution's victory in Caledon was first secured by the employer's deliberate exploitation of sectarian divisions, and then cemented through the creation of a discriminatory statelet, forged in a fire of orchestrated violence.

An analysis of the ideology propounded by Coote in South Tyrone, and by the UULA representatives in Belfast and across Ulster, points to a fusion of inherent concepts of Protestant supremacy linked to the colonial past, married with a more broadly derived imperial racism – a current already identified in Edwardian Unionism in Tyrone.[115] Similarly, the notion that the Unionist leadership espoused a liberal, democratic and secular ideology bears little or no relation to reality.[116] Irish Catholics were unable to enjoy liberty, as they occupied a 'profane space'. The most challenging aspect of lower-class Protestant involvement in trade unionism, as became apparent in Caledon, revolved around working-class Orangemen's willingness to open the 'sacred space' of freedom to their Catholic neighbours.[117] In short, the Unionist leadership employed a supremacist ideology to destroy anti-sectarian class solidarity by violence.

On the last day of May 1922, Lloyd George claimed that Mussolini's Fascisti served as an 'exact analogy' for the Ulster Specials, and that the initial attack and brunt of subsequent violence involved the 'murder of members of the [Catholic] minority', while Britain had armed 48,000 Protestants. In June 1922 the British civil servant, Stephen Tallents, arrived in Ulster to enquire into outrages against northern nationalists. The erstwhile leader of the Tyrone UVF, Ambrose Ricardo, admitted that the full-time 'A' Specials 'contained a large leaven of a bad type', had serious problems with 'drink and consequent indiscipline', and represented a 'distinctly partisan force'. Likewise, the part-time 'B' Specials were 'drawn from the Protestant section of the population and mainly from the more extreme side'. In Catholic areas, Ricardo claimed commandants had approached the leading nationalist with a list with 'his name at the top and he is told that if any "B" man is touched the list will be attended from the top'. Ricardo then stated that the 'N. Govt. is a very strict party machine which is influenced at the present time entirely by Belfast views of extreme type', concluding that 'the 26 counties [govt.] are not the only one that would benefit by a return to the Union and to impartial govt by the Imperial Govt'.[118]

Despite his contempt for Bates, Tallents whitewashed the Unionist regime. The British government would fully resource the USC, to the tune of over £6 million, for a further two years – a period of little or no violence in the north.[119] Ricardo hinted that the Specials partially solved the problem of chronic unemployment: 'Every man in N.I. who has lost his job or who is at a loose end has endeavoured to get into the "A"s and in many cases has succeeded.'[120] Ricardo also reported: 'Today the feeling against the Specials . . . is more bitter than against the Black & Tans – with this great difference – on the removal of the Black & Tans one side of the contending parties' had left the scene. In Tyrone, many killers had known their victims since childhood, establishing what Ricardo termed 'a group of personal blood feuds which will last for generations to come'.[121]

Recent intelligent analysis suggests the Unionist government maintained a 'moral economy of loyalty', rewarding supporters with patronage while discriminating against Catholics and trade unionists.[122] For instance, in 1925 Albert McClelland of Caledon, a 'B' Special struggling to find work, petitioned James Craig for compensation, arguing that his 'great service' during the 'time of trouble on the border' left him 'as entitled to compensation as any of the men about to be disbanded' – although he remained 'willing to accept whatever your Ministry of Home Affairs would think sufficient'.[123] Such patronage operated as the material basis for the Unionist elite's promulgation of a reactionary Orange populism, echoing post-war authoritarian and fascist movements in Europe and Britain. In Ulster, direct elite agency suppressed emerging progressive tendencies among working-class Protestants prepared to open the scared space of liberty to their Catholic neighbours and friends. Nevertheless, aspects of fascism, rather than returning to Europe as a 'colonial boomerang', had always shaped elite thinking in Tyrone's colonial society – both the British and European far-right apparently playing catch-up with their Ulster brethren.

6

Pogrom

> *Little in the following narrative is really new . . . but the latest, and most violent, perhaps, of a long series, the same in kind if differing in degree, which have blotched the story of that faction for well over a hundred years.*
>
> Fr John Hassan (a.k.a. G. B. Kenna), *Facts and Figures of the Belfast Pogrom*

Across the *longue durée*, the Tory Right and its natural allies in the British military, intelligence, press, and so on – not the Ulster Unionists – constitute the key agents in imposing and supporting partition, through violence, threatened or actual, and subversion. In his famous House of Lords speech, after the Anglo-Irish Treaty, Edward Carson lamented: 'What a fool I was. I was only a puppet, and so was Ulster, and so was Ireland, in the political game that was to get the Conservative Party into power.'[1] The British state sowed dragon's teeth in 1921, Lloyd George admitting: 'our Ulster case is not a good one'.[2] Nevertheless, the Welsh Wizard headed a reactionary and imperialist coalition that imposed partition, through which Ulster's Unionist leadership – with near unconditional state support – spawned a half-century of Orange supremacy in what Roy Foster euphemistically described as Britain's 'truculent and idiosyncratic offshoot'.[3]

This chapter contends that partition violently restored an older, harsher order. British rule in Ireland had, however reluctantly, begun to soften its anti-Catholic stance, seeking legitimacy through inclusion.

The establishment of a one-party Unionist government in Belfast definitively reversed this trend. In an era when democracy was steadily eroding older forms of authority, a newly manufactured Protestant majority instead created a system of intense sectarian control. British-backed Orange revanchism thus forged a polity that functioned less like a modern representative government than a *Herrenvolk* democracy, akin to apartheid South Africa.[4]

Northern Ireland also received a baptism in blood. While, in the south, violence overwhelmingly affected combatants, in the north-east indiscriminate sectarianism prevailed. Ó Corráin and O'Halpin's study of deaths from the Easter Rising until the Truce in July 1921 provides a civilian fatality figure in Antrim of 85 per cent, while the figures for comparably violent Tipperary and Cork range from 28 to 34 percent. Indeed, 'other than intercommunal violence in Derry and Belfast, it is impossible to assign sectarian or ethnic motives as the primary reason for individual killings between 1916 and 1921'.[5] After 1920, mobs drove 23,000, mostly Catholics, from their homes, and 50,000 had left the North by early 1923.[6] In Belfast between July 1920 and October 1922, Kieran Glennon has detailed 498 killings, including 266 from the Catholic quarter of the population and 181 Protestant civilians, or 90 per cent of all fatalities.[7] The expulsion of 10,000 workers (mostly Catholics, but also including Protestant trade unionists) from the city's shipyards and engineering works following the first working day after the annual Twelfth of July holiday is widely recognised as the spark that lit the bonfire.[8] Here the consensus ends, however.

Northern Ireland emerged from the resolution of three interwoven dilemmas, the pogrom effectively severing Unionism's Gordian knot. First, Carson needed to secure unity despite acceptance by the Ulster Unionist Council (UUC) of six-county partition under the 1920 Government of Ireland Act (GOIA). This decision effectively breached the 1912 Covenant and, as James Stronge put it, threw loyalists in Cavan, Monaghan and Donegal 'to the wolves with very little compunction'.[9] Secondly, Unionism then imposed its own discipline on the Protestant working class by crushing the nascent labour movement under the pretext of a refusal to tolerate Sinn Féin 'infiltration'. Thirdly, the reorganisation of the Ulster Volunteer Force (UVF) provided the means to this end – a strategy consummated by the imperial state's founding and funding of the Ulster Special Constabulary (USC).

An ultimately apologetic historiography strains to absolve the Unionist leadership of responsibility for the expulsions and resulting violence. Alan Parkinson, for instance, identifies 'a dearth of evidence' that the Ulster Unionist Council sponsored a 'systematic programme of sectarian attack', insisting that 'despite the virulence of political speeches, there was no "grand plan" involving senior politicians'.[10] Indeed, some historians portray Unionist leaders as hostages to their own extremists. Arguably, these positions rely on a failure to develop a full picture of the forces at work (particularly the three dilemmas already identified) and a misreading of the leadership structure – particularly the agency of Carson and, more significantly, Richard Dawson Bates.

Unionist Leadership and the British Radical Right

The Ulster Unionist Council laid the foundation for the Protestant statelet. Founded in 1905 by James Craig, the first northern prime minister, the council emerged from commercial élite desire for greater independence from British Toryism.[11] The UUC also consolidated Belfast's domination of Unionist politics – its secretary, Dawson Bates, the future Northern minister of home affairs, being the spider at the centre of Ulster Unionism's web.[12] Indeed, in November 1919 Craig asked the British cabinet if Bates could see the still-secret partition plans, as he 'knew the mind of Ulster almost better than anyone else'.[13]

Carson's appointment as Unionist leader in 1910 relied on his oratorical skills, access to the corridors of power and ability to exert pressure on executive policy. In fact, leaving aside propaganda events and UUC meetings, Carson spent very little time in Ulster. As Ronald McNeill admitted,

> A political campaign . . . could not be a success . . . however effective the oratory, unless the arrangements were based on good organisation. It was by general consent a triumph of organisation, the credit for which was very largely due to . . . Dawson Bates . . . Carson himself very wisely paid little attention to detail; happily there was no need for him to do so, for he had beside him in Captain James Craig and Mr Bates two men with real genius for organisation . . . [Bates] always knew what was going on in out-of-the-way corners, and where to turn for the right man for any particular piece of work.[14]

Carson formulated policy with an eye to influencing government, and expected Bates to manufacture consent. As he wrote himself, 'It is by unity alone that we can expect to maintain our position in the councils of the state and enforce our policy of obtaining for Ulster all that is thought essential.'[15]

Above all, Carson was a reactionary. After a legal career spent defending notorious landlords, attacking trade unions, justifying imperial aggression, and prosecuting Oscar Wilde, while in parliament Carson opposed a reduction in miners' working hours, disempowered trade unions, faced down ameliorative land legislation, protected the Anglican establishment, and opposed democratisation and franchise reform. During a 1912 Poor Law debate, he argued that 'the able-bodied paupers if well conducted might be placed in labour colonies, if ill-conducted in detention centres'.[16] The student of Irish history will likewise struggle to find any sustained treatment of the reactionary character of the British ruling class more generally.

After the war, David Lloyd George's coalition claimed it had no selfish interest in Ireland. Yet, above any other individual, Lloyd George remained politically indebted to Carson.[17] Indeed, the government was dominated by the very same Tories who had challenged parliament's sovereignty, openly supported the 'Curragh Mutiny' and funded the Larne gunrunning in 1914.[18] While in office, they enforced partition through legislation and financial subsidy for Belfast's security apparatus. In 1924, England and Wales had one police officer for 699 people, Scotland one for 751; meanwhile, Bates commanded one gendarme for every 160 inhabitants.[19] In fact, paramilitary police served to consolidate the Orange economy, and the state's eventually permanent suppression of British civil liberties under the 1922 Special Powers Act constituted perhaps the defining peculiarity of the one-party administration.

The British political elite supported partition to subvert Home Rule – or, failing that, to render any independent Irish state a virtual possession. During the Buckingham Palace Conference of 1914, Lord Milner advised Carson to 'stick out for the six counties as a minimum', although he added: 'There is no particular virtue in counties . . . as long as the excluded area is one solid block.'[20] While in South Africa, 'Milner's Kindergarten also helped develop the most formal, extreme and sophisticated form of racist governance in the modern world, apartheid'.[21]

Milner himself consciously promoted white supremacy as a means to settle the differences between the British and the Boers, at the expense of blacks.[22] His disciple, Lionel Curtis, who would play a leading role in Ireland, claimed that it was a 'false criterion' to take men like Gandhi and 'point to their educational superiority over the mass of white voters', since individual potentiality, from a social and political point of view, could 'only be measured by the potentiality of the race as a whole'.[23]

In a similar vein, Carson later opined that Irish Catholics were 'really far from civilised', and that 'the Celts have done nothing in Ireland but create trouble and disorder'.[24] During the Home Rule Crisis, Milner formed the Ulster Union Defence League to rescue 'the white settler colony of Ulster from submersion in a sea of inferior Celts'.[25] His chief ally, Walter Long, the former leader of Irish Unionist MPs, would head the parliamentary committee that drew up six-county partition under the GOIA. James Craig, himself a junior minister, informed Long that Unionists could not control, and did not want, nine counties.[26] Again, this policy revolved on an imperial pivot, which operated globally. Despite his crocodile tears following the Treaty, Carson had been settled on six-county partition since before the war. The polity that emerged bore many of the hallmarks of a *Herrenvolk* democracy.

Carson's familiarity with race patriots like Milner had significant implications for Belfast. In his introductory letter to Carson requesting 'a straight and confidential talk' in December 1913, Milner stressed that Ulster's position '*goes very deep with me*' (original emphasis), claiming that Ulster's 'uprising of unshakeable principles and devoted patriotism, of loyalty to the Empire and to the Flag', had stirred him from political retirement, as it went 'far deeper than ordinary party struggles' and required much more than 'mere talk'.[27] Both men played crucial roles in Lloyd George's appointment as prime minister in December 1916, and Carson apparently sought to transfer Milner's racist populism to Ireland.

While Milner funded the British Workers' League, which 'endeavoured to mobilise patriotic labour and counter the growing appeal of the Labour Party to the working class', Carson sat on its executive, and saw in the social imperialist body a blueprint for Unionist hegemony over labour politics.[28] As a leading historian of the movement observes, 'the term "National Socialist", if it had not acquired a special meaning in Germany, would be a fair summary of the opinions propagated by the League and its periodical at this period'.[29] Within this context, Carson created and promoted the Ulster Unionist Labour Association (UULA), which operated under the thumb of Dawson Bates, while John M. Andrews chaired this supposed labour organisation, whose four MPs then formed a group at Westminster with the National Democratic Party (the new name of the British Workers' League).

Many critical commentators mocked the notion of Andrews – far from a 'horny-handed son of the toil', but a millionaire and mill owner – chairing a labour organisation.[30] Indeed, when UULA representatives met a British Labour Party delegation to Ireland in January 1920, J. F. Gordon, branch secretary of the Amalgamated Society of Engineers, claimed that the body represented 80 per cent of the Unionist workers of Belfast, and further that the UULA constituted an independent working-class body, mockingly asking whether Labour members thought 'the workers of Ulster signed the Covenant because the employers asked them to do so'. The Labour leader, William Adamson, then politely replied by asking, if the UULA was a genuine labour organisation, why Carson was its president and Andrews its chairman.[31]

Carson's reasoning also reflected changing conditions in Belfast, where the independent trade-union movement challenged Unionist hegemony over the Protestant working class. Attempts by socialists to protest conscription in central Belfast in April 1918, for example, led to violent scenes, and spurred the re-emergence of the Belfast Protestant Association, led by Arthur Trew, 'the spokesman of the Tory working man'.[32] Inspired by Milner, Carson sought to equip Ulster Unionism for the democratic age by bringing the Protestant Association into the official party fold under UULA auspices. The UULA carried out the pogrom of July 1920. As a result, the Unionist leadership violently enforced its provincial hegemony in anticipation of the GOIA, marking indelibly the polity that emerged from the ashes. In effect, a hybrid of Orange colonial ideology and the wider post-war British radical right became deeply woven into the very fabric of Northern Ireland. Moreover, the imperial elite connived in this process, as Ulster Unionism reflected many of its own prejudices and strategic priorities.

The 1918 General Election and Belfast Forty-Four-hour Strike

The post-war boom sent employment in Ulster's key industries soaring. By 1919, linen manufacturing supported 90,000 workers, while the Belfast shipyards employed 30,000 people – nearly double the number of just five years earlier.[33] Under these favourable conditions, trade-union militancy flourished. While strike activity and economic demands appeared to be widespread, socialism seems to have been strongest among the unskilled, particularly female textile workers enfranchised by the Representation of the People Act, who voted consistently for the Belfast Labour Party, which objected to the Irish Labour Party's decision to abstain from the 1918 general election, and backed the British Labour Party's call (shortly to be cast aside by Ramsay MacDonald) for self-determination in a unified Ireland.[34] As early as October 1918, Bates wrote to Carson warning of the Belfast Labour Party threat.[35] Both promoted the UULA as 'a distinctive entity in the Loyalist movement in this country', with 'its origin in the brain of the greatest patriot and one of the greatest men this country ever saw – Lord Carson'.[36] At Carson's insistence, four UULA members stood as official Westminster candidates, providing a bulwark against those 'trying to set labour against capital and capital against labour'.[37]

At a rally for Samuel McGuffin, a UULA candidate in Shankill, Carson laid the foundation for the subsequent attack on labour and republicanism. McGuffin claimed that 'the cooperation of employer and employee, the capitalist and the worker', represented the best means to resolve labour issues. Carson, who doubted 'how far a great part of the increased enfranchised electorate had been politically educated', railed that 'the world was upside down'. He claimed that the Belfast Labour Party candidates disguised their Irish nationalism to secure Unionist votes under false pretences, before denouncing the 1916 Rising as the 'worst act . . . perpetrated by a treacherous and perfidious people' who 'stabbed us in the back . . . while we fought a world war for freedom':

> Sinn Fein was contesting every seat in Ireland, and I believe they have already had 26 unopposed returns. What does that mean? ('Bolshevism'.) You are about right . . . The whole thing [Irish Republic] is trash, but at the same time it is one of the most dangerous propositions ever put before the people so guided by sentiment as the people in the South of

> Ireland are. What are they coming to Ulster, to Belfast for? . . . [There was] never a greater insult offered to this great Imperial province [than] when they put a Sinn Feiner forward to contest every seat.[38]

In any event, McGuffin won easily, but a quarter of the electorate voted for Sam Kyle, suggesting that many trade unionists rejected the UULA's social imperialism. Carson had nevertheless characterised labour and republicanism as an unholy alliance within a global Bolshevik conspiracy bent on the Empire's destruction. This trope justified the subsequent pogrom, but in the period after the 1919 general strike, the Belfast Labour Party only consolidated its appeal among a significant minority of Protestant workers.

The Belfast Forty-Four-Hour or general strike of January 1919, which involved 60,000 people, at least demonstrated that 'workers wanted a shorter working week, were not fooled by the economic and political arguments of the employers and showed massive solidarity', which 'was not threatened in any way by communal tensions'.[39] Bates labelled the strikes' leaders Sinn Féiners, and one quarter of the strikers themselves 'socialists', expressing concern that these malevolent forces took 'advantage of some of the rank and file'.[40] In relation to the strike, Henry Patterson criticises the tendency to portray 'every economic conflict' as an opportunity for the working class to 'see through' Orange ideology, concluding that 'Unionist politicians in no way were clear-headed manipulators of ideology'.[41] Bates thus did not fear Russian-style revolution, but a repeat of 'the Belfast riots of 1886 between the Protestant workers and the police', 'the cunning bourgeoisie and its political representatives' operating as mere 'caricatures of reality'.[42]

Alternatively, at the end of January 1919, Bates noted that, after consulting with a few allies, Colonel R. H. Wallace, the Orange County grand master, drafted a manifesto. Bates opposed direct Unionist intervention, fearing workers might feel 'let down' and that, if Hacket Pain (the local British military commander and former UVF leader) intervened, embittered workers 'might join hands in a universal strike for the whole of Ireland . . . the consequences of which would be very far-reaching'.[43] The manifesto, therefore, aimed to separate 'decent men' from the 'Sinn Fein Bolshevik element'.[44] Bates also enclosed a leaflet linking republicanism to a global Bolshevik conspiracy seeking to infiltrate Ulster under a Labourite guise. Unionist leaders embraced these fears – one Fermanagh Unionist warned of an organised effort to flood Belfast with rebels, deploying young Catholics infiltrating shipyards to spread discontent. This 'class of man', he claimed, lay behind the Forty-Four-Hour and Red Clydeside.[45] Meanwhile, James Craig privately warned Lloyd George that Irish rebels were seeking to establish a republic hostile to Britain, collaborating with Bolshevik forces.[46] In this respect, Unionist rhetoric echoed British far-right conspiracy theories, from the Primrose League to the British Fascists.[47]

Likewise, the Wallace manifesto blamed the strike on malcontents who had 'taken advantage of a Trade dispute to bring discredit on the fair fame of Belfast'. Obviously in an allusion to the Belfast Labour Party, the manifesto continued that this group, 'smarting from the defeat they have suffered recently at the General Election', had sought to manoeuvre Belfast working men 'into a position from which in a short time they might find it very difficult to withdraw'.[48] Rather than passive observers, Unionist leaders coordinated a strike response based on the apocalyptic analysis of the viceroy, Lord French, and their own apparent weakness in the face of the popularity of the strike committee's demands during the post-war boom. Indeed, Bates sent James Craig a précis to that effect from Hacket Pain, so that he could understand the situation 'at a glance'.[49]

In the wake of the strike, Carson outlined Unionist strategy in a letter to Bates: the soft power of Unionist propaganda backed by the muscle of the UULA and the UVF. The way Bates dealt with each demonstrates how leadership and policy operated. Firstly, Carson returned to the issue of placing 'our organizations on the thoroughly democratic basis'. Bates should 'take care . . . that all classes and all views are thoroughly represented in all our local organizations'. Carson then regurgitated the radical right's conspiracy theory, concluding that 'our separatist opponents are working diligently both here and in America with a view to harnessing to their cause various elements of unrest in order to influence public opinion at home and abroad in favour of the policy of what is called an independent Ireland'. Carson therefore directed Bates to 'establish an active propaganda department'. He concluded by proposing the reorganisation of the UVF, since 'we should not shut our eyes to the serious condition of affairs existing in the south and west of Ireland', since 'the leader of the majority of the Irish people' demanded a republic. De Valera's

> undisguised threat . . . in the event of Ulster's refusal to abandon her loyalty to the King and her citizenship in the British Empire must bring home to each of us the necessity of being prepared for all eventualities. I have myself but a little trust in politicians or political parties in relation to Ireland and . . . in the last resort it will be found that we must rely upon ourselves, this I believe we are prepared to do.[50]

By June, Bates was warning: 'the Labour question is becoming acute in Belfast and the North of Ireland', before concluding: 'we have got to face this sooner or later'.[51] He subsequently urged Carson to strengthen the UULA, as 'many of the unions . . . are controlled by officials who hold Home Rule views' – a situation which 'leads the younger members of the working class to Socialist i.e., extreme, organisations run by the ILP [Belfast Labour Party] where they are educated in views very different to those held by our body'. Bates warned that 'if nothing is done the association will die, because its members will feel that it is not sufficiently progressive to meet an admittedly felt want'. Interestingly, he praised 'the vast bulk of thinking Employers, and those who have the interests of the Empire at heart', who realised that UULA advocacy had a 'most beneficial' effect.[52] Bates's letter reflected similar concerns from grassroots UULA members that 'some steps should be taken to enrol the younger members of the community who are liable to be influenced by opponents of the cause'.[53]

During the summer of 1919, the UULA and the Ulster Ex-Servicemen's Association (UESA) contacted Carson through Bates. Carson became UESA vice-president. Both groups wanted to discuss matters better left confidential. The UULA asked Carson for 'a private conversation with you at a time during your visit that would be most opportune'.[54] The UESA representative argued: 'if I had a private interview with you, I could explain more in person than in writing'.[55] While Carson's ill health prevented the meetings, around the same time, James Craig advised UVF gunrunner Fred Crawford to postpone his efforts temporarily. The Unionist leadership clearly shared grassroots concern for secrecy:

> When Peace is signed it will be for you to consult Dawson Bates and take whatever action the two of you deem judicious, but under no circumstances should either Sir Edward Carson or myself be

> implicated – we should know nothing whatever about it. I could talk more freely on this subject, but you will read between the lines.[56]

The UULA's Aims and Objects provide some insight into their intentions, which included 'getting employment for discharged and demobilised soldiers' by attempts to 'counteract and fight Sinn Fein organisations. Which are at present doing all they can to keep our men out of, and their own in employment.' They further emphasised the importance of 'harmony between Unionist Employers and workers', hoping that a branch be 'established in every town and village in Ulster'. Interestingly, they also proposed to start an 'Ulster Trades Council. The difficulties foreseen in this are that if this question were brought forward at Branch Meetings of Trade Unions there would be a complete rupture and the Sinn Fein element would likely break away and join the ITGWU, or perhaps, the "Big Union Movement" '.[57]

By September 1919, the UULA had identified the issues of ex-servicemen's jobs and Sinn Fein's 'infiltration' of Belfast as central to establishing Unionist hegemony over labour relations. The UESA and UULA constituted the dominant groups in the mass expulsion of Catholic and Protestant socialists the following summer. By that stage, the initial post-war boom had collapsed, wrecking labour's favourable bargaining position and facilitating a reactionary counterattack, the scarcity of work operating as a powerful lever for imposing political discipline. Nevertheless, while the Unionist leadership had long recognised the need to tackle trade unionists, the delicate issue of six-county partition precluded direct action until the summer. In short, Bates had to secure acceptance and the consequent betrayal of Unionists in the three border counties before dealing with labour in Belfast.

The 1920 Elections

Directly after the January 1920 urban elections, the *Newsletter* noted that 'the active supporters of the Labour candidates were jubilant after their success, and when Mr Kyle and some of his colleagues were leaving the City Hall grounds, they were surrounded by a crowd of enthusiasts who gave vent to their feelings by singing "The Red Flag" '.[58] Indeed, the influential, left-leaning, and Protestant Sinn Féiner, Willaim Forbes

Patterson, claimed that 'so deep and wide was the rift in the Orange Lodges' during the election 'that the Unionist leaders dared not bring out the Orange drums'.[59]

The results suggest that, at the time, the democratic legitimacy of even eventual six-county partition appeared questionable. Across urban, mostly Protestant Ulster, Labour won 19.8 per cent of the first preferences, compared with 14.9 per cent for the Nationalists, 8.9 per cent for Sinn Féin, and 52.6 per cent for Unionists. Protestants voted, in the number of at least 10,000, for Labour instead of for Unionist candidates. Furthermore, while Belfast Labour mainly attracted support from Protestants, around 20 per cent of Catholics supported the party as well. In Belfast, explicitly anti-partitionist parties won over 30,000 votes, while official Unionist parties won fewer than 50,000 in a city where Protestants made up three-quarters of the population – a hammer blow to Unionist prestige in the party's citadel. Elsewhere in Ulster, Labour candidates won 8,566 first preferences out of 50,346, and took 93 out of 505 seats.[60] In the June rural elections, Sinn Féin won 40 per cent of the seats in Ulster's nine counties, where anti-partition groups won 55 per cent.

The anniversary of the general strike gave organised labour another chance to show its strength, now bolstered by proportional representation (PR). Unionists quickly saw PR as a threat 'as far as the Belfast Corporation is concerned'.[61] Labour won twelve seats, maintaining its 1918 vote share – even in the Catholic Falls ward – suggesting an anti-sectarian constituency existed. Loyalists, however, had spent the past year branding them a republican Fifth Column. In Shankill, UULA's James Turkington now faced off against Kyle:

> Sinn Feiners, Socialists and Bolsheviks were going about today asking the people for their suffrages . . . There was a game going on, and socialists were running candidates in all the divisions of Belfast – men . . . pledged to a republic . . . With regard to the wages question, the socialists had opposed the granting of a living wage to the police, whom they had been fighting, and slaughtering throughout the country . . . to terrorise them in order that they could have a workers' republic in Ireland and rule Belfast, but that would never be. These people had also denied a living wage to the teachers because Sinn Feiners wanted education to be in the hands of the priests. In

conclusion, he said he was out against revolution, Bolshevism, and rampant Socialism.[62]

Thousands of Protestant workers nevertheless rejected the Sinn Féin blood libel, and Labour candidates consistently outpolled their UULA rivals. Turkington and his UULA running mate received fewer than 500 votes, while Kyle topped the poll with 2,082. Dawson Gordon secured a seat through transfers after earning 500 first preferences. Unionist voters largely favoured official candidates over the UULA. Despite a year of black propaganda, working-class politics proved resilient. The loyalist backlash would assume more bellicose form. Nevertheless, the delicate passage of six-county partition precluded direct action in the immediate aftermath of Belfast Labour's 'big stride'.[63]

Henry Patterson argues that the Belfast Labour Party's vote merely represented 'municipal politics with a vengeance', and that 'the minority of Protestant workers who voted for the Labour candidates had not revolutionised their politics'.[64] Unfortunately, this runs counter to contemporary Unionist opinion. The violently partisan *Newsletter* lamented the 'startling' results by the Belfast Labour Party in 'three divisions', which were 'undoubtedly a stronghold of working-class Unionism', concluding that there was 'something wrong with Unionist Labour as regards municipal politics'. Indeed, while the piece identified Unionist inability to 'answer the socialist propaganda', particularly around municipal issues, which 'had been much exploited by socialist labour from an extreme class point of view', it concluded that this did not 'account for the big changes which have been made in the personnel of the City Council by this election'.[65]

Partition

Despite Carson's pledges in 1919 to uphold the Covenant, he had accepted six-county partition as early as 1913.[66] He told a Tyrone Unionist that, if devolution became inevitable, Ulster should demand its own parliament.[67] Bates and Craig also quietly supported permanent six-county partition.[68] Before the general election, James Stronge criticised Bates for being too Belfast-focused, but ultimately accepted partition, reasoning that without allies south of the Newry Mountains, it was better to be 'West Britons' than Irishmen.[69] Tyrone UVF leader Ambrose Ricardo recalled Craig outlining his six-county plan in 1916, calling it madness.[70] Committed to equal imperial citizenship for all Ulster residents, Ricardo viewed partition and one-party rule as anathema. This underscores how elite manoeuvring shaped the discriminatory administration that followed. As a British cabinet official observed in Belfast in January 1920,

> most of the people . . . were of the opinion that the whole of the province would be excluded; but on the other hand, the people in the inner circles hold the view that the new province should consist of the six counties, the idea being that the inclusion of Donegal, Cavan and Monaghan would provide such an access of strength to the Roman Catholic Party, that the supremacy of the Unionists would be seriously threatened. Further with Home Rule not a vital issue, there is a real danger that on certain questions the Unionist Labour Party in Ulster might vote with the Roman Catholics.[71]

Carson's correspondence with Bates bears this out. Carson claimed that

> the situation with which we will be confronted will be the most difficult and critical one which has yet arisen and fraught with consequences for Ulster and the whole of Ireland in the future of such a character that any hasty or too ill-considered action is to be deprecated. I earnestly hope therefore that all our friends will keep an open mind.

He then outlined the wider imperial implications of six-county partition, which rested on 'not merely local or personal interests', asserting that Unionists should do 'our best for the United Kingdom and the Empire as a whole'.[72]

The UUC's acceptance of six-county partition on 10 March 1920 threatened to split Ulster Unionism. Cavan, Monaghan and Donegal loyalists naturally felt betrayed. Ricardo resigned in 'anger & disgust' as 'Carson on 10th [March] fell from the pedestal that many had placed him on'.[73] Elsewhere, he criticised 'the narrow Belfast clique' and claimed to speak for 'a strong minority of loyalists' who wished 'to prevent the Covenant being torn up'.[74] This led to much empty soul-searching. Yet, as UUC delegate John Gunning-Moore wrote privately, 'the whole question of "breach of Covenant" turns upon numbers . . . the whole nine will be such a rickety parliament that it must [almost] at once be absorbed into the Dublin one'.[75] Another UUC delegate, Barry Meglaughlin, argued:

> if the nine counties are included within five years there will be a nationalist majority, and this work has commenced already into a much more serious extent than most people imagine. There are funds provided in different centres for the purchase by nationalists of properties in or about the several towns of Ulster and even already nationalists from the midlands, south and west are being drafted in to such an alarming extent that even with the six counties alone, we would have to be constantly on the watch. It is asked by some of our people what is to prevent us doing to same, but I know from bitter experience that we cannot do so[;] we have not the power of the Church behind us to force our people to come . . . as you know the other side have 100 to every one of ours in the south and west on whom to operate.[76]

Indeed, Unionist leaders living on the 'right' side of the border recognised Carson's 'considerable triumph' in getting Tyrone and Fermanagh 'included in the Northern Pale', and that, 'if the whole thing is thrown back into the melting pot again, we may be the sufferers'.[77] A minority, however, shared the opinion of one female UUC delegate 'who no longer wish[ed] to be a member of a Council who deliberately and shamelessly broke the Solemn League and Covenant . . . It may have been expedient and statesmanlike to break it – it was not honourable.'[78]

That May, an emergency UUC meeting, attended by Carson, voted by 390 to 80 against the extension of the northern parliament's authority to nine counties. Clearly, in terms of the acceptance of six- over nine-county exclusion, the ultimate decision was 'not a question of ethics and honour, but a question of arithmetic'.[79] James Craig made his own position clear: 'the six counties are the citadel of Ulster Unionism. If we are unable to hold the outposts, must we refuse the offer of the undisturbed possession of the citadel? . . . The Covenant cannot be construed as a compact for suicide.'[80] Where room for a functioning democracy existed within this arrangement was a moot point.

Six-county partition was driven by Lloyd George's efforts to secure Ulster Unionism while crushing the IRA's 1920 campaign, thereby firmly entrenching wider strategic imperatives. With their new statelet secured, Unionist leaders cracked down on dissent, justified by outrage over alleged republican atrocities. As Parkinson notes, loyalists exaggerated these claims, using them to justify violent expulsions unseen anywhere in nationalist Ireland during the revolution.[81] Unionists watched in shock as the IRA's guerrilla warfare eroded British power, particularly through infiltration of the military and police. To them, the harsh response to southern violence and subsequent repression seemed justified – rooted in imperial loyalty, anxiety over their status, and a belief in Protestant supremacy. London fully aligned with these instincts. Bonar Law declared in 1920 that 'coercion was the only policy' since 'the Irish were an inferior race'.[82] These views helped fuel a very hot summer in Belfast.

The Pogrom

The defeat of socialism in Belfast rested on direct violent action by a loyalist aristocracy of labour. The UULA and UESA used the developing IRA guerrilla campaign to excuse the mass expulsion of Catholic and socialist workers from the city's main industrial centres. Despite elision by many historians, political Unionism, including Carson, inspired and directed these events, and went on to reap their reactionary dividends.

On 18 June 1920, the UESA sent Carson a telegram, pledging by 'all means in our power to restore law and order in Ulster'.[83] After violence between the IRA and a combined force of the UVF and the military in Derry, 'Belfast shipyard workers petitioned Carson to mobilise the UVF and take revenge'.[84] The UULA then arranged a meeting with Carson through Bates over the Twelfth, apparently to discuss the terms of the GOIA, but given Carson's subsequent rhetoric the upcoming expulsions also clearly made the agenda.[85] After meeting the UULA and UVF, Carson delivered an incendiary speech at the Twelfth field in Finaghy, despite his own disdain for a medium akin to 'the unrolling of a mummy. All old bones and rotten rags'.[86] Warning against Sinn Féin attempts to 'penetrate Ulster' by the 'insidious method' of 'tacking on . . . the Irish Republican question to the labour question', he claimed that 'these men who come forward posing as the friends of Labour care no more about Labour than does the man on the moon'. Carson concluded: 'we in

Ulster will tolerate no Sinn Fein . . . we will take matters into our own hands . . . And these are not mere words. I hate words without action.'[87]

An argument exists that this amounted to little more than irresponsible rhetoric, indicative of Carson's failure to lead effectively, and the assertion that he was urging loyalists to combat Sinn Féin through assaults on the labour movement is unsubstantiated by the historical record. This analysis rests on an untenable distinction between the Belfast (or Ulster) Protestant Association and the UULA. Nevertheless, each individual Morgan identified as a leading pogromist also held a prominent role in the UULA.[88] The elision here serves to obscure Bates and Carson's links to the pogrom. Others have chosen to downplay UUC 'wire-pulling' and 'plots', while simultaneously acknowledging that the UULA acted 'to "purify" the labour movement in Belfast'.[89] Elsewhere, Paul Bew claims that 'shipyard workers took matters into their own hands and expelled Catholic workers and "rotten Protestants" . . . Craig sent wary signals of support to angry Protestant workers but was fully aware of the dangers'.[90] In fact, Bates arranged a meeting between the UULA and Carson, who then gave an incendiary speech at the Orange field inciting his followers to expel Sinn Féin supporters and trade unionists. The UULA, a body Carson had created, and which Bates controlled, then carried out the expulsions.

Between Carson's speech and the reopening of the shipyards, the IRA assassination of Colonel G. F. Smyth in Cork on 17 July provided the excuse for loyalist 'action'. After Smyth's funeral, on 21 July, the first morning of full production after Carson's speech, a crowd of 'between two and five thousand' loyalists assembled outside Workman & Clark's to protest against the 'peaceful penetration' of Sinn Féin.[91] Loyalist workers then attended similar meetings at dinnertime, when 'the sudden ebullition of active hostilities against the Sinn Fein workers in the shipyards' erupted like 'a spark in a powder magazine', after one worker allegedly shouted out 'Up the rebels!'[92] A white terror swarmed through the two yards engulfing Catholics and Protestant trade unionists, some swimming for their lives under a hail of rivets. This ignited a series of expulsions affecting up to 10,000 people, including hundreds of Protestant trade unionists, as the terror rippled from the shipyards, reverberating through Belfast's foundries and factories.

After the initial frenzy, the UULA organised protests at City Hall against a motion by two Belfast Labour Party councillors (Campbell and

Baird) to reinstate the dismissed workers.[93] They then held a further dinnertime rally outside Harland and Wolff on 30 July, urging Unionist councillors to oppose the motion, and denouncing 'anyone in the works who is in alliance with the Sinn Fein party or policy, and the red flag of a mad revolution'. Speaking from the back of a lorry under a large Union Jack, James Connolly (not the socialist republican icon) challenged Sinn Féin and Labour councillors to condemn Smyth's murder, accused Jimmy Baird of falsely representing Harland and Wolff workers, and vowed that 'Sinn Féin blood money' would not corrupt the UULA. John Holness warned that loyalist workers' patience had reached its limit, and mocked de Valera as a 'hyphenated Spanish onion' who did not know who he was, prompting laughter and insults from the crowd: 'He's a Mongrel!' Holness urged workers to 'stand by their employers, and in return they could rely on their employers to stand by them'. John Crumlin declared that 'loyal workers in a loyal city' would never again work with 'disloyal' Sinn Féin supporters intent on toppling the British Empire. He evoked the sacrifices of the UVF at the Somme and their ancestors at Derry and the Boyne, denying hatred towards Catholics but blaming priests, 'the curse of Ireland', for poisoning their minds.[94] The Unionist chairman of Belfast Corporation refused the Belfast Labour Party request to postpone the meeting, leading to violent intimidation, in which loyalist shipyard workers packed City Hall, hurling projectiles, brandishing revolvers, spitting on Sinn Féin councillors from the gallery, and making death threats.[95]

The UULA organised the expulsions: they were not spontaneous. Crumlin and Connolly levelled internal disciplinary charges against UULA executive member Nicholas Gordon, which suggest that the UULA organised the meeting that had sparked the dinnertime expulsions. Indeed, the hearing asked the Ulster Protestant Association to attend. Gordon stood accused of failing 'to have a meeting at the Queen's Island when called upon'. This perhaps referred to the second dinnertime meeting on the day of the clearances, as Gordon also stood accused of not condemning a comment from a non-loyalist onlooker to the effect that 'the days of the Orange flag and the big drum were over'. More remarkably, Gordon also allegedly called Connolly and Crumlin, the two main UULA members behind the expulsions, 'the catspaw of the Official Unionist Party', while the two pogromists-in-chief accused Gordon of supporting 'red flaggers at the recent Municipal Elections'.

Crucially, before this dispute between members ended in an official UULA disciplinary hearing, Gordon first 'endeavoured to have this matter settled amicably' in a meeting with Dawson Bates at Old Town Hall to arbitrate; but Crumlin and Connolly made capital out of this initiative to insinuate that Gordon did not have the support of the Unionist hierarchy.[96]

Indeed, Connolly and Crumlin addressed loyalist meetings in East Belfast the week after the expulsions, when they outlined the steps taken to establish loyalist vigilance committees, which had 'put a nail in the coffin of Sinn Fein at the Queen's Island'. Connolly said 'they had struck Sinn Fein and red flag socialism the worst blow it had received in Belfast for thirty years', and 'planted the Union Jack at the East Yard', which 'would never come down'. Crumlin claimed that even Catholic ex-servicemen were disloyal, as 'once they had discarded the uniform their minds had been poisoned by Sinn Fein propaganda'. In a vote of thanks, John Holness confirmed that Connolly had organised the events of the past fortnight, and reiterated that 'any Roman Catholic who signed the declaration of loyalty and repudiated Sinn Fein should get back to his work, and they should all know that irrespective of creed every workman in Belfast shipyards was a Loyalist'.[97] Indeed, William Grant and other leading figures publicly admitted elsewhere that the UULA planned and carried out the expulsions.[98]

In short, the Unionist leadership left their fingerprints all over the pogrom. Bates wrote to Carson on 4 August, two days after the shipyard workers' public announcement of the vigilance committees, thrilled by the 'great exodus of Sinn Feiners'. He had 'never seen the temper of the men so strong in regard to their determination not to work along with Sinn Feiners any longer'. Tellingly, Bates added that the movement 'entirely lacks anything of an excited character and . . . is entirely different to the old spasmodic outbreaks, which used to take place now about the Twelfth'. This represented an organised assault that purported to 'exercise every possible self-restrain[t] and to prevent hooliganism breaking out among their ranks'.[99] On 7 August, Wilfred Spender addressed the UULA about the reorganisation of the UVF.[100] As the *Westminster Gazette* reported, 'It is common knowledge in Belfast, and frequently admitted by individual Unionists, that plans were matured at least two months ago to drive all Home Rule workmen in the shipyards out of their employment.'[101]

To present the Ulster Unionist leadership as fortuitous beneficiaries of spontaneous loyalist agency does not reflect the reality of events. Neither does Bates's rationale for the violence stand up to scrutiny. Loyalist claims that ex-servicemen suffered unemployment because republicans had peacefully penetrated the industrial centres to steal their jobs ignored Sinn Féin's weak support among Belfast nationalists and the enormous growth in wartime employment – it is very difficult to steal a job that did not previously exist.[102] Indeed, Belfast's Catholic community was also 'four times as likely to enlist as Catholics from other parts of Ulster', and proportionately contributed as many recruits as the city's Protestants.[103] In 1919, loyalists formed the UESA, 'all loyal Ulster men and 95% are Orangemen', in opposition to the Comrades of the Great War Association, as the latter accepted Catholic members.[104] In short, like a great deal of the radical right, Unionist paranoid rhetoric and conspiracy theories enjoyed a very tenuous relationship to the truth.

The targeting of socialists or 'rotten Protestants' likely played a greater role in the expulsions than fears of a rural Catholic influx, however. The UULA campaign ensured that the 'entire cadre of working-class leaders' suffered with their Catholic comrades. Jimmy Baird recalled that every trade-union activist 'had been absolutely driven from the island'.[105] Vigilance committees, launched in the shipyards on 28–29 July, enforced the expulsions, disregarding the service of many Catholics and trade unionists to king and country. Harland and Wolff even recognised these committees in failed negotiations with the Carpenters' Union to reinstate expelled workers.[106] With this exception, British trade unions singularly failed to challenge the expulsions, thereby facilitating loyalist control without severing ties to craft unions.[107] The cause of labour had ridden the wave of First World War production, which temporarily swelled in the early peacetime market, before crashing as a result of overproduction by the autumn of 1920. By December 1920, a quarter of Irish workers were idle.[108] By then, the UULA had achieved a key goal: depoliticising and effectively neutralising the trade-union movement.

The two leaders of Ulster Unionism then publicly backed the pogrom. On 14 October, James Craig's wife recorded in her diary how he 'unfurls a big Union Jack for them and makes a splendid speech' at the shipyards, 'that he approves of their action in not allowing the disloyal element in their midst'.[109] Carson subsequently told parliament: 'I am prouder of my friends in the shipyards than of any other friends I have in the whole world'.[110] Yet, with Bates operating as political fixer, there is prima facie evidence that both leaders anticipated the expulsions, as well as the reorganisation of the UVF, and that both pushed for a Special Constabulary in government.

From Ulster Volunteer Force to Ulster Special Constabulary

The British government then recruited pogromists en masse into the new Special Constabulary, providing further economic incentive for loyalty during the post-war depression. James Craig even coached a UULA delegation before it met Bonar Law to petition for their formation, in a meeting where William Grant passionately argued that loyalists had been 'at the mercy of rebels' and needed arms to support the police and military 'in protecting life and property'.[111] Ironically, on 14 July 1921, shortly after the Truce, Grant was shot while leading a loyalist mob against a Catholic enclave in East Belfast.[112] The Specials constituted the state sanction of the UVF. Fred Crawford noted in his diary that he had been mobilising them since March 1920 at Edward Carson's request.[113] Carson advised secrecy to avoid disrupting the GOIA, and by June 1920 the UUC had appointed Wilfred Spender as UVF organiser across Ulster.[114] Chief Secretary Hamar Greenwood privately approved, but warned against public acknowledgment.[115] In September 1920 the Tyrone UVF leadership admitted in a secret memo that the Specials would only enlist Protestants.[116]

Arguably, the Unionist leaders' appeals for British assistance operated against a deeply ingrained and condescending suspicion, not only of the rebels, but also of lower-class Protestants. Bew, Gibbon and Patterson argue that leadership ideology was 'not primarily Orange at all', but rather 'democratic', 'pro-imperialist' and 'secular'. But leaders struggled to control a 'populist strain within Protestant ideology'.[117] In reality, as we have seen, not only did elite rhetoric and agency chime with popular Orangeism, but Carson and Craig, through Bates, manipulated popular extremism to institute a white terror. Post-war Unionism constituted one element in an international counter-revolution, which included the allied invasions of Russia and subsequent civil war, radical right-wing paramilitaries across central and Eastern Europe, and the rise of Italian fascism.

The Unionist leadership merely echoed their own anti-democratic anxiety to the cabinet; the imperial government self-interestedly swallowed it whole. On 23 July 1920, a convinced James Craig told the British cabinet the USC would avert 'mob law' and 'prevent the Protestants from running amok'. In fact, Craig's UUC had sparked this violence through the UULA. General Tudor warned that the Specials' creation 'would show that the Government did differentiate between rebels and loyalists'. Lloyd George, however, did not consider such differentiation, but thought instead of 'releasing troops and police'.[118] Locked in a struggle to subvert the creation of a democratic Irish Republic, the imperial state employed Ulster loyalism as a colonial bulwark – a role Orangeism had filled since the 1790s.

Despite the disproportionate nature of loyalist violence, by 1922 the British government had stationed nineteen battalions and 48,000 Specials, and 'orders had been given to accede to Sir James Craig's request for arms and munitions to equip these'. Churchill warned that, 'at any moment, patience may be ruptured, and we shall find ourselves in an atmosphere where people see red'.[119] Apparently, if loyalists were not armed to the teeth, they might become violent. But partition, and Northern Ireland's illiberal exceptionalism within the British polity, pointed towards wider imperial objectives. In March 1920, Bonar Law ridiculed 'loose talk' about granting self-determination to Ireland, characterising the position as 'living in the world with his eyes shut'. Law further lamented the 'childish mistake' of ignoring Ireland's centrality to 'national security'. In short, self-determination for imperial possessions had 'never been adopted by any nation in the history of the world except after defeat and under compulsion'.[120] Even after the signing of the Treaty, Churchill speculated on contingency plans if 'Republican forces' triumphed in the south, which envisaged Northern Ireland's use as a base for reconquest.[121] Similarly, James Craig viewed the six-county area as 'an impregnable Pale', while other leading Unionists envisaged its use as 'a bridge head for the re-conquest of Ireland', if southerners declared a Republic.[122]

By the May 1921 elections, the loyalist stranglehold on working-class politics, and indeed on Belfast itself, appeared complete. When three Labour candidates booked the Ulster Hall, loyalists seized the building and telegraphed Craig: 'Mass meeting of loyal shipyard workers who have captured Ulster Hall from the Bolsheviks Baird, Midgley and Hanna request that you address them for a few minutes tonight.'

Craig replied: 'I am with them in spirit. Know they will do their part. I will do mine. Well done big and wee yards.'[123] Jimmy Baird told those assembled to hear the election returns that 'many seeking to vote were brutally assaulted' amid the 'worst intimidation' during a contest 'marked by wholesale impersonation'.[124] Loyalist direct action had crushed a growing labour constituency, in a campaign orchestrated by the UUC that the British state had sanctioned through the USC. This all operated within the remit of wider imperial interests. As Lord Birkenhead remarked in July 1921, the government was 'quite ready to be liberal to Ireland now that he and his friends had secured the safety of Orange Ulster'.[125]

The argument here is not that Unionism lacked popular support. Rather, the evidence challenges the widespread assumption that Ulster Protestants constituted a homogeneous group – a proposition typically deployed to legitimise partition. The local election results in January and June 1920 indicated a secure majority against partition and for independence across Ulster's nine counties. In the urban elections, nationalists captured Derry corporation, but anti-partitionists (including Labour) also secured unexpected victories in Lurgan, Dungannon, Carrickfergus, Larne, Limavady, Cookstown and Lisburn. In fact, anti-partitionist parties won over 55 per cent of seats across the nine counties, and over 41 per cent within the proposed Six Counties, including a majority in Fermanagh and Tyrone and half in County Armagh. Indeed, anti-partitionists won control of twenty-four of seventy-five local bodies in the Six Counties. A homogeneous Unionist Ulster was a fiction.[126]

Moreover, the general strike of January 1919 and municipal election results a year later pointed to the consolidation of an independent, anti-partitionist labour constituency in Belfast itself. In response, the Unionist elite employed mass reactionary violence to create the material conditions for a fabricated polity, Northern Ireland, which lacked any genuine democratic legitimacy – beyond rhetorical flourishes about self-determination designed to excuse imperial *force majeure*.

Through the UUC, the Belfast bourgeoisie played the decisive role in clamping down on the emergent socialist movement. While no serious observer disputes the presence of a reactionary Orange ideology within sections of the Protestant working class, long-prevalent assumptions about the immutability of sectarian antagonism in Ulster should be robustly challenged. For a brief period, a significant minority of working-class Protestants embraced a principled anti-sectarian egalitarianism. The triumph of Orange ideology relied on loyalist shock troops in the first instance, and its consolidation operated against the foundation of a discriminatory statelet, unconditionally backed by the imperial metropole.

An analysis of the politics propounded by UULA representatives in Belfast points to a fusion of concepts inherent in Protestant supremacy, linked to the colonial past, combined with a more broadly derived imperialist and racist discourse. Similarly, the notion that the Unionist leadership espoused a liberal, democratic and secular ideology bears little or no relation to reality. The very same week he parleyed with Belfast's pogromists; Carson praised the exploits of General Dyer at Amritsar.[127] The liberalism of British imperialists essentially excluded what George Orwell described as 'unpeople', or those 'unfit to enter history'.[128] Well into the nineteenth and early twentieth centuries, for many among the metropolitan elite, Irish Catholics ranked with other subject nations – those sullen peoples, half-devil, half-child. Such people could not enjoy liberty, as they occupied a profane space. Elites in Belfast and ultimately London looked on in genuine concern as significant numbers of Protestant workers stopped viewing their Catholic comrades as 'unpeople' and welcomed them through the sacred gates of freedom.[129] The Unionist leadership employed a supremacist ideology and promoted reactionary violence to breach this gap, in the process riveting extreme loyalism into the very structures of the Orange State.

A supremacist dimension formed part of the internal logic of loyalism and, rather than restraining this tendency from running amok, the structures of the Unionist bloc encouraged conceptions of Protestant superiority and Catholic inferiority, thereby justifying violence. Indeed, separate republican and Free State intelligence reports in 1924 claimed that elements of the USC had formed branches of the Ku Klux Klan. In April 1924, the IRA reported: 'The KKK has been formed about three months ago in Belfast under the title of the "Gay Crusaders". Members consist of Specials officers and recently the ordinary rank and file have been admitted.'[130] On 4 January 1923, the *Newsletter* carried an article on the Klan and Italian fascism, which asserted that, while 'undemocratic' at root, it would be 'absurd to underestimate the significance of such movements, or to ignore what is noble in their intentions. Their strength springs from the genuine desire . . . to make life sweeter and more wholesome.' Fortunately, here, government rested on 'the will of the people, rather than on the symbolism of White Hood or Black Shirt'.[131] In 1934, Craig himself boasted that members of the 'Orange Order, the Black Brotherhood or the B Specials could substitute as Fascists'.[132]

This ideology underpinned a material reality of scarcity within a *Herrenvolk* democracy. Certainly, Craig himself claimed that the Stormont government's main function was 'to distribute the bones'.[133] The payoff for preferential treatment in employment – whether a position in the 'A's or a job in foundry, factory or local government – was that working-class Protestantism was thereby 'stripped of [its] progressive elements'.[134]

But the Unionist establishment and bourgeoisie constituted the net beneficiaries of the Orange economic order. Belfast went from being the most militant centre of trade-union activity in Ireland in 1919 to the quietest, failing to engage in the British engineering lockout of 1922 and abstaining from any industrial action in 1923 when, after the end of its civil war, southern Ireland witnessed an explosion of popular militancy. The Labour Ministry report (1923) noted that (in Belfast) 'no material stoppage occurred in the shipbuilding and engineering industries or in the transport trades. The linen trade generally was also free from serious trade dispute.'[135]

The UULA perhaps served a similar function to other corporativist groupings on the radical right, which gave some expression to working-class politics, but within the carefully demarcated confines of cross-class solidarity based on ethnic or national distinction – a position that typically reinforced capital's dominance over labour. The UULA Westminster MPs always voted against organised labour and sided with the National Democratic Party, former Labour MPs who supported Lloyd George's coalition. McGuffin himself publicly admitted: 'If [the UULA] had not been much in the limelight of oratory they had been diligent in their support of the Government.'[136] These social imperialists all became members of the British Empire Union, another grouping that shared an affinity with emergent fascist ideology in Europe.[137]

In the wake of the pogrom, the ITGWU's *Watchword of Labour* claimed that the UULA and UWU were both 'founded, financed, and directed by the Unionist capitalists for the purpose of killing the ordinary non-sectarian and non-party trade unions'. The UULA, therefore, constituted 'the bosses' organisation . . . the instrument which was used to begin the pogroms in the Belfast shipyards in July'.[138] Certainly, the

Unionist elite deliberately manipulated a form of reactionary Orange populism to subvert far more progressive, and developing, currents among working-class Protestants, which employed the liberal aspects of Orange ideology in a universalist fashion to include non-Protestants. Indeed, this Faustian bargain formed the very basis of the new Orange State, but *cui bono*? In short, on yet another turn of the dreaded historical spiral, Ulster's ruling elite, in its own class interests, deliberately instituted a system of sectarian privileges to define and maintain its position. The consequences appeared negative all round: not just for lower-class Catholics, but for the mass of Protestant workers too, whose true class interests stood in sharp opposition to those of a regional elite that remained beholden to, and buttressed by, a supremacist imperial centre.[139]

7

The 'Miracle of Coalisland'

> *That Ulster which they pictured in their dreams and prayed for in their prayers . . . promoted by the energy and enterprise of their capitalists working in friendly cooperation with their industrious workers.*
>
> John M. Andrews, 1924

In January 1923, the *Northern Whig* published 'Ulster Coal for Ulster', in which 'Old Fogey' waxed lyrical on the potential of the Tyrone coalfield, recently acquired by millionaire coal importer Sir Samuel Kelly: 'Although nibbled at for 200 years by the people of the locality, the Coalisland deposit had never been tested at a deep level'. The article predicted that the mine's 'vast' reserves would revolutionise Ulster's fuel supply, with enough coal to meet its needs for years.[1] Elsewhere, the *Whig* envisioned Tyrone as the 'Staffordshire of Ulster' and Coalisland as its industrial hub, 'the prospect opened out by the wonderful enterprise and energy of one man – an Ulsterman'.[2] In April, James Craig's cabinet declared that the 'whole economic situation in Ulster will be changed', the area becoming 'the home of many new industries', providing 'employment on a very large scale'.[3]

As a devolved, one-party Unionist administration created under the 1920 Government of Ireland Act (GOIA), Northern Ireland was less an effort to resolve the Irish question than to settle the Ulster question.[4] But when Unionist politicians spoke of 'Ulster', they did not mean the historic nine-county province, or even the truncated Six Counties of

Northern Ireland. Andrew Horner, for instance, argued that Ulster was 'more a people than a place' and that 'imaginary boundaries between counties had nothing whatever to do with [the] British settlers . . . the forefathers of the Ulster Covenanters of today'.[5] Yet Tyrone, the largest of Northern Ireland's two majority-Catholic counties, remained a persistent challenge. The 'dreary steeples of Fermanagh and Tyrone' had long frustrated British partition plans, and Churchill ruefully noted that 'the integrity of their quarrel is one of the few institutions that has been unaltered in the cataclysm which has swept the world'.[6]

Indeed, Article XII of the 1921 Anglo-Irish Treaty anticipated the creation of a Boundary Commission, which would redraw the border 'in accordance with the wishes of the inhabitants, so far as may be compatible with economic and geographic conditions'. Accordingly, a sword of Damocles hovered over local Unionists' heads, until the Commission's ignominious collapse in December 1925. In the intervening period, Craig's government consolidated its control over the two counties, establishing the Leech Commission, which gerrymandered electoral boundaries, abolished PR, and inserted a rateable valuation clause in the Local Government Act (1922), thereby guaranteeing Unionist control of local government and the crucial patronage that entailed.[7] When the British state objected to this flagrant breach of the GOIA, Craig threatened to resign, and London averted its gaze.

Furthermore, in 1924, when extremists complained that disloyal Catholics received government positions in preference to loyal Protestants, Craig ordered a full-scale investigation.[8] In 1969, the Cameron Commission reported that, across majority-nationalist areas, Unionists had consistently manipulated electoral boundaries to control local government, and then 'use their power to make appointments in a way which benefited Protestants' in housing and employment.[9]

But Unionist claims to Tyrone ultimately rested on force. As the GOIA passed through parliament, the British government sanctioned the creation of the Ulster Special Constabulary (USC), a paramilitary police force for the new jurisdiction.[10] In September 1920, Tyrone's three UVF commanders – Ambrose Ricardo, Robert Stevenson and John Knox McClintock – assured the rank and file that the USC represented Carson's army reincarnate.[11] On 15 March 1922, the minister of home affairs, Richard Dawson Bates, introduced the Civil Authorities (Special Powers) Bill, which amounted to the total suspension of civil liberties.

Amid this febrile atmosphere, Samuel Kelly attempted to conjure an industrial revolution in Tyrone.

Samuel Kelly

Kelly acquired the Coalisland (or Annagher) pit from the eccentric landlord and watercolourist Robert Ponsonby Staples, known as the 'barefoot baronet' for his refusal to wear shoes, believing they would insulate him from the Earth's magnetic field. The land and mining rights formed part of the Castle Stewart estate during the 1609 Ulster Plantation, eventually becoming the 'joint property of the Caulfield and Staples family'.[12] A liberal Protestant Home Ruler, Staples recounted his futile efforts to attract investment from the Unionist elite: 'Would Belfast merchants help in such mineral developments at their own door? No! "Well," said to me one of them in 1911, "If as you say it's a Nationalist district, I won't touch it." Ned Carson, as some here call him, was equally indifferent to my promoting spirit.' Staples then turned to the revolutionary Sinn Féin government, Dáil Éireann, which confirmed the potential of the Coalisland fields but, with six-county partition on the cards, conceded that it could not help 'in what is to be a new Orange Free State'.[13]

Then, in March 1919, Staples approached Kelly, who made his fortune as Ireland's leading coal merchant and the largest owner of coastal steamers in Britain. Kelly also owned coalmines at St Helens and Whitehaven, in north-west England, and commissioned his Whitehaven manager, Thomas Durham, to bore for coal and plan a 'moderately extensive colliery'.[14] Durham predicted that Coalisland might produce '100,000 tonnes per annum over an estimated life of 40 years', speculating that the Lough Neagh basin contained 200 million tonnes.[15]

Staples hoped that Kelly, 'a Belfast boy with a genius for finance and certainly on the business plane with wide vision', might 'in a few years do more to help complete Irish unity than Carson, Griffith [and] De Valera rolled together'.[16] In fact, Kelly was a leading financial contributor to the Unionist Party's secret arms committee, established in 1912, which included the future prime minister, James Craig; his permanent secretary, and then UVF quartermaster, Wilfred Spender; George Clark of the 'Wee Yard', Workman & Clark's, Belfast's second-largest shipyard;

the millionaire stockbroker, James Cunningham; and the aforementioned Dawson Bates.[17] Indeed, prior to and during the abortive general strike of 1926, Kelly sat in on cabinet meetings and advised on policy.[18] As a Unionist insider, Kelly assured the minister for finance, Hugh Pollock, that he was 'practically sure' the Lough Neagh basin could produce at least 120 million tonnes: 'You can appreciate what this will mean to Ulster both from an economic standpoint and in providing employment.'[19]

In addition to the two mine shafts, Kelly planned to build 300 houses for English and Scottish miners. Moreover, he purchased the Ulster Fireclay Works, which produced a range of kiln-fired piping products, and the Tyrone Brickyard on the road between Coalisland and Dungannon. Kelly bought the bankrupt Roan Spinning Mill and, in cooperation with Christopher Beatty, the local Unionist JP and manager at Clark's now defunct weaving factory, he established the Coalisland Weaving Factory Limited. Beatty had known Kelly from his time as a manager at Ewart's Spinning Mill in Belfast.[20]

The Unionist government provided Kelly with a guaranteed loan to build the houses, and Dawson Bates pressured the local Rural District Council (RDC) to construct the necessary infrastructure; the UULA chairman and new minister for labour, John M. Andrews, provided £40,000 for the project, secured from the London exchequer. When the pit officially opened amid great fanfare in July 1924, Andrews described Kelly as a 'public spirited, patriotic Ulsterman' who 'had found for them a coal supply of their own, within their own boundaries, and within the loyal county of Tyrone.' It was 'through industry and industry alone' that they could create 'that Ulster which they pictured in their dreams and prayed for in their prayers': industry 'promoted by the energy and enterprise of their capitalists working in friendly cooperation with their industrious workers.'[21]

Andrews' characterisation appeared questionable on two key points. Firstly, the loyalty of majority-nationalist Tyrone rested on shaky ground. While the Dungannon RDC, where Coalisland lay, had a slim enough nationalist majority, the town itself was overwhelmingly Catholic.[22] Indeed, under the ambiguous terms of Article XII, Tyrone nationalists widely, but wrongly, anticipated that the entire county would transfer to the Irish Free State.[23] Furthermore, the recent and subsequent history of the Coalisland area indicated little in the way of 'friendly cooperation' between capitalist and worker. Indeed, Kelly's intervention exacerbated existing sectarian tensions, which the employers often manipulated to serve their own ends. The best historical treatment of the Kelly scheme has concluded that 'Northern Ireland's natural disadvantages overcame both the enterprise of its leading coal merchant and the enthusiasm of the Ministry of Commerce.'[24]

In this chapter I will explore why the new Unionist government supported Kelly, and how complex issues of class and sectarianism played out on the ground when Ulster's leading capitalist confronted a majority-nationalist workforce in an area whose constitutional future appeared to hang in the balance.

Above all, the Coalisland story sheds light on the sectarian underpinnings of Unionist rule in Tyrone, and across the North more generally, wherein the elite institutionalised discrimination in the allocation of scarce economic resources and deliberately manipulated a form of reactionary Orange populism to maintain working-class Protestant support. The chapter concludes by exploring an unprecedented display of working-class solidarity in 1926, when Protestant and Catholic workers united after the much-heralded Coalisland miracle turned out to be little more than pie in the sky.

Government Assistance

Kelly's Whitehaven pit manager hinted that Newtownkelly also made sense from 'the national standpoint', as the operation would 'very shortly' require a 'large and steady' stream of English and Scottish miners. Within the context of a sectarian electoral headcount and the impending Boundary Commission, the influx of hundreds of British workers obviously bolstered Unionist claims to this contested territory. Interestingly, Durham admitted that it had 'only been possible to obtain our existing staff because of the industrial depression in other mining areas', and that, 'if trade conditions improve in their home areas, we are very likely to lose a good many valuable men'. He therefore advised Kelly to 'lay out a modern colliery village properly sewered and with an adequate domestic water supply'.[25] Subsequent events suggested that many of these Scottish miners carried significant political baggage with them that not only partially explained their unemployment at home, but also rendered them peculiar candidates for the Orange colonisation of nationalist Tyrone.

While Kelly invested at least £100,000 of his own money, he also lobbied hard for government assistance to build miners' homes, fund local infrastructure, and eventually subsidise coal production. Pollock was 'in full sympathy' with Kelly regarding housing, since the enterprise presented 'possibilities of a wonderful mineral future for Ulster'.[26] Indeed, he warned cabinet that it would be well 'for the government to have some interest in the matter and to give some form of concrete encouragement to the enterprise and courage of a citizen who has taken great personal risks, merely, I believe, animated by a high sense of public duty'.[27] Pollock then petitioned the 'very sympathetic' chancellor of the exchequer, Stanley Baldwin, for a £1.5 million extension of the Trade Facilities Act – legislation designed to enable companies to borrow money for projects which would create employment, with the state guaranteeing the capital and interest.[28] Indeed, while London ended its series of Trade Facilities Acts in 1926, Stormont persevered with their Loans Guarantee Act until 1934, as it kept Belfast's largest shipyard afloat – 'crucial not only for the industrial survival of Northern Ireland but also for the political survival of the Unionist government'.[29]

Andrews, Bates and Craig formed a populist faction within the cabinet, blending sectarian and democratic tactics to secure loyalist support.[30] With Coalisland in mind, Bates pushed for a clause in the Housing Bill to grant industrial centres in rural areas the same benefits as urban districts. This allowed the government to provide a partial subsidy to housing at Newtownkelly, with additional funding from Ulster Bank under the Guaranteed Loan Act (1922).[31] Water supply, sanitation and road transport remained under local government control, however. Andrews secured a British-funded grant for Dungannon RDC's water scheme, but criticised delays, admitting that Bates's Ministry of Home Affairs had 'probably gone further than they ought in putting pressure upon the local authorities to exercise their powers'.

Despite divisions within cabinet between Craig's sectarian populists and Pollock's fiscal conservatives, both backed the Coalisland project. By January 1923, Pollock detailed the extensive government support for Kelly's coal venture: easy financing under the Trade Facilities Act, £60 per house built, and labour assistance through the Unemployment

Scheme. In short, 'the government had done everything that was possible, taking into account the present financial position'.[32]

The latter referred to ongoing negotiations between Belfast and London to revise the GOIA's financial terms: Craig's government did not wish to appear 'more generous than the Imperial Government in such matters as this would embarrass his negotiations with the Colwyn Committee'.[33] More than once, Craig threatened London with resignation, and convinced Baldwin to establish the Northern Ireland Special Arbitration, or Colwyn, Committee in winter 1922 to revise the terms of Belfast's imperial contribution, the funding of its social services, and payment for the USC.

The second Colwyn report, in 1925, effectively abolished the imperial contribution, which the Belfast government redirected into the sinkhole of unemployment relief.[34] Furthermore, Westminster would provide 'ongoing financial support', but 'total public expenditure per capita in Northern Ireland' was capped 'to the average level in Britain, despite greater demands on public expenditure, particularly unemployment' in the North. This inevitably led to 'a lower standard of public services, with opportunity costs in the areas of education, housing, and industry and infrastructure'.[35]

Certainly, the passion for Kelly's enterprise appeared to be fuelled by the hope, no matter how vain, that Craig's cabinet could square the circle between its self-image as an industrious imperial province and the stark reality of Northern Ireland's inexorable economic decline. Yet, while the Stormont regime's threat of long-term bankruptcy receded, the Coalisland colliery's prospects appeared less secure. Kelly soon petitioned the government for 'a subvention in aid of wages . . . in order to place the colliery on parallel lines with those in Great Britain', as, without help, it 'would have to close down'. While an alarmed Andrews 'thought it would be disastrous if the colliery had to close', the frugal Pollock 'expressed doubt as to the view Lord Colwyn would take'. Ultimately, Craig insisted: 'we should obtain our proper proportion of' the Treasury subsidy to British mines, later adding that he 'did not want it suggested that the owners had to close down the mine owing to lack of support'.[36]

In the meantime, James Craig, with his wife and son, paid an unofficial visit in May 1924, by 'special train', and Kelly personally 'conducted the party . . . through the various departments'.[37] Craig remarked that 'Coalisland had a great future', predicting that 'it would be the first town in County Tyrone'.[38] Indeed, Kelly made Craig's son, also James, 'a humble worker' at the colliery, the nationalist *Irish News* retrospectively sneering that Kelly had handpicked young Craig 'for the post on the assumption that the venture was going to be a gigantic success'.[39]

Due to the prime minister's illness, Lady Craig officially opened the Colliery in July 1924 during a 'luncheon for 2000 guests', who arrived by two special trains from Belfast, Lisburn, Portadown and Dungannon. Kelly expressed his 'gratification' at 'having done something for his native province', and promised that this day marked 'only the beginning of a great era of industry and progress'. Lady Craig described the occasion as 'a red-letter day in the history of Ulster', while the mayor of Belfast, William Turner, claimed that the ceremony that day 'marked an epoch not only in the life of Sir Samuel but also in the history of the imperial province of Ulster'.[40]

A standard propaganda piece with photographs appeared in all the major Unionist dailies and weekly regional papers, proclaiming the 'Gigantic Ulster Enterprise – the Miracle of Coalisland – the Romance of Newtownkelly'. The celebratory tone portrayed Kelly as an industrial titan, who, 'by his foresight, courage, and enterprise in the face of many difficulties', had 'won through, and the colliery and town bearing his name will be looked upon by every Ulsterman as work well done by a patriotic and noble son of the province'. In short, 'Ulster's industrial life will be completely revolutionised' and, 'with a reduction in the cost of their fuel, northern manufacturers should be able to beat their foreign competitors'.[41] Elsewhere, Kelly strode the Ulster stage as an 'Alexander of Industry', who, 'once committed to an enterprise[,] never permits consideration of expenditure to stand in the way of successful achievement, especially when . . . the desired consummation is fraught with vital influence upon the economic destiny of his native Province'. The same article continued that the colliery would produce 100,000 tonnes per year, and that 'the value to the economic life of Ulster of a thriving and productive coalfield within her own borders is incalculable'. Likewise, the Ulster Fireclay Works exuded 'an air of prosperity and progressiveness' that generated 'infectious optimism'. Indeed, the workers' homes or 'palaces', built with government assistance, boded well for a future where, in 'a few years, a population of some 25,000 should find ideal conditions in this new urban community, whose location will be marked on future maps by the new and magic name of Newtownkelly'.[42]

A contemporary opinion piece by the nationalist *Irish News* avoided much of the hyperbole, however, noting that it was 'unfortunate that the houses are not yet ready for occupation, the delay being due to a wages dispute between Messrs Collen Bros (Portadown) the contractors for the water and sewage scheme and their workers'. The reporter opined that the men's 'reasonable [demands] should have been met in a spirit of conciliation by the contractors, who apparently assumed that they had the sole right to fix the wages, and that the men are bound to take what they get'.[43]

Class and Sectarianism in the Coalisland Coalfield

Managers across Kelly's businesses in Coalisland manipulated sectarianism to undermine the bargaining power of labour. In several instances, they locked out workers and replaced them with strike-breakers recruited from the part-time 'B' Special Constabulary. Interestingly, when Craig first approached Baldwin in 1922 regarding the eventual Colwyn award, the chancellor quickly identified the funding of the USC as the 'sole exception . . . to be reserved for separate consideration'.[44] In 1925, one Liberal MP wryly pointed out that Craig wielded an armed force larger than the armies of Austria or Bulgaria.[45] While Craig lobbied hard for additional funds for 'the present magnificent system of Special Constabulary', the Treasury in London hinted that the force served as 'a means of providing for unemployment'.[46]

Three classes of Special Constabulary existed. The full-time 'A' Specials were either attached to Royal Irish Constabulary (RIC) or Royal Ulster Constabulary (RUC) barracks, or formed independent platoons. The part-time 'B' Specials each had a rifle and Webley revolver, and mobilised once a week and during emergencies. The local 'C' Specials comprised the less physically able members of the old Ulster Volunteer Force (UVF). By 1924, Tyrone contained 3,630 'B' Specials. Constables on full patrol received a £10 annual bounty, while those on half patrol got £7, and 7s per day in event of mobilisation. In short, 'B' Specials received an increment on their ordinary salary, funded by a British government grant of £1,250,000 for the 1924 financial year alone.[47]

In June 1922, Dungannon mill owner, former Irish rugby international and local 'B' Specials commander, Major Robert Stevenson, wrote a scathing confidential report about the USC's sectarianism, which came 'right down through from the politicians on top'. Stevenson claimed that the 'B' force represented 'the ordinary Protestant countryman and in many cases corner boy', being 'supplied with arms and clothing by his Government and "authorised" to get "on top", as it were, of his [Roman Catholic] neighbours'.[48] He concluded: 'North of Ireland Protestants are not saints, they have always been taught to hate [Roman Catholics] and it is against all reason to expect that untrained, undisciplined, and almost wholly without supervision, they can be armed, uniformed, and entrusted with police duties – human nature cannot rise to that right away!'[49]

After an attack on the Police Barracks in Coalisland on 3 May 1922, the IRA shot dead local 'B' Special Constable Robert Cardwell.[50] A party of USC, two of them 'unable to stand they were so drunk', then killed two nationalist civilians in reprisal.[51] While Stevenson published a public letter warning the Specials about their future conduct, the RIC district inspector (DI), Henry Jordan Walshe, described USC violence as par for the course: 'until the [IRA] gunmen were banished', he declared, 'those people [Catholics] would have to bear the consequences'.[52]

In addition to the local religious breakdown, the Coalisland and Dungannon nexus represented one of the most republican areas in Ulster. The Irish Republican Brotherhood remained strong locally through the late nineteenth and early twentieth centuries, and exhibited a strong strain of working-class labourite politics. Indeed, local republicans had been central to strikes at the failed Congo colliery, on the southern side of Coalisland, in the late 1890s. More recently, local trade unions had ridden the wave of industrial militancy that swept Ulster in the late war years and just prior to the post-war economic slump. The same slump formed the background to the defeat of labour politics in Tyrone and Ulster more generally in the wake of the July 1920 shipyard expulsions in Belfast, and the consolidation of the new Unionist one-party regime. Within this context of depression and demoralisation, the Dublin-based Irish Transport and General Workers' Union (ITGWU) vied with the British-based Workers' Union for the fragments of local trade unionism. Ironically, many of the same activists had cooperated during Ulster's red wave, but a return to the successful militancy of 1918 and 1919 seemed a distant prospect.

Just prior to the signing of the Treaty in 1921, the local ITGWU's organiser reported that talk of an eight-hour-day or half-holiday on

Saturday would be condemned as 'Bolshevik' by the local Unionist elite, concluding that, 'in Dungannon[,] the Fatherhood of God is proclaimed, although the Brotherhood of Man may be non-existent'. He continued: 'the boss is merely pulling the strings in his own interests', unconcerned 'as to whether a man is Catholic or Protestant, black or white, providing his labour is cheap; And that it is, sir, cheap in Dungannon'. In Coalisland, the organiser claimed that 'the philanthropist [Kelly] is giving local labour a chance, of course at the philanthropist's price! The men are showing signs of discontent with the pittance and before long there will be an improvement or a stoppage.' He concluded: 'while Coalisland is more hopeful than Dungannon . . . with prosperous times ahead, if the workers mean to share that prosperity, they must of necessity combine'.[53]

At Kelly's Tyrone Brickyard, workers joined the ITGWU, while the union competed against the Workers' Union to secure members in the Ulster Fireclay Works and the large clay pit that served it. John McMahon chaired the ITGWU branch at the Brickworks, and Patrick Skelton acted as secretary. Both men were republicans, and very likely also members of the Old Engine branch of the IRB.[54] They were also the sons of local miners, who appeared to have spent considerable time working in Scotland as well as the then-defunct Congo mine.[55] At a large meeting, the local 'representative of the cross channel [Workers'] union', Neal O'Donnell, 'was present, but neither questions nor criticisms, although cordially invited, were forthcoming, and a good meeting ended in the appointment of shop stewards and a committee of organisers'.[56]

O'Donnell, however, clearly resented the ITGWU's attempts to poach members in Coalisland, especially given the much-heralded prospect of industrial revival. While the ITGWU carried the day at the Brickyard, the two unions appeared 'at loggerheads' in the Ulster Fireclay Works. The employer apparently sided with O'Donnell and the Workers' Union, however, and would not 'allow any ITGWU men into the works'.[57]

Kelly had therefore set upon developing his industry in an area riven by sectarian and class divisions. At the beginning of 1923, the ITGWU's *Voice of Labour* sarcastically remarked: 'one would think the golden age at last was dawning. Alas! The facts are at present [that] some 120 employees of Sir Samuel Kelly's clay pit, brickyard, and pipe [Ulster Fireclay] yard are out on strike against a 5-shilling cut in wages.' It continued that 'those who have toiled through the muck of a clay hole in winter, or sweated in a kiln in summer, will understand best the ideas which some people hold as regards prosperity'.[58]

At the Ulster Fireclay Works, Patrick Quinn, Con O'Neill and Joseph Quinn 'accosted' John Davis for crossing a picket line. The magistrate and local Orangeman, Robert Newton, warned that the workers

> had been getting on shaky ground, but as the strike was now settled the magistrates would dismiss the case. Sir Samuel Kelly was a wealthy man, one of the few who had made his money in Ireland . . . They had their first taste of labour trouble in Coalisland, and the magistrates hoped it would be the last.[59]

The fifty men at the Tyrone Brickyard worked over fifty hours for 40s in continuous day-and-night shifts, producing 100,000 bricks per week. Indeed, the firm admitted 'they [made] a profit on the brick-yard, but wages must come down, although [they refused] a proposal to accept 37s 6d for 48 hours' from the men. The piece continued that, 'when Sir Samuel Kelly was plain Mister, we found him the best and most reasonable man amongst the hard-faced men of the Belfast coal ring. Whether the knighthood has changed him or the coal discovery, or that he has handed his power over to his managers, we cannot say but hope to learn this week'. Nevertheless, the local ITGWU pledged to 'stand firm against an injustice, determined that if Coalisland is to be prosperous, it will be real prosperity, as found in the strong healthy bodies of free men and free women, not in the dwarfed and stunted bodies of slaves'.[60]

The following week, the *Voice* noted the appearance of 'imports from Belfast', a city notorious for sweated labour, which also manufactured 'the blackleg species'. Similarly, at the clay pit, 'the blacklegs were introduced under the protection of the Specials, who, to give them credit, do not relish the task, for there's streaks of loathsomeness about the scab which makes honest men shun them'. The piece noted: 'there are still a few rebels in Coalisland against attempts to exploit them in the interests of the wealthy', concluding, 'no matter who rules, the worker intends to secure a living wage'.[61] After a conference with Kelly himself, the firm agreed to implement a smaller reduction, to be reviewed in July at the Ulster Fire Clay and Tyrone Brick yards, although the men in the clay pit held out for better terms.[62]

The ITGWU then alleged that O'Donnell had attempted to frustrate their efforts by siding with the employer for more favourable terms.[63] The *Voice* alleged that 'to be in the Irish Transport Union in Coalisland not only gets a man in the black books of the Unionist employers but good nationalists are also seeing to it that there's no work for the members of the ITGWU'.[64] After O'Donnell apparently poached back members at the Clay Pit, the ITGWU described him as the 'hidden hand of a management which hates the Transport Union', who got among 'members of the Transport out on strike', warning that, 'if ever a boomerang was made, the firm and the Workers Union will discover this pact as one, and it will not be long ere it whirls back with renewed force and smashes the unholy combination'.[65]

A local republican and ITGWU supporter, John Quinn, criticised O'Donnell for protesting 'against the action of certain employers importing labour from country districts, while fifty or sixty men were signing the unemployment register in the town'. Quinn alleged that the blame lay with O'Donnell, who connived with employers.[66] Apparently, having marginalised the ITGWU in favour of the Workers' Union, local employers then used mostly Protestant labour from outside Coalisland to undermine O'Donnell, leading to his eventual arrest in July.[67]

At this point a relative of Constable Robert Cardwell wrote to the local Unionist *Mid-Ulster Mail* to challenge nationalist complaints that Kelly's firms employed too many 'outsiders'. David Cardwell, from the Unionist townland of Ballynakilly, just outside Coalisland town, claimed that Protestants had previously been unable to get jobs in the Fireclay Works, before Kelly bought the business, but that now things were gradually changing. Cardwell had 'lived in this district' and his 'forebears' before him, and could never get a job in the town, but he trusted 'the time is at hand when this will be changed'. Indeed, it appeared 'near time there was a change in a class of hands', as the Catholics 'were always on strike and quarrelling with their masters'. Alluding to the dispute between the Workers' Union and ITGWU, Cardwell mocked how 'they could not even agree amongst themselves, and were shifting from one agitator to another, whichever one would threaten the bosses the most, and it is not long since they went into the yard and threatened the manager'. He concluded that there was no use 'complaining about bringing Englishmen over here to do work which the local men refused to do', and that 'the handwriting is on the wall' for local Catholics looking for work from Sir Samuel Kelly.[68]

Having displaced the ITGWU from the Ulster Fireclay Works and the Clay Pit, O'Donnell then sought a standard local rate for workers employed in building miners' cottages. The main building contractors were Teggart, from Belfast, and Collen Bros from Portadown – both Protestant firms. After a strike and negotiations, Collen Bros agreed to the local rate, but Teggart held out, paying 2s 6d per week less. During a picket of the site, Teggart employed local 'B' Specials as strike-breakers. Workers' Union organiser Robert McClung alleged that the RUC had acted 'in a very offensive manner . . . using violence towards the wives and children of our members, who are on dispute there'. He wrote to Bates that members had 'the right to peacefully picket during a trade dispute, and as the police know every man, woman and child in the Coalisland area, we do not think it is necessary . . . to use violence in the slightest degree'. He then warned that it would be a 'very unfortunate thing for everybody if our members get out of hand owing to the violence of the RUC'.[69]

The local RUC denied using violence, and reported that a 'crowd of about 250 persons including women were outside the works . . . booing and their attitude was intimidatory'. When the sergeant told O'Donnell they would have to move on, he replied: 'we can stay as long as we like as long as we don't assault anybody'. The police 'ordered the crowd to disperse and after some persuasion' the Constable apparently 'got them away'.[70] On this occasion, the workers knew the law and the Trades Disputes Act better than the police, and the Ministry advised the RUC 'to avoid, if possible, coming into conflict of any sort with the strikers'.[71] Bates's department also directed the RUC to monitor the Workers' Union in a similar fashion to the ITGWU.

Then, on 27 July, while Teggart paid the strike-breakers, O'Donnell approached him to ask for wages owed to men who had worked a partial week before going on strike. Teggart got the police to remove him, and O'Donnell then told another large crowd in earshot of the strike-breakers: 'If you had the spirit of a dog you wouldn't work for Teggart. You are yellow dogs anyway.' The police arrested him for a breach of the peace. At O'Donnell's trial, one of the 'B' Specials claimed that O'Donnell 'came into the building ground [and] called him bad names for not coming out on strike along with the rest'. When John Skeffington, O'Donnell's solicitor and a local Hibernian or constitutional nationalist leader, questioned Teggart as to his failure to pay the local rate, D.I. Walshe interjected in the proceedings, shouting: 'Don't answer that question!'[72]

Two witnesses – McClung and Henry Hughes, a local Catholic labourer – then testified that Teggart had in fact assaulted O'Donnell. D.I. Walshe asked Hughes whether he was 'a very peaceful citizen'. Hughes replied: 'I belong to Coalisland (Laughter).' Walshe then added: 'Coalisland has a bad name. (More laughter).' Skeffington interjected: 'We will see now if the workman will get the same justice as the employer.' The JP claimed that 'it was a scandal to see so much opposition to' Kelly, 'a man . . . prepared to spend so much money in promoting employment. It was playboys such as they had heard about that day that were destroying trade and creating trouble'.[73] He then fined O'Donnell £5 – a sentence overturned on appeal.[74] The dispute lasted four months. In October, the RUC reported that the strike was 'fizzling out', and that Teggart still 'employed' the USC 'strike breakers'.[75]

Nevertheless, in April 1924 the *Belfast Telegraph* reported that 'the labour dispute at Coalisland appears to be spreading'. Even before the pit officially opened, some British miners joined local workers in demanding improved conditions.[76] Ominously, the issue at the colliery revolved around 'faults' and 'varying strata conditions', which meant that sinkers in Shaft 2 did not meet their quota, and management docked their pay. The men in Shaft 1 then went out on sympathy strike.[77] The miners struck at the same time as workers, also employed by Collen Bros (Portadown), on the Coalisland Water Supply Scheme, which had received a £40,000 grant from Andrews to service Newtownkelly. The Dungannon RDC hired two contractors, one working at the Coalisland end of the scheme and the other at the Washingbay on Lough Neagh, nine miles to the east. A local nationalist won the Coalisland contract, while the RDC granted Collen Bros (Portadown), which had paid the local rate at Newtownkelly in 1923, the contract for Washingbay. Under the grant's terms, only workers with a 'green ticket' from the Unemployment Exchange could gain employment. Collen Bros complained that, as the strikers had not 'made any attempt to return to work', they proposed to employ 'an entirely new set of men regardless of the green ticket man and get on with the work without further delay'. Nevertheless, the conditions of the grant meant that they could not employ whom they wished.[78]

The employer then spread the rumour that the Washingbay strike hinged on the appointment of 'a new gaffer', who alleged that his position as 'a member of the C Special Constabulary' represented the real reason for the strike. Once again, the newspapers noted: 'a strong force of police has arrived under District-Inspector Walshe, Dungannon'. Collen Bros, who had previously paid the local rate, appeared emboldened by Teggart's success at Newtownkelly, paying workers at the Lough shore end of the scheme 25s, while men employed in Coalisland Town by the local nationalist contractor, McNally, were receiving 33s 6d. The Workers' Union called both teams out, demanding the local rate of 35s. Similarly, carters at the Ulster Fireclay Works and the Colliery, who received 24s, struck demanding 'the local standard wage'. Collen Bros then informed its building workers at Newtownkelly that they would be cutting wages from 35s to 32s 6d. The Unionist *Newsletter* lamented the inconvenience caused by the strikes, since the 'Coalisland streets are all "up" for the laying of the water main through the town, and they are dangerous to traffic'.[79] It might help to note that the average weekly income of a labourer in Britain in 1905 exceeded what Collen Bros paid workers on the Lough shore in 1924, and that the average wage for a British labourer in 1925 sat at 55s 7d, while a bricklayer could expect 73s 6d.[80]

The contractor for the Coalisland end of the Water Scheme eventually paid the local rate, and it was 'expected that the laying of the line of pipes from Annagher will speedily be completed'. Collen Bros then agreed to pay the 'district rate of wages' at Newtownkelly, and it was 'expected that the first eighty houses will be ready for occupation in a few weeks'. The carters at the Fireclay Works and Colliery and the thirty sinkers agreed to return to work, with 'terms of pay . . . left to the management and the union officials for final settlement'. This agreement was reached after face-to-face meetings between Robert McClung and Kelly at the latter's office in Station Street, Belfast.[81] Negotiations 'broke down', however, when Collen Bros maintained its belligerent attitude at Washingbay.[82]

The Workers' Union headquarters in London duly sent a £107 strike fund at the beginning of May.[83] Collen Bros then recruited three strikebreakers from Stewartstown, nine miles north-west, for the Washingbay end of the Water Scheme – each with a 'green ticket'. One morning, three union members armed with bludgeons held them up a mile from the works. 'They were told that if they crossed a line that had been drawn across the road they would do so at their peril. The men thought discretion was the better part of valour and went to Coalisland by a circuitous route', returning to work 'under police protection'.[84] After arranging an identity parade, Walshe arrested three strikers. One of the men, Peter Douglas, described the strike-breakers as 'three right blackguards . . . It would not be so bad had they been there before the strike'.[85]

At this stage, several hundred people attended another 'big labour demonstration' in Coalisland Square, which pledged 'fealty to the men out on strike'. Speaking from the back of a motor car, McClung claimed the three prisoners were only guilty of 'asserting their right in a trades labour dispute'. These men were 'working in mud and slush and dirt' for the 'miserable wage' of 6d per hour. 'The Workers Union did not advocate strikes, but sometimes, as in the case of the Water Scheme at Washingbay, they are unavoidable.' Bob Getgood said: 'it was quite evident that there was something radically wrong at Coalisland'. The employer 'was certain to have his pound of flesh while you have the bone. (Laughter)'.[86] The RUC reported that the meeting generated 'considerable enthusiasm', and O'Donnell resolved to 'call out' Collens's workers at Newtownkelly 'in sympathy with the men [at Washingbay], who were working for the same firm'.[87]

Across 1923–24, the Workers' Union alleged that the police acted under the direction of local bosses.[88] Sam Kyle complained to the Ministry of Home Affairs of police 'exceeding their duty in treating members of the Workers' Union as if they were members of a secret society', and asked that police not visit the homes of union officials and question their relatives, but instead acquire information on the union from the regional office in Belfast.[89] Managers and subcontractors across Kelly's enterprises developed a policy of reducing wages, falsely claiming the Catholic workers were sectarian, and then appointing part-time members of the USC to act as strike-breakers, while the RUC and full-time USC backed the employers. The tension between the Workers' Union and ITGWU rapidly dissolved, and trade-union organisers, mostly Protestant socialists from Belfast, cooperated in a struggle against a deliberately sectarian policy instigated by the employers and supported by the police.

For instance, while O'Donnell and the Workers' Union struggled to gain the local rate for labourers at Newtownkelly and on the Water Scheme, conflict re-emerged at the Tyrone Brickyard. Here, forty-three ITGWU men downed tools because 'six additional men were taken on' despite an agreement with managers that Transport members who had previously been made redundant would be re-hired. The *Northern Whig* reported that the yard then continued with 'voluntary labour under police protection, and these men are being conveyed to and from their work by motor under police escort'.[90] The ITGWU organised large meetings in Coalisland and Dungannon, addressed by William McMullen, the trade union's secretary, and Dawson Gordon. McMullen rejected allegations by the employer that the strike had a 'religious and political side', as 'they were both Protestants and strongly contended that there was nothing of a religious or a political taint in the fight for an honest wage'. Indeed, 'the 43 men who were out on strike were replaced by 50 Protestants'. The management desired to make it 'a religious quarrel' with their 'deep-rooted designs' to divide the workers.[91]

On the other hand, the local police fully backed the employer's line, claiming that the ITGWU's 'real grievance is that the six men are imported Protestants, practically all the workers hitherto being Roman Catholics. The management have decided to take this strike to the finish, and already they have 24 strike-breakers (all Protestants) engaged'. The report continued that the men were 'working under ample police protection and all precautions necessary for the protection of life and property have been taken. The works have been picketed by the strikers, but up to the present no intimidation has taken place'.[92]

The ITGWU branch then hired John Skeffington to demand a correction from the *Northern Whig* about its published account of the strike.[93] According to the workers, when management ended the night shift in March 1924 because of improved mechanisation, eight workers lost their jobs. The manager agreed that 'if extra men were required those dispensed with would get first preference'. Nevertheless, he then appointed seven Protestant workers 'without any notice whatever to the branch officials'. He eventually told McMahon and Skelton of the ITGWU, 'That is my business; Your business is to go on with your work.'

The branch committee then apparently convinced the new workers to 'stop operations immediately until the members of the union who were paid off' gained reinstatement, and that these men would be given next preference at the yard. The seven men duly 'came out with the other 43 men', but the Unemployment Bureau informed them that 'unless they went back to work, they would not be entitled to any further benefit'. The management then sent a motor car to the seven workers' homes, and they crossed the picket line.[94]

The manager, Cooper, then replaced the entire workforce with 'a similar number of demobilised "Specials" – Orange and Protestant to a man.'[95] The ITGWU alleged that management had spread a false rumour that the workers downed tools 'against the employment of Protestants – a clever, calculated perversion of the truth, told in the atmosphere where it has most likelihood of bearing fruit'. These Orange 'scabs' were brought 'to and from their work in motors' and 'paid 5s per week more than the old employees (dirty money) and have the company of armed protection'. The union concluded that, 'for crucifying their comrades, as usual, they are receiving the usual Judas fee':

> religion, thank God, is never a bone of contention in the One Big Union [ITGWU] . . . our members struck for the reinstatement of Protestant and Catholic alike – religion was not mentioned until the scab-hunters introduced the word. We believe that Sir Samuel Kelly would not stand for a pogrom being started in Tyrone, but we know that there are others who have not his tolerance or broad mindedness, and we know that, with the boundary question once more acute, there are many who would do much to see every Catholic cleared out of the county.[96]

The police noted: 'a certain amount of bitterness has now crept into this dispute', and that the ITGWU had covered the area with 600 posters, labelling the strike-breakers 'spineless jellyfish who live by scabbery'. When the ITGWU organiser 'attempted to address the strike-breakers when entering and leaving work', he 'was subjected to much cross-examination and would have been assaulted were it not for the presence of a large posse of police'. All told, the manager employed 'eleven more men . . . than before the strike. The men are brought to and from their work, under police protection, in motor cars supplied by the firm.'[97] The strike collapsed on 21 August 1924, with pickets withdrawn the following day. One local republican described the struggle to a comrade interned on the prison ship *Argenta*: 'The strike at the brickworks still continues and looks very blue. We are down and out all through the signing of the f**king Treaty!'[98]

Indeed, the *Voice of Labour* declared: 'No Catholic need apply!', adding that 'when God made the earth and placed coal in the Dungannon district, apparently, He placed it there to be worked by Protestants only, this, at least, seems to be the opinion of Sir Samuel Kelly's manager at the pit'.[99] Similarly, the *Irish News* reported that 'a religious test was being applied to men seeking employment at the new coal mine at Coalisland and other works in the same district'. The 'overwhelming evidence' apparently proved that 'under the cloak of industrial developments the Ulster Unionist leaders are carrying out a new plantation. The Catholic majority in Tyrone has always been a bitter pill to the Unionists, and plans were made immediately after the passing of the Government of Ireland Act to gain the balance of power'. After citing the gerrymandering of electoral boundaries as 'the first step in the conspiracy', the paper alleged that Craig's government had promoted the coal industry as 'another big effort to accomplish their purpose'. The employer apparently took care that the Cumberland and Scottish miners 'were all Protestants'. However, 'two of the Scotch miners, preferring to have working by their side men they knew, sent to Lanarkshire for two of their old [Catholic] mates'. These men signed a statement that they were refused work on religious grounds. The article alleged that 'this was not an isolated instance but was part of a considered policy to exclude Catholics, as far as it was possible to do so, from benefiting by the industrial development'.[100]

The Coalisland Colliery Lockout

Then, less than four months after its July opening, the Colliery management locked workers out twice in two months. The causes can be traced back to already apparent issues with faults in the steep seams, and with the workers themselves. The manager of the pit later privately confided that the lockout's 'real object . . . was to get rid of some undesirable men'.[101] Across Kelly's enterprises, local managers had deployed a religious test to undermine workers' demands for fair pay and conditions. Indeed, some Unionists clearly hoped that the influx of solidly Protestant miners from Scotland and northern England might even tip the demographic balance in East Tyrone. Nevertheless, the unemployed miners attracted to Coalisland contained a hard core of militant trade unionists. It is likely many happened to be unemployed in their own districts because they were already blacklisted.

The RUC reported how, due to continuing underproduction, the management informed the workers that, from 27 October 1924, 'they would be paid by output (or piecework) instead of at certain rates per shift as at present'. The Scottish miners 'do not belong to any trade union in this country', and 'all necessary protection is being afforded to the police, but it is feared that further strike trouble is brewing in Coalisland and district'.[102] The workers faced a 25s-a-week cut precipitated by the dawning realisation that 'Kelly has been greatly disappointed in the results so far of the new enterprise, the output of coal not being anything like what he expected. Several of the seams which promised to yield enormous quantities of coal stopped short, while others were gradually reduced in size until they would not pay the working'.[103]

The 150 men duly formed a branch of the Miners' Federation, 'and all those employed at the colliery, except the engine and pump engineer, left their work'. The RUC noted that 'the owner of the colliery is prepared to make a stand against the men's demands'.[104] The resulting negotiations proved 'so unsatisfactory' that the management instituted a lockout on 28 October. The workers not only insisted on the old rate, a half holiday each Saturday, and overtime for work on weekends, but demanded that 'the management should meet a committee of the men each week, to "discuss the running of the mine"'. Regarding this 'as purely communistic', management 'refused to consider it'. The police identified 'several very doubtful characters' among the miners who were 'absolute Bolshevists in their attitude and are a source of danger in the locality', including a miner named Shaw from Durham, who 'is an out-and-out Communist'.[105]

After another meeting, the miners sent a deputation, which management rejected. The workers complied, sending a 'peace' deputation, and management insisted they return to work before discussions could take place. Most miners agreed, while some, dissatisfied, worked a week's notice and returned to Scotland.[106] The dispute flared again a month later, when further wage cuts prompted another strike. On 29 November, Kelly suspended operations, prompting many remaining miners to leave for England and Scotland. The RUC reinforced its presence in the district following the closure.[107] Kelly, having lost confidence, locked out workers to pave the way for a skeleton crew of forty men to maintain the mine as long as the government's coal subsidy lasted. The RUC reported that only about ten locked-out miners and their families remained in Coalisland, and 'the local branch of the Coalminers' Union' had effectively disbanded.[108] The *Irish News* noted that many laid-off miners filed unemployment claims, which Andrews's Ministry of Labour delayed pending investigation – though it was widely expected they would be denied.[109]

Clearly, estimates of daily tonnage predicted in Unionist propaganda bore little relation to the hard facts on the coalface. By March 1925, the colliery was only producing fifty tons per day – the largest daily output across the period being eighty. The miners were working in 'broken ground and then about half the places they are crossing faults and that is the cause of the reduced output'. The seams were also too steep for conventional mining techniques, and many of the Scottish and English miners quickly returned home, as they were not 'accustomed to' working under such conditions.[110]

By July 1926 the nationalist *Irish News* speculated that 'a series of roads through the mine' needed to be built to access the fragmented seams, and that 'this would not only involve the expenditure of a large sum of money but would stop all mining operations at the pit'.[111] By this stage, the operation was receiving regular inspections as part of the Coal Mines Act.[112] That spring, the inspector did 'not think the colliery will work much longer', Kelly's dreams being 'doomed to disappointment' because the seams appeared badly affected 'by faults and washouts'. The report advised against 'hanging on' while 'steadily losing their money', concluding: 'if I was the owner, I should abandon the place and sell up'.[113]

The *Irish News* derived clear *Schadenfreude* from reporting James Craig Jr's appointment as a director of Kelly's St Helens Colliery Company in January 1927, hinting at 'strange stories' about efforts to portray the Coalisland mine as profitable. The paper mocked the Unionist government for exaggerating the venture's success, and painting it as the dawn of Ulster's industrial revolution. It also noted, with biting sarcasm, that Kelly's Coalisland Housing Company had yet to repay its secured loan for the miners' so-called palaces at Newtownkelly.[114]

Eventually, Craig's government conceded defeat and ended the coal subsidy – three times higher than in Britain – since the mine still operated at a greater loss than any British counterpart. Even with financial support, the accounts never balanced, and the mine shut down in April 1927.[115] As long as Kelly lived, the Ulster Bank refrained from enforcing timely payments on the housing loan. By 1937, the Ministry of Finance expressed 'relief' that the £200,000 government-backed loan had been repaid without loss, emphasising its resistance to repeated attempts to link the debt to the mine and absolve Kelly of liability.[116]

Postscript

By January 1926, Kelly's mine was no longer a going concern. The *Mid-Ulster Mail* wrongly guessed that 'the boundary question has something to do with the matter'.[117] The Unionist government could comfort itself, however, with the knowledge that the failure of the Commission the previous month had secured Coalisland and all of Tyrone's place within the boundaries of Craig's 'Ulster Pale'. With the threat to the south gone, however, the British Exchequer appeared less inclined to support the earlier extravagant funding for the USC. On 22 December, the Ministry of Home Affairs paid off the 600 'A' Specials in Tyrone. Similarly, after 1 April, the full- and half-patrol rates for the 'B' Specials ended, members now being left to manage on a £3 reserve annual bounty.[118] In 1926, unemployment in the North stood at 24.2 per cent – over double the figure in Britain. Furthermore, Craig's Unionist Party had achieved a less than impressive 55 per cent of the popular vote in the 1925 elections to the Northern parliament, and Sam Kyle of the Workers' Union led the recently formed Northern Ireland Labour Party (NILP) to a respectable 4.7 per cent, and three seats. When Craig added the four independent populist loyalist MPs to the equation, the result pointed towards some fraying at the edges of the cross-class Orange alliance.

In this context, the nascent NILP held a meeting of 500 people at Coalisland Picture House in a follow-up to a similar meeting at Dungannon on 28 December 1925. Robert Brown, a Scottish coal-miner resident in Newtownkelly, took the chair. Neal O'Donnell addressed the meeting, as did veteran socialist, Dublin-born Quaker and recently appointed NILP senator, Bob Dorman. The Workers' Union procession, which marched through the town carrying pit lamps, 'was headed by the Coalisland Brass Band and the Coalisland Pipers Band', while the worshipful master of the Orange Lodge and president of the Ancient Order of Hibernians 'marched in the procession and IRA ex-internees marched behind "B" Special Constabulary Pipers'. The perplexed secretaries of the Ministry of Home Affairs described this as an 'extraordinary gathering', whose 'composition . . . must, I should think, be unique in N. Ireland'.[119]

At the meeting itself, Brown protested the Ministry of Labour and the Employers' Committee decision to disallow 'a large number of our members' from unemployment benefit on 7 January, since they were 'not genuinely seeking work, when there is none to be had'. Dorman then pointed to 'two members of the RUC who were present, with good clothing, and clean hands, who were guaranteed a living, so long as they behaved themselves, and their health allowed them to perform their onerous duties'. The NILP

> wanted a similar guarantee for the working man. He asked those present to sink all differences and let North and South unite – Catholics and Protestants – Union Jack and Tricolour. He hoped the audience would do nothing by force. The Labour Party were out to do all by constitutional means – to stand together and use the vote.

The RUC inspector general, Charles Wickham, described the meeting as 'an extraordinary mixture, showing unanimity between Orangemen, Hibernians, and Sinn Feiners. "B" men marched with ex-internees and Scottish miners with local labourers'.[120] Dawson Bates's ministry felt particularly affronted by loyal 'B' Specials attending a socialist meeting, 'a practice which would appear to be altogether objectionable'.[121] Wickham claimed that the men were not in uniform and, therefore cautioned against drawing 'a distinction between this and an ordinary political meeting', since 'any action taken as regards one would have to govern that taken as regards the other'.[122] Wickham clearly implied that if 'B' men were banned from NILP meetings, then they presumably could not attend Unionist ones either!

The Unionist reflex was instinctively sectarian. In 1929, Craig abolished PR for elections to the Northern parliament in favour of first-past-the-post. He did this not to discriminate against nationalists, as that had already been effectively achieved by the 1922 local government gerrymander. Rather, abolishing PR halted electoral momentum based on working-class Catholic and Protestant support for the NILP, since, as Craig admitted, the 'old-fashioned plain and simple system' returned 'men who are for the Union on the one hand, or who are against it and want to go into a Dublin parliament on the other'.[123] When the Great Depression further stripped the meat from Stormont's bones and the working-class temporarily combined in the Outdoor Relief Strikes, the Unionist elite doubled down on sectarianism.

In the context of permanent British-imposed dependency and baseline austerity, and within the constraints of a supremacist Orange ideology, prominent Unionist leaders clearly adopted 'sectarian rhetoric', and endorsed 'exclusivist practices that actively discriminated against Catholics'.[124] This practice, however, had marked the northern polity from its birth, and efforts to provide a more granular or nuanced impression of Unionist rule tend to emphasise the particular over the general, and risk adopting a resigned indifference to the plight of the northern nationalist minority.

I have suggested that the Unionist government gave the maximum support possible to Samuel Kelly due to his history as a UVF gunrunner and his personal connections to Craig and Bates in particular. Furthermore, the government hoped that Kelly's success would alleviate their structural dependence on British subvention and chronic unemployment. The sectarian employment practices across Kelly's enterprises, and the protection they received from the police and judiciary, suggests that the new industrial revolution would benefit the Protestant population at the expense of Coalisland's considerable Catholic majority. Furthermore, the enthusiasm and considerable financial support for the homes at Newtownkelly partly relied on the desire to increase the local Protestant population, adding substance to Unionist rhetoric about 'loyal' Tyrone.

Therefore, while 'ideological diversity and complexity' did exist within Unionism, it is necessary to emphasise that those most prominent within the sectarian populist faction occupied the apex of Unionist politics for four decades, from Craig through Andrews and onto Basil Brooke. By 1933, Andrews was challenging those who claimed that Catholic porters outnumbered Protestants at Stormont's recently opened parliament buildings, adding: 'I have investigated the matter, and I find that there are 30 Protestants, and only one Roman Catholic there temporarily.'[125] When, that very year, Basil Brooke told assembled Orangemen at the Twelfth Field that he did not have a Roman Catholic about his own place, Craig subsequently supported him at Stormont, and claimed that 'there is not one of my colleagues who does not entirely agree with him.'[126] Indeed, the following month, he notoriously told the same body: 'I am an Orangeman first and a politician and Member of this Parliament afterwards', and that Stormont was a 'Protestant Parliament and Protestant State'.[127] In short, the Orange social contract underpinning Northern Ireland's foundation and continued miserable existence required a material basis in discrimination.

Yet, Unionism's determination to keep majority nationalist areas like East Tyrone within Craig's impregnable Pale, plus the Orange populist character of its discriminatory rule, created the long-term conditions for its eventual demise. The Tyrone Brickyard lay on the road between Coalisland and Dungannon. On 24 August 1968, the first Civil Rights march went down that very road, when the children and grandchildren of the striking workers discussed in this book engaged in one of those small acts which, when multiplied, can transform the world.[128] Bernadette Devlin joined the march from '90% Republican' Coalisland, which descended from a carnival atmosphere to one of 'passive anger' when an RUC cordon blocked the marchers' entry into Dungannon. Afterwards, in a pub not far from the empty shell of Coalisland colliery, Devlin criticised 'out of touch' politicians who 'thought they could come down, make big speeches, and be listened to respectfully'. It was then that 'the people all got out together' and 'turned round and said in effect to the politicians, "Clear off, you don't even think the way we think" '.[129] Here once again, for any historian willing to see, in the same place among descendants of the same people, 'the same aspirations, fears, and tensions are there', but 'in a new context, with new language and arguments, and a changed balance of forces'.[130]

Conclusion

Recall the song of the weavers, that bold call to struggle, in which there is not even a mention of hearth and home, factory or district, but in which the proletariat at once, in a striking, sharp, unrestrained and powerful manner, proclaims its opposition to the society of private property.

Karl Marx, 1844

Writing in 1914, from his home on Belfast's Falls Road, James Connolly famously predicted that partition would betray 'the national democracy of industrial Ulster' and herald 'a carnival of reaction both North and South' that 'would set back the wheels of progress . . . destroy the oncoming unity of the Irish Labour movement and paralyse all advanced movements whilst it endured'.[1] During the next decade, thousands of Irish workers heroically but in vain, challenged the forces of capital and empire, in a struggle informed by Connolly's own synthesis of the social and national questions. Until recently, however, these women and men appeared lost to posterity. This book has sought to retrieve one strand of this big story, charting the agency of a significant Protestant minority in Ulster politics that opposed partition and sectarianism, and promoted socialism to the extent that parts of the linen triangle appeared pregnant with revolutionary possibility – until Unionist reactionary violence fulfilled its half of Connolly's grim prophecy.

Certainly, with James 'Dongaree' Baird and other 'Rotten Prods' in the vanguard, Emmet O'Connor shows that hundreds of radical working-class Protestants broke with the labour aristocracy in Belfast's shipyards and foundries.[2] This book casts the net wider, to include the precariat of the city's mills and docks, and indeed mid-Ulster's rural proletariat, during socialism's heyday between the Armistice and the slump. Baird's Belfast Labour Party colleagues formed an activist hub which spread their anti-sectarian gospel across this Red Triangle, organising 40,000, mostly female, linen workers by 1919. Furthermore, while they clearly acted as 'catalysts of strike activity', the evidence suggests that complaints by bosses and police alike about the 'agitator theory of strikes' or 'the alleged manufacture of discontent' ignored how their socialist message fell 'on receptive ears', because workers had genuine 'grievances and justifiable demands to agitate about'.[3]

I have concentrated on how Dawson Gordon guided the Flax Rougher's Union from a semi-skilled benevolent society of 400, typically men, in 1914, to a 10,000-strong general union of mostly female linen spinners. Indeed, Sam Kyle and his comrades similarly organised the weavers through the Workers' Union, which mushroomed from having no local organiser and less than a thousand members before the war to 128 branches and 20,000 members across Ulster by 1920, also encompassing general labourers in shipyards, and factories and farms in Belfast and across rural east Ulster.[4]

In terms of strike activity and electoral support, by 1920, anti-partitionist Ulster Labour posed a genuine challenge to Unionist hegemony. The period this book has explored saw a series of strikes across the network of small regional towns from Armagh, Portadown and Lurgan to Cookstown, Dungannon and Coalisland in Tyrone. Indeed, strike fever spread rapidly to small satellite mills and factories in villages such as Donaghmore, Caledon and Gilford, while municipal workers and farm labourers also succumbed to the contagion, as militancy radiated from Belfast, rippling westwards across the surface of the Lough Neagh basin – out from the towns and into the countryside. Likewise, in the January 1920 urban elections, 'Protestants voted, to the number of at least 10,000, for Labour instead of Unionist candidates' in Belfast, returning Kyle and Gordon for Shankill, while 20 per cent of Catholic voters had switched to the ITGWU's Denis Heuston and Labour on the Catholic Falls. Across Ulster, Labour won almost 20 per cent of the UDC vote. As Baird ruefully told British trade unionists in the pogrom's aftermath, 'the workers were becoming class conscious . . . of course we had been defeated, but we were still making progress'.[5]

Northern workers – men and women, Catholic, Protestant and Dissenter – formed one part of a stillborn revolution across Ireland. O'Connor noted how, 'never since has the working class confronted the rationale of capitalism so profoundly or so extensively'.[6] Militancy and class consciousness flourished, with some advocating 'socialism from below'.[7] This energy materialised in the hundred soviets that emerged, including eighty in Munster alone in 1922. The revolution failed, however, due to the Labour leadership's timidity and the ferocity of its opponents. Despite their Connollyite roots, Tom Johnson and William O'Brien mastered the art of 'rhetorical extremism and practical quietism'.[8] During the independence struggle, the ILP&TUC deferred to Sinn Féin, sidelining itself from key decisions. Though Congress called four general strikes that paralysed the country, these remained largely symbolic, tied to the National Question rather than class struggle.[9] In short, the strikes showed massive working-class power, but did not look to achieve power for the working class. Kieran Allen concludes that Ireland's 'only became an aborted revolution because no political force emerged which could fuse national and social demands'.[10] Or, as Stefano Bartolini argued, 'Irish socialism lost a war that it never fought.'[11]

After the post-war boom had collapsed into overproduction by late 1920, and paranoid fears about Fenian invasion helped fuel the northern counter-revolution, the southern working-class struggle soon faced similar challenges. Jim Larkin returned to Ireland in April 1923, and by autumn 20,000 trade unionists were on strike in the Free State.[12] But the reactionary die had been cast. That February, one Cork employer openly wished for 'another Mussolini arising in this country'.[13] He would not wait long. Kevin O'Higgins, who dismissed the Democratic Programme as 'mostly poetry', swiftly crushed the labour movement, boasting in 1923: 'We are the most conservative-minded revolutionaries that ever put through a successful revolution.'[14] O'Higgins and a coterie of well-heeled Catholic public-school boys led the Party of Order, determined to 'vindicate the idea of law and ordered government, as against anarchy'.[15] Fellow Clongowes alumnus Patrick McGilligan bluntly declared: 'It is not the function of the Dáil to provide work and the sooner this is realised the better'. Consequently, 'people may have to die in this country of starvation'.[16] Ironically, Jimmy Baird, already scourged by the loyalist backlash, suffered the sharp end of the southern carnival of reaction as an ITGWU organiser for the hard-fought Waterford farm strike; the rural workers' struggle eventually crushed by Free State White Guards and abandoned by William O'Brien.[17]

Mike Davis argued that revolutionary class consciousness emerges at moments of convergence, when activists unite diverse demands and strategically synthesise proletarian grievances within specific crises.[18] By the early twentieth century, disillusionment with parliamentary politics and bureaucratic unions fuelled revolutionary syndicalism. In Belfast, activists embraced Connolly's fusion of republicanism, socialism and feminism as the Great Labour Unrest spread through the Welsh Valleys, the Liverpool Docks and Dublin's slums. The period from 1916 to 1920 saw escalating class struggle, driven by wartime devastation and impoverishment. By 1917, mass mutinies, bread riots and strikes had erupted across Europe, culminating in the October Revolution, while, in Belfast and the linen triangle, anti-sectarian socialists organised thousands in a doomed effort to create a fairer future.

During the European Revolution (1917–21), metalworkers in munitions plants and shipyards led rank-and-file revolts against war and exploitation, from Liebknecht in Berlin to Willie Gallacher on Red Clydeside. Confronted with the decline of craft regulation, many in the labour aristocracy embraced radical workers' control, sparking revolutionary consciousness in Petrograd, Glasgow, Turin and Berlin. In Belfast, however, much of the skilled labour aristocracy clung to craft exclusivity, reinforced by sectarian chauvinism. James Hinton described these 'labour aristocrats' as posing 'as the authentic spokesmen of the working class as a whole: but it was a pose. So long as they held to the exclusive character of their trade unionism the aristocrats could never genuinely embrace the working class.'[19] As Eric Hobsbawm noted, they simultaneously formed both 'the most active cadres of the workers' collective self-defence' across revolutionary Europe and 'the main prop of middle-class social control and industrial discipline' in the Anglosphere.[20]

This book has shown how elements of the Belfast labour aristocracy served as a tool of elite Unionist power. Across the long nineteenth century, Belfast grew from 20,000 to 387,000 residents, while skilled British migration intensified sectarianism. These migrants brought craft union traditions – and anti-Irish prejudice, partly mirroring Roediger's analysis of the formation of American contemporary 'whiteness'.[21] In

Belfast, anti-Catholicism reinforced Protestant supremacy, as 'the natural position of the white, like that of the Protestant, is on the higher steps of the social pyramid'.[22] Belfast's craft unions mirrored US 'craft and race unions', excluding unskilled workers and deepening sectarian division. Socialists struggled to foster class solidarity in a *Herrenvolk* democracy that reassured Protestants wary of loss of status. As in the United States and South Africa, sectarian labour divisions mirrored racial hierarchies, Catholics being relegated to the lowest-paid jobs. During the counter-revolution outlined in this book, the Unionist elite and their imperial allies reinforced these 'wages of whiteness' through a toxic mix of pogromist violence, sectarian job discrimination, and imperial economic subvention for a colonial gendarmerie. This formed part of a worldwide Thermidor, outside Russia, where the counter-revolution prevailed, backed by Entente forces, Freikorps, and paramilitaries.

This history of working-class militancy nevertheless proves that the two communal blocs, Protestant Unionists and Catholic Nationalists, appeared more fluid in their political sensibilities than revising hindsight has allowed. Yet partition led to the consolidation of two conservative regimes, North and South, compatible with the interests of both Irish petty capitalism and British imperialism. Indeed, the panicked and violent response of northern business interests to the emergence of tentative class-based unity in Belfast in 1907 and 1919 – and, for that matter, during the Outdoor Relief Strikes of 1932 – underscored the extraordinary measures deployed to shore up sectarianism.[23] Furthermore, partition in Ireland was an imperial construct – as in Palestine, India and Cyprus – where Britain ruled through the exacerbation of existing or emerging ethno-religious tensions, which formed the basis of a geographical division on the terms of their favoured community. Indeed, Sir Ronald Storrs, first military governor of Jerusalem, argued revealingly that any new Zionist homeland 'would form for England "a little loyal Jewish Ulster" in a sea of potentially hostile Arabism'.[24]

Lloyd George's coalition (December 1916–October 1922) may have said it had no selfish interest in Ireland; but the same Tories who dominated his government had already challenged parliament's sovereignty on the Irish Question, openly supported the 'Curragh Mutiny', and funded the loyalist Larne gunrunning in 1914.[25] We have already seen how Lord Milner intervened to rescue 'the white settler colony of Ulster from submersion in a sea of inferior Celts'.[26] While in office, these race patriots steadfastly reinforced partition, through both legislative instruments and massive financial support for Dawson Bates's security apparatus. Furthermore, along with Tory leader, Bonar Law, Milner tried to cut a deal with 'the patriot section of the Labour Party' to stymie the broader British trade-union movement.[27] His close ally, Edward Carson, employed a similar tactic in Belfast, aping Milner's proto-fascist British Workers' League by forming the UULA.

In this context, Unionist employers consciously manipulated sectarianism, deploying the UULA to smash local trade unionism. These tactics reached their peak in Tyrone in 1919, when 220 workers struck at Fulton's woollen mill at Caledon. In many respects Belfast replicated the rural pattern of revolution and reaction, but the close urban environment acted as a catalyst for communal confrontation, and there the sectarian bonfires burned much brighter and more intensely. The UULA invoked the threat of the IRA's guerrilla campaign to justify the mass expulsion of Catholics and committed socialists from the city's shipyards, foundries and factories. Contrary to the accepted historical narrative of spontaneous sectarian violence, this analysis reveals Bates and Carson as puppet masters: their hands deep in the mechanisms of violence, pulling the strings that animated the mob and, ultimately, orchestrating the tragedy. When one weighs the evidence, no question remains about who manned the controls – whatever agency the marionettes themselves possessed.

When the IRA assassinated District Inspector Oswald Swanzy on 22 August in Lisburn, loyalist mobs turned on the Catholic population, torching their homes and driving them from the town in a repeat of earlier scenes in Dromore and Banbridge. Viewing the aftermath of this ethnic cleansing, Fred Crawford wrote in his diary that Lisburn resembled 'a bombarded town in France [with] only four or five RC families left'. The only drawback came in the form of 'some very hard cases in which Unionists lost practically everything they had by the fire of a house of Catholics spreading to theirs'.[28] The London *Daily News* described events in east Ulster that summer as 'five weeks of ruthless persecution by boycott, fire, plunder and assault, culminating in a week's wholesale violence, probably unmatched outside the area of the Russian or Polish pogroms'.[29] That October, the left-wing *Daily Herald* argued that big business had engineered the expulsions as part of a policy of divide-and-conquer in what the editorial called 'Helfast'.[30]

Both Carson and Craig then publicly backed the pogrom, while the British state provided retrospective sanction by enlisting the loyalist perpetrators into the Specials, the paramilitary body set up as a key part of the coercive apparatus of the northern statelet. In fact, the force also served to underwrite the Orange economy, as the temporary (eventually permanent) suppression of British civil liberties under the 1922 Special Powers Act became the defining peculiarity of the one-party Unionist regime. Partition, imposed by a British imperial power as a means of extending its control over the whole island, looked to undermine any drift towards social revolution during a period of remarkable upheaval. It established a new set of political arrangements through which capitalism and an imperial order would continue to dominate Ireland, drawing into the fold an emerging conservative comprador ruling class in the South, while reinvigorating the foundations of a system of colonial sectarian supremacy in the North.

The imperial logic behind partition found expression in the career of Lord Londonderry – the most moderate member of Craig's cabinet, yet a future fascist and confidant of Hitler. Londonderry, Craig and the Unionist leadership stood as fully fledged members of an imperial elite, which manipulated plebeian loyalism to frustrate Irish self-determination. In 1922, Londonderry privately bemoaned 'the narrow and selfish Belfast spirit', and admitted that, once he had carried out his 'mission', he intended to 'return where I came from and leave Belfast to run the Six Counties'.[31] This book has challenged the ludicrous picture of Ulster Unionist plutocrats as hostages to their extremist grassroots, tossing and turning across feather beds and silk sheets in their stately homes and Mayfair apartments for fear of reprimand from the warren of red-bricked terraces on the Shankill Road and Sandy Row, with their outside toilets and weather-worn mural of King Billy on the nearest gable wall.

By retrieving the small stories of working-class struggle across the Red Triangle, this 'history from below' has sought also to tell three bigger and related stories. Firstly, after the First World War a significant minority of working-class Protestants in north-east Ireland embraced an egalitarian ideology, which formed a northern upsurge in a national wave pregnant with revolutionary potential. Secondly, reactionary violence in Belfast in 1920 and across southern Ireland in 1922–23 smashed this nascent democratic groundswell. Ireland witnessed a failed social revolution, involving tens of thousands, which, in its most advanced stage, promoted workers' control and the demand for a Co-operative Commonwealth. The revolution lacked genuine national leadership, relied on spontaneous workers' militancy fuelled by revolutionary expectancy, and remained distinct from and antithetical to conservative elements within the Sinn Féin movement; meanwhile, it suffered massively at the hands of a reactionary Ulster Unionist leadership integrated into the British imperial elite. Nevertheless, a widespread democratic struggle for socialism took place in Ireland, and it can do so again.

Thirdly, this book has sought to argue that, across the *longue durée*, Ulster's colonial ruling elite, in its own class interests, deliberately instituted a system of sectarian privileges to define and maintain its position: a dispensation that left ruin in its wake – for lower-class Catholics most visibly, but also, inevitably, for the Protestant workers who had been led to believe they would be its beneficiaries.[32] This analysis flies in the face of much of the accepted 'common sense' surrounding Northern Ireland. The two-warring-tribes thesis, however, relies on a partial reading, and a failure to view history itself as a process of both continuity and change. As David Lloyd has recently noted of loyalist supremacism: 'what appear as primordial identities are in fact politically significant only', persisting 'through performatively maintained structures of power' which 'do not survive the withdrawal of the material support that sustains them'; or, as Des Bell likewise argues, 'the primary responsibility of progressive politics in Ireland is neither to "understand" nor "accommodate" unionism, as if this was the magic key to opening a locked door barring the way to reunification'.[33] The Unionist statelet stood as an historical expression of settler-colonial supremacism; its consignment to the dustbin of history will benefit no segment of the island's population more than the Northern Protestant working class itself.

Sectarian division – the straitjacket of Orange and green – is neither inevitable nor immutable. The reader is already aware of the 1907 Dockers' and Carters' strike, so brilliantly illuminated by John Gray, when 2,600 British troops occupied the docks to protect scab, or 'free', labour crossing the picket lines, while 100,000 workers, led by Orange and Hibernian flute bands, marched down the Shankill Road.[34] Indeed, this book began with Dawson Gordon recounting to Ruth Russell how, as the war dragged, in a remarkable shift, Catholics began attending labour meetings in Orange Halls and vice versa – a new spirit captured in processions where Orange and Hibernian bands marched together in perfect harmony.[35] Nevertheless, on each occasion, the forces of reaction, backed by the state, shattered working-class solidarity in Belfast. Between 'Big Jim' Larkin's entry into Belfast's docks and Dawson Gordon's interview, remarkably similar scenes took place a few hundred miles to the east, in a city with a similar history of sectarian conflict, a thriving dock, and its own shipyards: Liverpool.

During Liverpool's great 1911 General Transport Strike, radical trade unions confronted the city's conservative political establishment. Mirroring Belfast, Britain's second-largest port thrived on casual dock and transport labour, where workers endured poor pay and conditions under employers fiercely hostile to union activity. Local syndicalist activists led by Tom Mann showed how 'explosive, militant and aggressive strike action could erupt and collective union organisation . . . gain a strong foothold'.[36] The following account of a workers' parade during the strike echoed the detail and harmony of their comrades and kin in Belfast:

> From Orange Garston, Everton and Toxteth Park, from Roman Catholic Bootle, and the Scotland Road area, they came. Forgotten were their religious feuds . . . The Garston band . . . drum-major proudly whirled his sceptre twined with orange and green ribbons as he led his contingent band, half out of the Roman Catholic band, half out of the local Orange band.[37]

As Ralph Darlington relates, for nearly three months Liverpool's workers resisted intense pressure from employers, local authorities, and police and military forces, ultimately winning significant concessions. Through this struggle, they transformed one of the country's key industrial regions – a place with virtually no stable unions – into its best-organised port.[38]

Liverpool obviously sat in the Metropole, Belfast in Britain's first and last colony. As Robert Fisk rightly argued, 'the border of Northern Ireland was a sign of imperial decline, the frontiers of the Middle East a last attempt by Britain and France to hold imperial power'.[39] Trapped in a mausoleum of ossified sectarianism, Belfast's socialists watched on enviously while Liverpool gradually took the path of social democracy. By the time Beatlemania rocked the swinging sixties, Northern Ireland looked to many outside observers like a filthy colonial anachronism.[40]

This book ends where it began – in 1919 – with Ruth Russell's fact-finding Irish tour. Ominously, Dawson Gordon warned the Chicago journalist how, despite burgeoning class consciousness and anti-sectarian solidarity, 'there will always be a chance of disunion until the political question is settled'. As a result, 'Ulster labour decided to assist in that settlement. So, it killed Carsonism. And now it is trying to lay . . . the ghost of Carsonism by the permanent settlement of the Irish political question'. This aspiration led 'Ulster labour' to back 'the rest of the Irish Labour party' in asking for the 'free and absolute self-determination of each and every people in choosing the sovereignty under which they shall live'.[41] In retrospect, Gordon, through Russell, spoke far too soon. Carson's ghost still haunts the politics of Ireland's north-east to the present day.

Yet, Carson's malevolent spectre aside, other, more benign spirits dwell in the liminal space between the Orange State and the tantalising prospect of a different future. In her recent book, the sociologist Claire Mitchell charts 'a personal exploration of an absence in my own identity. A ghost limb.' Mitchell argues forcefully that the 'radical heart of the Protestant north still beats'. Like this history from below, her book looks back to the United Irishmen, and tells 'stories which take power away from the straitjacket of orange and green. Which unlock a tumbling, radical, dissenting Protestant history'.[42]

Likewise, when we rescue the poor hemstitchers, the soap-wrappers, the utopian railwaymen, all followers of the Red Flag, from the enormous condescension of posterity, we realise, like Mitchell, that 'the roots of anti-sectarianism may be hidden from view, but they run deep through the earth beneath our feet. Through time and place. These roots can anchor us, if we let them. We have all the tools we need to dream a new reality into being'. Like their forbears in the United Irish movement, the women and men of the Red Triangle stood at an historical juncture – a 'portal', in Mitchell's words, to an unrealised democratic, egalitarian and anti-sectarian future.[43]

Acknowledgements

This book began to take shape shortly after I started my current position at St Mary's University College, Belfast. I am deeply grateful for the support I received there, especially from Damian Knipe and the Research Department.

I would also like to thank Verso, and particularly Tom Hazeldine for his encouragement and assistance throughout the project. Some of the research presented here first appeared in a collection that I co-edited with Francy Devine for Umiskin, a collaboration that helped crystallise many of the ideas developed in this book.

The staff of every archive I consulted were generous with their time and expertise, but I would like to give special thanks to the Linen Hall Library and to my former colleague in St Mary's Library Ciaran Crossey, whose help in locating first-hand accounts was invaluable. Naomi Shewan at the University of Warwick provided tremendous assistance with the Workers' Union archive, while the staff at PRONI could not have been more helpful. Gò háirithe Saul, Ailbhe agus an iardhalta s'agam Meagan – níor shíl mé ariamh go mbeadh deis agam Gaeilge a labhairt le foireann na cartlainne sin.

I am also indebted to Terence Bowman for granting me access to the McClung Papers.

My thanks are due as well to friends and comrades who read drafts of the manuscript, offered criticism and encouragement, and discussed the project over a few pints: Peter Collins, Brian Kelly, Michael McCann, Dónal Ó Dálaigh, Cathal Murtagh, and Paddy Smylie.

I owe a particular debt of gratitude to Kerby Miller, who, as always, was unstinting in his support, advice, and generosity. Emmet O'Connor, John Cunningham, Chris Loughlin, and Adrian Grant also responded generously to queries and requests for information.

Any errors or shortcomings that remain are, of course, entirely my own.

Ba mhaith liom buíochas a ghabháil le Séamus, Pádraig Fia, Síobhra, Ciarán agus Feargal a léigh cuid den tsaothar agus le mo chomhghleacaithe, Seán, Padaí agus Teresa a spreag mé lena gcairdeas sa choláiste. I also need to thank my comrades in Dash who fuelled the long writing sessions with the best Báinín in Belfast.

Thar aon ní eile, tá an leabhar seo tiomnaithe do mo chlann, do mo bhean ghrámhar, ghalánta agus do mo pháistí, go bhféacha siad Éire shaor shóisialach lá den tsaol agus go léirí siad an misneach, meas agus daonnacht chéanna is atá le feiceáil i measc na mban a sheas ar son an chirt sa scéal seo.

Notes

Introduction

1. Walter Benjamin, 'The Storyteller', in his *Illuminations* (New York, 1969), pp. 83–109.
2. Ruth Russell, *What's the Matter with Ireland?* (New York, 1920), p. 146.
3. Ibid.
4. The latter figure referenced the total number of workers across trade unions in the Textile Federation.
5. 'Orange' refers to the Orange Order, a Protestant organisation founded in 1795 in Armagh. Hibernian, in this context, refers to the Ancient Order of Hibernians (Board of Erin), a Catholic organisation led by West Belfast MP Joe Devlin. Ibid, p. 150.
6. Jonathan Bardon, *A History of Ireland in 250 Episodes* (Dublin, 2008), p. 272.
7. Cited in Anne Cadwallader, *Lethal Allies: British Collusion in Ireland* (Cork, 2013), p. 15.
8. One of the loudest acoustic instruments, the Lambeg drum is played with Malacca canes during Orange Order parades.
9. Quoted in Brendan O'Leary, *A Treatise on Northern Ireland, Volume I* (Oxford, 2020), p. 378.
10. Ibid., p. 107.
11. Kyla Madden, *Forkhill Protestants, Forkhill Catholics, 1787–1858* (Liverpool, 2006), p. 6.
12. E. P. Thompson, *The Making of the English Working Class* (London, 1963), p. 9.
13. Denis O'Hearn, 'Irish Linen: A Peripheral Industry', in Marilyn Cohen, *The Warp of Ulster's Past: Interdisciplinary Perspectives on the Irish Linen Industry, 1760–1920* (London, 1997), p. 177.

14. Sarah-Anne Buckley, 'Women, Labour, and Class in the 1920s: A Historiographical Overview', in Francis Devine, Sarah-Anne Buckley and Olivier Coquelin, eds, *Retreat from Revolution* (Dublin, 2024), p. 38.
15. This paraphrases Thompson's famous passage in *Making of the English Working Class*, p. 13.
16. 'But history, in general, treats the working class as the manipulator of politics treats the working man – that is to say, with contempt when he remains passive, and with derision, hatred and misrepresentation whenever he dares evince a desire to throw off the yoke of political or social servitude. Ireland is no exception to the rule'. James Connolly, *Labour in Irish History* (Dublin, 1922), p. 1.

1. Land, Linen and Liberty

1. Geoffrey Elton, *England Under the Tudors* (London, 1955), p. 388.
2. John Gillingham, 'The Beginnings of English Imperialism', *Journal of Historical Sociology* 5: 4 (1992), pp. 392–409, cited in O'Leary, *Treatise*, p. 450.
3. Geoffrey Elton, *The Practice of History* (London, 2001), p. 170.
4. Gerard Farrell, *The 'Mere Irish' and the Colonisation of Ulster, 1570–1641* (London, 2017), p. 8.
5. Aimé Césaire, *Discours sur le colonialisme* (Paris,1955), pp. 12–15.
6. Jane Hiddleston, 'Aimé Césaire and Post-colonial Humanism', *Modern Language Review* 105: 1 (January 2010), p. 88.
7. W. T. Wolfe Tone, *The Life of Theobald Wolfe Tone* (Dublin, 1998), p. 51.
8. Nancy Curtin, 'The Origins of Irish Republicanism', PhD, University of Wisconsin, 1988, p. 54.
9. Kevin Whelan, *The Tree of Liberty* (Cork, 1996), p. 119.
10. Theodore Allen, *The Invention of the White Race*, vol. 1 (London, 1994), passim.
11. C. L. R. James, *The Black Jacobins: Toussaint L'Ouverture and the San Domingo Revolution* (London, 2001), p. 230.
12. Eric Williams, *Capitalism and Slavery* (London, 2022), p. 103. 'Dreaded spiral' is a term of David Harvey's – see *A Companion to Marx's Grundrisse* (London, 2003), p. 492.
13. Author's translation, from Máire, *Saol Corrach* (Baile Átha Cliath, 1981), pp. 71–2.
14. Máire, *Saol Corrach*, p. 80. The song in question was 'Úirchill an Chreagáin', by Art Mac Cumhaigh (1738–73), which appears again in this chapter in eighteenth-century south Armagh.
15. James Connolly, *Labour in Irish History* (Dublin, 1922, p. 4.
16. David Edwards, 'Tudor Ireland' in Cathie Carmichael and Richard C. Maguire, eds, *The Routledge History of Genocide* (London, 2015), p. 23.

17. Christopher Maginn, *William Cecil, Ireland, and the Tudor State* (Oxford, 2012), pp. 90–6.
18. John Davies, *A Discovery of the True Causes Why Ireland Was Never Entirely Subdued* (Shannon, 1969), p. 265.
19. Quoted in Farrell, *'Mere Irish'*, p. 81.
20. Caroline Elkins, *A Legacy of Violence* (London, 2022), p. 15.
21. Jane Ohlmeyer, *Making Empire: Ireland, Imperialism, and the Early Modern World* (Oxford, 2023), pp. 73, 91.
22. Quoted in Katherine Simms, 'Late Medieval Tír Eoghain: The Kingdom of "The Great Ó Neill"', in Charles Dillon and Henry A. Jefferies, eds, *Tyrone: History and Society* (Dublin, 2000), pp. 149–50.
23. Quoted in Clare Carroll, 'Spenser and the Irish Language', *Irish University Review* 26: 2 (Autumn–Winter 1996), p. 283.
24. Hiram Morgan, 'Hugh O'Neill and the Nine Years War in Tudor Ireland', *Historical Journal* 36: 1 (1993), p. 22. See also, James O'Neill, *The Nine Years War, 1593–1603: O'Neill, Mountjoy and the Military Revolution* (Dublin, 2017).
25. Hiram Morgan, *Tyrone's Rebellion: The Outbreak of the Nine Years War in Tudor Ireland* (Rochester, 1993), p. 3.
26. Ibid., p. 189.
27. Diarmaid Ó Doibhlín, 'Tyrone's Gaelic Literary Legacy' in Dillon and Jefferies, *Tyrone*, p. 408.
28. Brendan Bradshaw, *The Irish Constitutional Revolution of the Sixteenth Century* (Cambridge, 1978), pp. 276–82.
29. Fynes Moryson, *An Itinerary, vol. 3* (Glasgow, 1908), p. 283.
30. John McCavitt, *Sir Arthur Chichester: Lord Deputy of Ireland 1605–16* (Belfast, 1998), pp. 10–12.
31. Nicholas Canny, *Imagining Ireland's Past* (Oxford, 2021), p. 73.
32. Raymond Gillespie writes of 'the replacement of a Gaelic lordship economy by an English-style market economy': Raymond Gillespie, 'Explorers, Exploiters and Entrepreneurs: Early Modern Ireland and its context, 1500–1700', in B. J. Graham and L. J. Proudfoot, eds, *An Historical Geography of Ireland* (London, 1993), p. 136. Nicholas Canny, however, argued that the new colonists 'brought little knowledge of agricultural methods that was not already familiar to the native population in Ulster': Nicholas Canny, 'Migration and Opportunity: Britain, Ireland and the New World', *Irish Economic and Social History* 12 (1985), p. 27. Aidan Clarke likewise suggests that 'there was a quickening, and an increasing commercialisation, but the aim of replacing Gaelic pastoralism by a more civilised arable economy was not quickly achieved': Aidan Clarke, 'The Plantations of Ulster', in Liam De Paor, ed., *Milestones in Irish History* (Cork, 1986), p. 66.
33. Philp Robinson, 'The Ulster Plantation and Its Impact on the Settlement Pattern of Co. Tyrone', in Dillon and Jefferies, *Tyrone*, pp. 240, 256.

34. See 'County Settlement Map for Eighteenth Eentury Armagh', in D. W. Miller, 'The Armagh Troubles 1785–1795', in S. Clark and J. S. Donnelly, eds, *Irish Peasants, Violence and Political Unrest, 1780–1914* (Wisconsin, 1983), p. 160. The original Plantation Precincts appear in Farrell, *'Mere Irish'*, p. 5.
35. William Macafee, 'Movement of British Settlers into Ulster in the 17th Century', *Familia: Ulster Genealogical Review* 8 (1992), pp. 94–111.
36. Micheál Ó Siochrú, *God's Executioner: Oliver Cromwell and the Conquest of Ireland* (London, 2008), p. 29.
37. Raymond Gillespie, 'Owen Roe O'Neill', in G. O'Brien and Peter Roebuck, eds, *Nine Ulster Lives* (Belfast, 1992), p. 162.
38. Ohlmeyer, *Making Empire*, p. 91.
39. Ó Siochrú, *God's Executioner*, pp. 85–8.
40. Ibid., pp. 73, 92.
41. Macafee, 'Movement of British Settlers into Ulster', p. 96.
42. Cormac Ó Grada, *Ireland: A New Economic History, 1780–1939* (Oxford, 2001), p. 282.
43. Both quotes from Denis O'Hearn, 'Irish Linen: A Peripheral Industry', in Marilyn Cohen, ed., *The Warp of Ulster's Past: Interdisciplinary Perspectives on the Irish Linen Industry, 1700–1920* (London, 1997), pp. 164, 161.
44. Anne McKernan, 'The Dynamics of the Linen Triangle: Factor, Family and Farm in Ulster, 1740 to 1825', PhD dissertation, University of Michigan (1990), pp. 328–30.
45. For the historical origins of the 'Ulster Custom', which included security of tenure and free sale with the landlord's approval, see the testimony provided by Lord Lurgan's agent to the Devon Commission (1844), in W. F. Bailey, *The Ulster Tenant-right Custom: Its Origin, Characteristics, and Position under the Land Acts* (Dublin, 1894), p. 16.
46. McKernan, 'Dynamics of the Linen Triangle', pp. 331–4.
47. Quoted in Harry Gribben, 'The Irish Linen Board, 1711–1828', in Cohen, *Warp of Ulster's Past*, pp. 84–5.
48. C. F. McGleenon, 'Lord Gosford Versus the "Patriots"', *Seanchas Ardmhacha: Journal of the Armagh Diocesan Historical Society* 17: 2 (1998), p. 55.
49. J. Greer, 'Average of Sales of Brown Linens in the Markets of the Province of Ulster' 1784 (PRONI, D562/5596).
50. Ó Grada, *Ireland: A New Economic History*, p. 282.
51. Quoted in Marcel Boldorf, 'The Ulster Linen Triangle: An Industrial Cluster Emerging from a Proto-Industrial Region', in J. Czierpka, K. Oerters and N. Thorade, eds, *Regions, Industries, and Heritage* (London, 2015), p. 28.
52. McKernan, 'Dynamics of the Linen Triangle', p. 335.

53. For flax cultivation by 1796, see William J. Smyth and Kevin Whelan, *Common Ground: Essays on the Historical Geography of Ireland Presented to T. Jones Hughes* (Cork, 1988) pp. 234–52. For the extent and nature of commercial handloom weaving around 1810, see W. H. Crawford, *The Handloom Weavers and the Ulster Linen Industry* (Belfast, 1994), p. 5.
54. Quoted in Jim Smyth, *The Men of No Property: Irish Radicals and Popular Politics in the Late Eighteenth Century* (Dublin, 1998), p. 48.
55. Smyth, *Men of No Property*, p. 47.
56. Miller, 'Armagh Troubles', p. 168.
57. Brendan McEvoy, 'The Peep of Day Boys and Defenders in the County Armagh', *Seanchas Ardmhacha: Journal of the Armagh Diocesan Historical Society* 12: 1 (1986), p. 128.
58. Miller, 'Armagh Troubles', p. 171.
59. Ibid., pp. 171–4.
60. Smyth, *Men of No Property*, pp. 30–1.
61. Vincent Morley, *The Popular Mind in Eighteenth-Century Ireland* (Cork, 2017), p. 313.
62. Quoted in Kyla Madden, *Forkhill Protestants, Forkhill Catholics, 1787–1859* (Liverpool, 2006), pp. 17, 23.
63. Ibid., p. 21.
64. Ibid., p. 7.
65. Miller, 'Armagh Troubles', pp. 176–8.
66. Morley, *Popular Mind*, p. 306.
67. Breandán Ó Buachalla 7rl. 'Peadar Ó Doirnín Agus Lucht Scríte a Bheatha', *Studia Hibernica* 5 (1965), pp. 123–54.
68. Tomás Ó Fiaich, 'Art Mac Cooey and His Times', *Seanchas Ardmhacha: Journal of the Armagh Diocesan Historical Society* 6: 2 (1973), pp. 217–50.
69. Quoted in Morley, *Popular Mind*, pp. 212–13.
70. George Rudé, *Ideology and Popular Protest* (London, 1980), pp. 9–30.
71. Breandán Ó Buachalla, 'An Cúlra Idéolaíoch', in Gearóid Ó Tuathaigh, ed., Éirí Amach 1798 in Éirinn (Indreabhán, 1998), p. 34.
72. Morley, *Popular Mind*, pp. 179–80.
73. Ibid.
74. Ibid., pp. 186–90.
75. Domenico Losurdo, *Liberalism: A Counter-History* (London, 2011), p. 25.
76. William Lecky, *A History of England in the Eighteenth Century*, 8 vols (London, 1883–88), Vol. 1, p. 288.
77. Liz Curtis, *The Cause of Ireland: From the United Irishmen to Partition* (Belfast, 1994), p. 4.
78. Morley, *Popular Mind*, p. 195.
79. Ibid., p. 187.
80. James, *Black Jacobins*, p. 100.
81. Ó Grada, *Ireland: A New Economic History*, p. 283.
82. Jonathan Bardon, *A History of Ulster* (Belfast, 2005), pp. 217–20.

83. Ibid., pp. 214–17.
84. Nancy Curtin, 'Ideology and Materialism: Politicization and the Ulster Weavers in the 1790s', in Cohen, *Warp of Ulster's Past*, p. 114.
85. Ibid., pp. 125.
86. Morley, *Popular Mind*, p. 242.
87. Ibid., p. 278.
88. Quoted in Thomas Bartlett, David Dickson, Daire Keogh and Kevin Whelan, eds, *1798: A Bicentenary Perspective* (Dublin, 2003), p. 417.
89. Whelan, *Tree of Liberty*, p. 86.
90. Smyth, *Men of No Property*, p. 46.
91. Ibid., p. 97.
92. Cavan magistrate quoted in Curtin, 'Ideology and Materialism', p. 114.
93. The 'Battle of the Diamond', like Dolly's Brae more than half a century later, would be more aptly called the 'Massacre of the Diamond'. The Peep-o'-Day Boys were heavily armed, the Defenders almost entirely unarmed.
94. Quoted in Whelan, *Tree of Liberty*, p. 127.
95. Ibid., p. 165.
96. Smyth, *Men of No Property*, pp. 112, 119.
97. Quoted in Morley, *Popular Mind*, p. 253.
98. Whelan, *Tree of Liberty*, p. 119.
99. Miller, 'Armagh Troubles', p. 188.
100. Peter Gibbon, *The Origins of Ulster Unionism: The Formation of Popular Protestant Politics and Ideology in Nineteenth-Century Ireland* (Manchester, 1975), pp. 22–66.
101. Curtin, 'Ideology and Materialism', pp. 118–20.
102. The Vendée was a British-backed counter-revolutionary conflict in northern France, 1793–96.
103. Ibid., p. 126.
104. Whelan, *Tree of Liberty*, p. 125.
105. Ibid., p. 124.
106. Thomas Bartlett has questioned the reliability of figures over 10,000, but contemporary reports all provide figures of more than 20,000. Thomas Bartlett, 'Clemency and Compensation: The Treatment of Defeated Rebels and Suffering Loyalists After the 1798 Rebellion', in Jim Smyth, ed., *Revolution, Counter-revolution and Union* (Cambridge, 2000), p. 100.
107. James, *Black Jacobins*, p. 229.
108. Moya Wylie, 'Moygashel Mills: A Brief History', *Dúiche Néill* 16 (2007), pp. 180–4.
109. Quoted in Fergal McCluskey, 'Unionist Ideology in Tyrone, 1911–1914', *Clogher Record* 21: 1 (2012), pp. 65–89.
110. James, *Black Jacobins*, p. 197.
111. Ibid., p. 224.

2. Belfast Beginnings

1. James Connolly to William O'Brien, 7 December 1911 (NLI, William O'Brien papers, MS 13,908/1/51).
2. Philip Ollerenshaw, 'Industry, 1820–1914', in Liam Kennedy and Philip Ollerenshaw, *An Economic History of Ulster, 1820–1939* (Manchester, 1985), p. 62.
3. Denis O'Hearn, 'Irish Linen: A Peripheral Industry', in Marilyn Cohen, ed., *The Warp of Ulster's Past: Interdisciplinary Perspectives on the Irish Linen Industry, 1700–1920* (London, 1997), p. 163.
4. Quoted in Kerby A. Miller, 'Belfast's First Bomb, 28 February 1816: Class Conflict and the Origins of Unionist Hegemony', *Éire-Ireland* 39: 1 (2004), pp. 262–80.
5. Ollerenshaw, 'Industry, 1820–1914', p. 286.
6. Miller, 'Belfast's First Bomb', p. 270.
7. Ibid., p. 275.
8. Alvin Jackson, *Ireland, 1798–1998: War, Peace and Beyond* (West Sussex, 2010), p. 39.
9. Gustave de Beaumont, *L'Irlande, sociale, politique et religieuse*, 2 vols, cited in Domenico Losurdo, *Liberalism: A Counter-History* (London, 2011), pp. 116, 299.
10. Gerard Mac Atasney, *'This Dreadful Visitation': The Famine in Lurgan/ Portadown* (Belfast, 1997), p. xvi.
11. Figures from Official Census of Ireland for the years 1841–1901.
12. John Mitchel, *The Last Conquest of Ireland* (Knoxville, Tennessee, 1858).
13. Theodore Allen, *The Invention of the White Race: Volume One,* (London, 2005), p. 131.
14. David Bleakley, *Saidie Patterson: Irish Peacemaker* (Blackstaff, 1980), p. 15.
15. William Topping, *A Life in Linenopolis: The Memoirs of William Topping, Belfast Damask Weaver, 1903–56* (Belfast, 1992), pp. 4–5.
16. Betty Messenger, *Picking Up the Linen Threads: A Study of Industrial Folklore* (Austin, TX, 1978), p. 22.
17. Topping, *Linenopolis*, pp. 5–6.
18. Messenger, *Picking Up the Linen Threads*, p. 121.
19. O'Hearn, 'Irish Linen', p. 179.
20. John P. Lynch, *An Unlikely Success Story: The Belfast Shipbuilding Industry, 1880–1935* (Belfast, 2001), pp. 1–7.
21. The figures are based on respective census returns, 1861–1911. I would like to thank Kerby Miller for his help in providing these statistics.
22. Karl Marx to Sigfrid Meyer and August Vogt, 9 April 1970, *Selected Correspondence* (Moscow, 1975), p. 220.
23. David R. Roediger, *The Wages of Whiteness* (London, 1991), p. 116.

24. Quoted in John Gray, *City in Revolt: James Larkin and the Belfast Dock Strike of 1907* (Belfast, 1985), p. 18.
25. Roediger, *Wages of Whiteness*, p. 243.
26. Ibid., p. 170.
27. Bill Rolston, 'The Limits of Trade Unionism', in Liam O'Dowd, Bill Rolston and Mike Tomlinson, *Northern Ireland: Between Civil Rights and Civil War* (London, 1980), pp. 71–2.
28. Roediger, *Wages of Whiteness*, p. 113.
29. Allen, *Invention of the White Race*, p. 132.
30. Robert McClung, 'Recollections of the Belfast Labour Movement' (1929), McClung Papers, Terrence Bowman's Private Collection, p. 1.
31. Ibid., p. 2.
32. Quoted in Roy Jenkins, *Asquith; Portrait of a Man and an Era* (New York, 1964), p. 398.
33. Gray, *City in Revolt*, p. 3.
34. Quoted in Emmet O'Connor, *Rotten Prod: The Unlikely Career of Dungaree Baird* (Cork, 2022), p. 36.
35. Quoted in Gray, *City in Revolt*, p. 13.
36. O'Connor, *Rotten Prod*, p. 4.
37. Gray, *City in Revolt*, p. 6.
38. Ibid., p. 23.
39. Geoffrey Bell, *The Twilight of Unionism* (London, 2022), pp. 71–2.
40. Gray, *City in Revolt*, p. 204.
41. Helga Woggon, *Ellen Grimley (Nellie Gordon): Reminiscences of Her Work with James Connolly in Belfast* (Dublin, 2000), p. 20.
42. Robert 'Bob' Getgood memoir, Jim Larkin radio file, PRONI, D3358/1.
43. Henry Pelling, *A History of British Trade Unionism* (London, 1992), p. 89.
44. Gray, *City in Revolt*, p. 5.
45. John Newsinger, *Rebel City: Connolly, Larkin and the Dublin Labour Movement* (London, 2003), p. 13.
46. Thomas Johnson, Bureau of Military History, Witness Statement [BMH, WS], 1755, p. 1.
47. Anthony Gaughan, 'Johnson, Thomas Ryder', *Dictionary of Irish Biography* (2009), at dib.ie.
48. *The Times*, 30 November 1905.
49. Gray, *City in Revolt*, p. 48.
50. Robert 'Bob' Getgood memoir.
51. Ralph Darlington, *Labour Revolt in Britain 1910–14* (London, 2023), p. 3.
52. Gray, *City in Revolt*, p. 89.
53. Emmet O'Connor, Big Jim Larkin: Hero or Wrecker? (Dublin, 2015), p. 33.
54. Gray, *City in Revolt*, p. 209.
55. Ibid., pp. 207–8.
56. Quoted in ibid., p. 238.

57. Peter Collins, 'Belfast Trades Council, 1881–1921', PhD dissertation, University of Ulster (1988), pp. 22–6.
58. *Forward*, 3 June 1911.
59. Gray, *City in Revolt*, p. 205.
60. Ibid., p. 43.
61. Ibid., p. 212.
62. Ibid., pp. 207–8.
63. *Forward*, 3 June 1911.
64. O'Connor, *Rotten Prod*, p. 16.
65. McClung, 'Recollections of the Belfast Labour Movement', p. 25.
66. O'Connor, *Rotten Prod*, p. 17.
67. Terry Cradden, 'Labour in Britain and the Northern Ireland Labour Party, 1900–70', in P. Catterall and S. McDougall, eds, *The Northern Ireland Question in British Politics* (London, 1996), p. 72.
68. See Mike Mecham, 'The Revolution Thwarted: Northern Labour Through Its Press', in Francis Devine, Sarah-Anne Buckley and Olivier Coquelin, eds, *Retreat from Revolution* (Dublin, 2024), p. 211.
69. O'Connor, *Rotten Prod*, pp. 19–20.
70. Collins, 'Belfast Trades Council', pp. 185–6.
71. Ibid., p. 194.
72. Ibid., p. 197.
73. Quoted in Myrtle Hill, 'Margaret McCoubrey, 1880–1956: Suffragist and Labour Activist', in Devine, Buckley and Coquelin, *Retreat from Revolution*, p. 338.
74. Dawson Gordon to D. R. Campbell, 16 October 1916 (NLI, Thomas Johnson papers, MS 17,115/3).
75. Copy of draft manifesto by ILP&TUC opposing conscription in Ireland, October 1916 (NLI, Thomas Johnson papers, MS 17, 115/5).
76. *Workers' Republic*, 25 March 1916.
77. DI Belfast, February 1918 (CO904/105).
78. *Voice of Labour*, 20 April 1918.
79. DI Belfast, April 1918 (CO904/105).
80. Brian Feeney, *Antrim, 1912–25* (Dublin, 2021), p. 49.
81. *Voice of Labour*, 19 October 1918.
82. For corporation meeting, see *Watchword of Labour*, 31 January 1920; *Belfast Newsletter*, 23 January 1920. For a recent analysis of Baird as a 'rotten prod', see Conall Parr, 'Expelled from Yard and Tribe: The "Rotten Prods" of 1920 and Their Political Legacies', in *Studi Irlandesi: A Journal of Irish Studies* 11 (2021), pp. 309–11.
83. Emmet O'Connor, *Syndicalism in Ireland, 1917–1923* (Cork, 1988), p. 173.
84. Workers' Union Annual Reports 1915–20.
85. Flax Roughers' and Yarn Spinners' Trade Union Balance Sheets for 25 September 1915 and 30 March 1918.

86. *Cork Examiner*, 2 December 1918.
87. Between 1913 and 1920, Irish wages in most sectors more than doubled, but the increases did not significantly outpace the rising retail price of food. Interestingly, nearly every ship in the German fleet, sunk at Scapa Flow, was equipped with Sirocco fans sold by the violently partisan anti-trade unionist and sectarian bigot Sir Samuel Davidson. Mackie's textile machinery works turned most of their production over to munitions. See Collins, 'Belfast Trades Council', p. 233.)
88. McClung, 'Recollections', pp. 17–20.
89. Richard Hyman, *The Workers' Union* (Clarendon, 1971).
90. Annual Report of the Workers' Union, 1916 (Modern Records Centre, Warwick University, MSS126/WU/4/1/12), p. 27.
91. Annual Report of the Workers' Union, 1918 (Modern Records Centre, Warwick University, MSS126/WU/4/1/14), p. 37.
92. The research involved creating a branch database formed from Workers' Union Annual Reports 1915–20, held at Warwick University, cross-referenced with the local press, the 1911 Irish census and the online index of Irish townlands.
93. Annual Report of the Workers' Union, 1916 (Modern Records Centre, Warwick University, MSS126/WU/4/1/12), pp. 11–13.
94. *Tyrone Courier*, 15 May 1919.
95. *Freeman's Journal*, 29 January 1917. For Gordon's position on the ILP&TUC, see *Evening Herald*, 29 May 1917.
96. Flax Roughers' and Yarn Spinners' Trade Union [FR&YS] minute book, 4 April 1917 (PRONI, D1050/7/3).
97. *Voice of Labour*, 17 August 1918. For Lurgan, see *Voice of Labour*, 8 December 1917; *Hansard*, House of Commons, 24 June 1918, vol. 107, cc 815–16.
98. Hyman, *Workers' Union*.
99. FR&YS minutes, 29 March 1916.
100. *Hansard*, House of Commons Debate, 22 December 1916, vol. 88, cc 1862–7.
101. Flax Roughers' and Yarn Spinners' Trade Union Balance Sheets for 25 September 1915 and 30 March 1918 (PRONI, D1050/7/3).
102. ITUC Annual Report 1920, p. 147.
103. Robert 'Bob' Getgood memoir.
104. Woggon, *Ellen Grimley*, pp. 19–21.
105. Robert 'Bob' Getgood memoir.
106. Committee of Production meeting for Irish Linen manufacturers and trade unions,1917 (PRONI, D2088/27/1).
107. FR&YS minutes, 3 January 1917.
108. 1918 PRONI, D2088/27/3.
109. Committee of Production to Kyle, republished in *Northern Whig*, 19 November 1918.
110. FR&YS minutes, 4 July 1917.

111. FR&YS minutes, 3 October 1917.
112. FR&YS minutes, 31 October 1917.
113. FR&YS minutes, 30 January 1918.
114. FR&YS minutes, 1 May 1918.
115. FR&YS minutes, 3 July 1918.
116. FR&YS minutes, 31 July 1918.
117. FR&YS minutes, 4 September 1918.
118. FR&YS minutes, 2 October 1918 and 30 October 1918.
119. Annual Report of the Workers' Union, 1918 (Modern Records Centre, Warwick University, MSS126/WU/4/1/14), p. 268.
120. FR&YS minutes, 4 April 1917.
121. FR&YS minutes, 5 February 1919.
122. FR&YS minutes, 30 June 1920.
123. FR&YS minutes, 29 March 1916, 28 June 1916 and 3 January 1917.
124. FR&YS minutes, 10 April 1918.
125. FR&YS minutes, 4 September 1918 and 2 October 1918.
126. FR&YS minutes, 30 October 1918 and 2 April 1919.
127. FR&YS minutes, 30 April 1919.
128. FR&YS minutes, 5 October 1919.
129. FR&YS minutes, 29 October 1919.
130. FR&YS minutes, 3 March 1920.
131. FR&YS minutes, 29 September 1920.
132. O'Connor, *Syndicalism in Ireland*, p. 168
133. Ibid., pp. 168–70. O'Connor cites a ratio of 3-to-1. Patterson writes that, in July 1914, a labourer's weekly rate of pay in shipbuilding and engineering was 51 per cent of a plater's and 54 per cent of a fitter's. By July 1918, those proportions were 67 per cent and 69 per cent, respectively. Henry Patterson, *Class Conflict and Sectarianism: The Protestant Working Class and the Belfast Labour Movement, 1868–1920* (Newtownards, Co. Down, 1980), p. 95.
134. *Belfast Newsletter*, 20 January 1922. For the 'fascist' character of the UULA and a detailed examination of its role in the 1920 pogrom, see Fearghal Mac Bhloscaidh, 'The Belfast Pogrom and the Interminable Irish Question', *Studi Irlandesi* 12 (2022).
135. *Voice of Labour*, 2 August 1919.
136. *Watchword of Labour*, 28 August 1920.
137. *Watchword of Labour*, 24 January 1920; *Portadown News*, 17 January 1920.
138. *Watchword of Labour*, 28 August 1920.
139. *Irish Times*, 19 January 1920.
140. O'Connor, *Rotten Prod*, p. 14.
141. Ibid., p. xv.
142. *Voice of Labour*, 22 February 1919.
143. Bates to Craig, 31 January–2 February 1919 (PRONI, D1507/A/29/7–8).
144. W. Chaine to Edward Carson, 17 June 1919 (PRONI, D1507/A/30/6).

145. "Practically all the Roman Catholic vote was given to Hanna . . . The Ulster Protestant Home Ruler still exists, though in small numbers, but they can make a lot of mischief" (Bates to Captain Craig, 18 June 1919, PRONI, D1507/A/30/3).
146. CI Antrim, January 1920 (NAL, CO904/111).
147. Quoted in O'Connor, *Rotten Prod*, p. 24.
148. *Portadown News*, 3 July 1920.
149. Mike Davis, *Old Gods, New Enigmas: Marx's Lost Theory* (London, 2024), p. 56.
150. This section adapts Jeffrey B. Perry's summation of the argument from the introduction to the second edition (2010) of Allen, *Invention of the White Race*, vol. 1 (p. xviii).

3. Women, Weavers and the Workers' Union

1. From Æ (George William Russell), *The National Being* (Dublin, 1916), p. 18.
2. David Bleakley, *Saidie Patterson: Irish Peacemaker* (Belfast, 1980), pp. 13–15.
3. James Connolly, *To the Linen Slaves of Belfast: Manifesto of the Irish Textile Workers' Union* (Belfast, 1913).
4. Helga Woggon, *Ellen Grimley (Nellie Gordon): Reminiscences of Her Work with James Connolly in Belfast* (Dublin, 2000), pp. 17, 12.
5. Connolly, *To the Linen Slaves of Belfast.*
6. A Belfast bap is a round, crusty loaf with a burnt top which protected the bloomer beneath from the mills' suffocating atmosphere. See Mats Greiff, '"Marching Through the Streets Singing and Shouting": Industrial Struggle and Trade Unions Among Female Linen Workers in Belfast and Lurgan, 1872–1910', *Saothar* 27 (1997), p. 29.
7. Ibid., p. 30.
8. Robert McClung, 'Recollections of the Belfast Labour Movement' (1929), McClung Papers, Terrence Bowman's Private Collection, pp. 7–8.
9. Greiff, '"Marching Through the Streets"', p. 39.
10. Ibid., p. 30.
11. Woggon, *Ellen Grimley*, p. 19.
12. Penny Holloway and Terry Cradden, 'The Irish Trade Union Congress and Working Women, 1894–1914', *Saothar* 23 (1998), p. 52.
13. Ibid., p. 51.
14. Ibid., p. 55.
15. Woggon, *Ellen Grimley*, p. 23.
16. W. P. Ryan, *The Irish Labour Movement*, quoted in *Workers' Republic*, 29 October 1921.

17. *Northern Whig*, 5 May 1919.
18. David Fitzpatrick, 'Strikes in Ireland, 1914–21', *Saothar* 6 (1980), pp. 37–8.
19. *Irish Citizen*, 6 March 1915.
20. Kyle is listed as Belfast district organiser of the Workers' Union during the 44-hour strike: *Derry Journal*, 19 February 1919; *Belfast Newsletter*, 2 December 1919.
21. Copy of draft manifesto by ILP&TUC opposing conscription in Ireland, October 1916 (NLI, Thomas Johnson papers, MS 17, 115/5).
22. I have employed the spelling McKeag throughout, although McKeague often appeared in newspaper reports. Sam Kyle would go on to be ITUC president in 1940 and 1950. D. R. Campbell was congress treasurer, 1913–18: Donal Nevin, *Trade Union Century* (Cork, 1994), pp. 437–41
23. *Irish News*, 27 November 1918.
24. *Irish News*, 9 November 1918.
25. *Ulster Examiner*, 22 November 1919.
26. Ruth Russell, *What's the Matter with Ireland?* (New York, 1920), pp. 146–7.
27. Annual Report of the Workers' Union, 1918 (Modern Records Centre, Warwick University, MSS126/WU/4/1/14), p. 270.
28. FR&YS minutes, 3 March 1915.
29. FR&YS minutes, 1 September 1915.
30. FR&YS minutes, 28 June 1916.
31. FR&YS minutes, 5 October 1919.
32. See McCoubrey's article in *Irish Citizen*, 6 March 1915.
33. *Lisburn Standard*, 27 June 1919.
34. FR&YS minutes, 30 October 1918.
35. FR&YS minutes, 31 December 1919.
36. CI Down, October 1918 (CO904/107); *Portadown News*, 16 November 1918.
37. McClung, 'Recollections of the Belfast Labour Movement', pp. 24–5.
38. *Banbridge Chronicle*, 14 June 1919.
39. *Banbridge Chronicle*, 11 October 1919.
40. *Voice of Labour*, 17 August 1918.
41. Annual Report of the Workers' Union, 1919 (Modern Records Centre, Warwick University, MSS126/WU/4/1/15), p. 7. Donnan is listed as a Catholic living at 18 Fisherman's Row in 1911; no D. Curdy is listed in the 1911 census for Ireland, but Ulster contained three D. McCurdys with two Daniels or Domhnalls listed as Catholic Irish-speaking farmers from Rathlin island, off the Antrim Glens coast, and Daniel McCurdy, an Anglican apprentice cobbler from Belfast.
42. FR&YS minutes, 31 December 1919.
43. FR&YS minutes, 28 May 1919.
44. FR&YS minutes, March 1920.

45. Robert A. Newland, *PR Urban Elections in Ulster, 1920* (London, 1972), p. 61.
46. NA, 'Reprisals against Catholics in Lisburn and environs, July–August 1920', *History Ireland* 20 (January 2012).
47. *Watchword of Labour*, 2 October 1920.
48. Henry Patterson, *Class Conflict and Sectarianism: The Protestant Working Class and the Belfast Labour Movement, 1868–1920* (Newtownards, Co. Down, 1980), p. 125.
49. Peter Collins, 'Belfast Trades Council, 1881–1921', PhD dissertation, University of Ulster (1988), p. 233.
50. IG July 1918 (NAL, CO904/106).
51. Emmet O'Connor, *Syndicalism in Ireland, 1917–1923* (Cork, 1988), pp. 168–9.
52. Ibid., p. 179.
53. Sam Kyle would go on to be ITUC president in 1940 and 1950. D. R. Campbell was congress treasurer, 1913–18. Nevin, *Trade Union Century*, pp. 437–41.
54. The RIC IG noted the ITGWU's unpopularity in North-East Ulster (IG July 1919, NAL, CO904/109).
55. CI Armagh, September 1918 (CO904/107).
56. *Freeman's Journal*, 29 September 1918.
57. *Belfast Newsletter*, 1 November 1918; CI Armagh, October 1918 (CO904/107).
58. CI Armagh, November 1918 (NAL, CO904/107).
59. From an Anglican background, Getgood would lead the anti-partitionist wing of the NILP and also chair the ITUC in 1944.
60. CI Armagh, December 1918 (NAL, CO904/107).
61. *Voice of Labour*, 8 March 1919.
62. *Northern Whig*, 26 April 1919.
63. *Lurgan Mail*, 10 May 1919.
64. *Freeman's Journal*, 25 October 1919.
65. The research involved creating a branch database formed from Workers' Union annual reports from 1915 to 1920, held at Warwick University, cross-referenced with the local press, the 1911 Irish census and the online index of Irish townlands.
66. *Frontier Sentinel*, 29 November 1919.
67. FR&YS minutes, 3 October 1917.
68. FR&YS minutes, 30 March 1920; *Ulster Examiner*, 27 March 1920.
69. FR&YS minutes, 30 March 1920. For McKinstry's position, see *Banbridge Chronicle*, 6 October 1917.
70. *Northern Whig*, 24 May 1919.
71. FR&YS minutes, 2 July 1919.
72. *Pall Mall Gazette*, 31 July 1919.
73. *Frontier Sentinel*, 30 August 1919.

74. FR&YS minutes, 5 October 1919.
75. FR&YS minutes, 29 October 1919.
76. FR&YS minutes, 3 December 1919.
77. FR&YS minutes, 27 November 1919.
78. '"Many Lurgan Workers Down": Influenza in Lurgan and Portadown' in Patricia Marsh, *The Spanish Flu in Ireland: A Socio-Economic Shock to Ireland, 1918–1919* (London, 2021), p. 201.
79. W. H. Crawford, *The Impact of the Domestic Linen Industry in Ulster* (Belfast, 2005), pp. 140, 149.
80. Jim McIllmurry, 'Lurgan Weaving Industry', at lurganancestry.com.
81. Greiff, '"Marching through the streets"', p. 36.
82. Ibid., p. 30.
83. Ibid., p. 41.
84. CI Armagh, January 1913 (CO904/89).
85. ITUC Annual Congress, Cork, 1913, p. 24.
86. Details of the strike come from Ken Austin, 'The Lurgan Weavers and Winders Strike, 1913', at lurganancestry.com.
87. *Portadown News*, 17 November 1919.
88. *Voice of Labour*, 8 December 1917. For the hemmers' and veiners' strike, see *Portadown News*, 30 June 1917. As mentioned above, Charles Duncan MP raised this case in parliament the following summer, the *Belfast Newsletter* noting a wages dispute in the local Gas Works in Lurgan, and reporting Duncan attacking the UDC partly on account of its attitude towards the Workers' Union, but chiefly because of its refusal to reinstate the strikers or agree to arbitration (6 June 1918).
89. *Voice of Labour*, 8 December 1917; *Northern Whig*, 21 November 1917; *Belfast Newsletter*, 22 November 1917.
90. CI Armagh, June 1919 (NAL, CO904/108).
91. CI Armagh, February 1918 (NAL, CO904/105).
92. *Belfast Newsletter*, 25 February 1918.
93. CI Armagh, March 1918 (CO904/105).
94. CI Armagh, April 1918 (CO904/105).
95. *Belfast Newsletter*, 9 April 1918.
96. *Voice of Labour*, 20 April 1918.
97. *Belfast Newsletter*, 15 April 1918.
98. FR&YS minutes, 1 May 1918.
99. CI Armagh, June 1918 (CO904/106); *Portadown News*, 1 June 1918.
100. CI Armagh, August 1919 (NAL, Co904/109).
101. CI Armagh, October 1919 (NAL, CO904/110).
102. CI Armagh, November 1919 (NAL, CO904/110).
103. *Watchword of Labour*, 31 January 1920.
104. *Watchword of Labour*, 13 January 1920. Lurgan UDC Results: North Ward: Felix McCluskey (N), Henry Cummins (Lab-Presbyterian), Robert Levin (Lab-Catholic), Thomas Brady (Lab-Catholic), Wm. O'Neill (Lab-Catholic)

and John Mahaffy (U); South-West Ward: Edward Lunn (Ind. Lab.), Edward Mullen (Lab-Catholic), George Ferguson (U.), Henry Maxwell (Lab-Methodist), Joseph Holland (U), Thomas Cordner (Lab-Christian); South-East Ward: James Burke (Lab-Catholic), Crozier Wilson (U), George Anderson (U). See *Portadown News*, 24 January 1920.

105. *Belfast Newsletter*, 7 February 1919.
106. IG Mar 1919 (NAL, CO904/108).
107. *Belfast Newsletter*, 7 March 1919.
108. Portadown News, 24 September 1920.
109. *Watchword of Labour*, 31 January 1920.
110. Robert Lundy was the military governor of Derry who offered to surrender the city to Catholic forces during the 1688–89 siege. His effigy is burnt annually to commemorate the shutting of Derry's gates in 1688, and his name has become synonymous among loyalists with treachery.
111. *Lurgan Mail*, 25 September 1920.
112. *Portadown News*, 26 January 1918.
113. Conor McCabe, 'The Irish Labour Party and the 1920 Local Elections', *Saothar* 35 (2010), pp. 7–20. James McIlhagga, NUR and future UDC, told a crowd at Harryville, including Campbell and Gordon, that 2,000 workers were attached to the Ballymena Trades Council: *Belfast Newsletter*, 9 September 1918. For Turkington's intervention in Doagh and Ballymena, see *Watchword of Labour*, 21 August 1920.
114. *Watchword of Labour*, 17 July 1920.
115. *Watchword of Labour*, 31 July 1920; *Portadown News*, 31 July 1920.
116. Head Office ITGWU select Vennard as a railway organiser: *Voice of Labour*, 17 February 1923. See also *Voice of Labour*, 9 and 23 June 1923; Vennard 'spreads the light': *Voice of Labour*, 23 May 1924; *Irish Worker*, 25 March 1925; *Voice of Labour*, 4 April 1925.
117. *Portadown News*, 2 February 1918.
118. *Portadown News*, 15 September 1917, 6 October 1917 and 9 February 1918.
119. *Portadown News*, 9 February 1918.
120. *Portadown News*, 16 February 1919
121. *Portadown News*, 23 February 1918.
122. CI Armagh, February 1918 (NAL, CO904/105); CI Armagh, March 1918 (NAL, CO904/105).
123. CI Armagh, October 1918 (CO904/107).
124. Ibid.
125. *Portadown News*, 26 October 1918.
126. *Portadown News*, 25 October 1919.
127. *Portadown News*, 7 December 1918.
128. *Portadown News*, 3 January 1920.
129. Vennard, Skelton, Yeman, Greenaway and Dell were listed as five Labour returns: *Portadown News*, 24 January 1920.
130. *Portadown News*, 24 April 1920.

131. McCabe, 'Irish Labour Party and the 1920 Local Elections', p. 15.
132. *Portadown News*, 25 October 1919.
133. *Portadown News*, 24 April 1920.
134. *Portadown News*, 24 April 1920; CI Armagh, June 1920 (NAL, CO904/112).
135. McClung, 'Recollections of the Belfast Labour Movement', card. 18.
136. *Portadown News*, 28 August 1920.
137. *Northern Whig*, 29 May 1917.
138. Quoted in David Fitzpatrick, *The Two Irelands, 1912–39* (Oxford, 1998), p. 239.
139. *Weekly Freeman*, 2 June 1917.
140. Bob Getgood referring to the 1932 Outdoor Relief Strikes, in Recollections of Joe Devlin (PRONI, D3358/2).
141. Quoted in Maurice J. Casey 'Irish Women and Radical Internationalism: From Suffrage to Antifascism, 1916–1939', PhD dissertation, Oxford (2019), p. 133.
142. The final sentence paraphrases E. P. Thompson's famous passage from *The Making of the English Working Class* (London, 1978), p. 13.

4. Tyrone: Revolution Among the Bushes

1. Fergus Campbell, *Land and Revolution: Nationalist Politics in the West of Ireland, 1891–1921* (Oxford, 2008), p. 284.
2. Ibid., p. 282.
3. Conor Kostick, *Revolution in Ireland: Popular Militancy, 1917 to 1923* (London, 1996), p. 110.
4. Kevin O'Shiel (BMH WS 1770/1, p. 60).
5. E. P. Thompson, *The Making of the English Working Class* (London, 1963), p. 76.
6. James Connolly, *Labour in Irish History* (London/Dublin, 1922), p. 59.
7. Report of the 1911 census: province of Ulster, County Tyrone (London, 1911), pp. 68–72.
8. Philip Robinson, *The Plantation of Ulster: British Settlement in an Irish Landscape, 1600–1670* (Belfast, 1984), pp. 84–94, 119.
9. Alice Milligan quoted in *Irish University Review* 33 (1970), p. 86.
10. This is a reference to the Caledon Lockout – see *Watchword of Labour*, 13 December 1919.
11. Alice Milligan, *Shan Van Vocht*, August 1897.
12. Catherine Morris, *Alice Milligan and the Irish Cultural Revival* (Dublin, 2013), p. 43.
13. Helga Woggon, *Ellen Grimley (Nellie Gordon): Reminiscences of Her Work with James Connolly in Belfast* (Dublin, 2000), p. 25.

14. Quoted in Morris, *Alice Milligan*, p. 181.
15. CI Tyrone, July 1913 (NAL, CO 904/90).
16. Brendan McEvoy, 'The United Irishmen in Co. Tyrone', *Seanchas Ard Mhacha: Journal of the Armagh Diocesan Historical Society* 3: 2 (1959), p. 309.
17. Kevin O'Shiel (BMH WS 1770/1, p. 26).
18. David Fitzpatrick, *The Two Irelands, 1912–39* (Oxford, 1998), p. 11.
19. 1911 census for Tyrone, pp. 68–72.
20. David Fitzpatrick, 'The Geography of Irish Nationalism, 1910–1921', *Past and Present* 78 (1978), pp. 138–9.
21. Montgomery to Farnham, 25 March 1919 (PRONI, Montgomery papers, D627/437/62).
22. John Gray, *City in Revolt: James Larkin and the Belfast Dock Strike of 1907* (Belfast, 1985), p. 5.
23. Henry Pelling, *A History of British Trade Unionism* (London, 1992), p. 101.
24. Elaine McFarland, 'The Making of an Irishman: John Ferguson (1836–1906) and the Politics of Identity in Victorian Glasgow', *Immigrants and Minorities* 27: 2–3 (2009), pp. 194–211; Patrick Maume, 'Richard McGhee', *Dictionary of Irish Biography*, at dib.ie.
25. *Tyrone Courier*, 24 March 1894.
26. *Tyrone Courier*, 21 January 1893.
27. *Tyrone Courier*, 4 January 1896.
28. *Tyrone Courier*, 3 February 1894.
29. *Tyrone Courier*, 3 March 1894.
30. *Tyrone Courier*, 7 January 1893.
31. *Irish News*, 11 June 1897; *Dublin Weekly Nation*, 3 July 1897.
32. The arrested strikers were Peter Harte, John McMahon, Bartley Finney [*sic*: Fenney], Daniel Ferguson, John Devine and George Madden. See *Northern Whig*, 17 December 1897.
33. *Mid-Ulster Mail*, 18 December 1897.
34. The strikers Charles McMahon, John Dunne and Peter Harte, Jr, attacked Patrick Magee. See *Portadown News*, 29 January 1898.
35. *Dungannon News,* 20 January 1898; *Tyrone Courier*, 20 January 1898; four of the men arrested – Hart, McMahon, Devine and Feeney – were INF members: *Dungannon News,* 23 December 1897. The RIC reported that there was neither boycotting nor intimidation in the county 'except some slight stir in connection with the Congo Colliery strike. A number of men have been returned for trial to the assizes for unlawful assembly and others have been sentenced to one month's imprisonment for assaulting men who continued to work': CI Tyrone, 27 January 1898, NAI, DCCI Box 8.
36. On Slean's position in Dungannon INF, see *Tyrone Courier*, 9 January 1897). On public letters, see *Tyrone Courier*, 6, 13, 20 January and 3 February 1898.

37. Four hundred people assembled in the centre of the town in support of the strikers and a 'living wage': *Irish News*, 30 May 1917; *Tyrone Courier*, 5 November 1917.
38. Information from Coalisland Museum and Heritage Centre, *A History of Coalisland Weaving Company* and *Roan Spinning Mills* – both available in pdf at coalisland-lnp.com.
39. FR&YS minutes, 15 December 1915.
40. FR&YS minutes, 27 September 1916.
41. *Hansard*, House of Commons Debate, 28 June 1917, vol. 95, cc 529–30.
42. FR&YS minutes, 4 July 1917.
43. *Belfast Newsletter*, 11 June 1920.
44. *Freeman's Journal*, 24 October 1917.
45. FR&YS minutes, 3 October 1917.
46. FR&YS minutes, 31 October 1917.
47. FR&YS minutes, 21 November 1917.
48. *Dungannon Democrat*, 15 August 1917.
49. *Tyrone Courier*, 4 October 1917.
50. *Tyrone Courier*, 15 November 1917.
51. IG, December 1917 (NAL, CO904/104).
52. Tyrone CI, January 1918, NAL, CO904/105.
53. See Fergal McCluskey, *Tyrone: The Irish Revolution, 1912-23* (Dublin, 2014), p. 108.
54. C. L. R. James, *The Black Jacobins: Toussaint L'Ouverture and the San Domingo Revolution* (London, 2001), p. 28.
55. FR&YS minutes, 3 April 1918.
56. FR&YS minutes, 4 September 1918.
57. FR&YS balance sheet, 30 March 1918.
58. *Irish Opinion*, 21 September 1918.
59. The research involved creating a branch database formed from Workers' Union annual reports from 1915 to 1920, held at Warwick University, cross-referenced with the local press, the 1911 Irish census and the online index of Irish townlands.
60. Emmet O'Connor, *Syndicalism in Ireland, 1917–1923* (Cork, 1988), pp. 168–9.
61. The analysis of the tendencies within Derry comes from Adrian Grant, *Derry, 1912–23* (Dublin, 2018), pp. 145–6.
62. Anton McCabe, 'The Stormy Petrel of the Transport Workers', *Saothar* 19 (1994), p. 43.
63. O'Connor, *Syndicalism in Ireland*, p. 39.
64. For a short profile of each man's role in the Independent and then Belfast Labour Party, see Austen Morgan, *Labour and Partition: The Belfast Working Class, 1905–1923* (London, 1987), pp. 251–2.
65. O'Connor, *Syndicalism in Ireland*, p. 33.
66. CI Tyrone, March 1918. For the number of workers, see CI Tyrone, April 1918 (NAL, CO904/105).

67. *Belfast Newsletter*, 12 April 1918.
68. *Voice of Labour*, 13 April 1918.
69. *Mid-Ulster Mail*, 4 May 1918.
70. *Dungannon Democrat*, 15 May 1918.
71. *Dungannon Democrat*, 5 June 1918.
72. *Dungannon Democrat*, 22 May 1918. For details of the second round of prosecutions regarding the Donaghmore strike, see *Tyrone Courier*, 25 April 1918.
73. McCluskey, *Tyrone*, p. 75.
74. IG, September 1918 (NAL, CO904/107).
75. Nicholas Smyth, 1952 (BMH, WS 7210, p. 3).
76. McCluskey, *Tyrone*, p. 75; CI Tyrone, August 1918 (NAL, CO904/106).
77. *Ulster Herald*, 27 April 1918.
78. CI, July 1918 (NAL, CO904/106).
79. The Inspector also mentioned a female textile workers' strike in Omagh, CI Tyrone, August 1918 (NAL, CO904/106).
80. *Dungannon Democrat*, 4 September 1918.
81. *Strabane Chronicle*, 31 August 1918.
82. *Irish Times*, September 1918; O'Connor, *Syndicalism in Ireland*, p. 32.
83. *Dungannon Democrat*, 18 September 1918.
84. *Dungannon Democrat*, 25 September 1918.
85. *Strabane Chronicle*, 14 September 1918.
86. *Dungannon Democrat*, 30 October 1918.
87. Annual Intelligence Notes for County Tyrone 1918 (NAL, CO903/19/4).
88. Kostick, *Revolution in Ireland*, p. 70.
89. *Dungannon Democrat*, 2 October 1918.
90. *Ulster Herald*, 23 November 1918.
91. *Strabane Chronicle*, 29 March 1919.
92. For criminal cases, see *Strabane Chronicle*, 3 May 1919, 17 May 1919 and 28 June 1919.
93. *Strabane Chronicle*, 27 September 1919.
94. *Tyrone Courier*, 15 May 1919.
95. *Irish Independent*, 28 April 1919.
96. *Tyrone Courier*, 15 May 1919.
97. For Turkington's involvement in Donaghmore, see *Watchword of Labour*, 28 August 1920.
98. *Tyrone Courier*, 22 May 1919.
99. *Tyrone Courier*, 29 May 1919.
100. *Ulster Herald*, 15 March 1919.
101. *Ulster Herald*, 14 June 1919 and 12 July 1919.
102. *Ulster Herald*, 10 May 1919.
103. *Strabane Chronicle*, 6 December 1919.
104. *Ulster Herald*, 9 August 1919.
105. *Tyrone Constitution*, 19 September 1924.

106. *Ulster Herlad*, 23 March 1920.
107. *Ulster Herald*, 19 April 1920.
108. Michael Laffan, *The Resurrection of Ireland: The Sinn Féin Party, 1916–1923* (Cambridge, 1999), p. 253.
109. Arthur Mitchel, *Revolutionary Government in Ireland. Dáil Éireann, 1919–22* (Dublin, 1995), p. 166.
110. *Ulster Herald*, 11 October 1919.
111. *Ulster Herald*, 25 October 1919.
112. CI Tyrone, July 1920 (NAL, CO 904/112); *Ulster Herald*, 24 July 1920.
113. CI Tyrone, December 1920 (NAL, CO 904/113).
114. IG, August 1921 (NAL, CO 904/116/367).
115. NAI, Department of the Taoiseach, S. 600, quoted in Claire Fitzpatrick, 'Flexing the Muscles of a Fledgling State: The Irish Postal Workers' Strike of 1922', in Francis Devine, Sarah-Anne Buckley and Olivier Coquelin, eds, *Retreat from Revolution* (Dublin, 2024), p. 106.
116. O'Connor, *Syndicalism in Ireland*, p. 184.
117. Ibid., p. 87.
118. See McCluskey, *Tyrone*, pp. 83–4.
119. Peter Hart, *The IRA at War, 1916–1923* (Oxford, 2003), p. 21.
120. Campbell, *Land and Revolution*, p. 284.
121. IG, April 1918 (NAL, CO 904/105); *Ulster Herald*, 27 April 1918.
122. CI Tyrone, February 1920 (NAL, CO 904/111).
123. O'Connor, *Syndicalism in Ireland*, p. 114.
124. Kostick, *Revolution in Ireland*, p. 146.
125. Morgan, *Labour and Partition*, pp. 270, 276.

5. The Caledon Lockout

1. The village is made anonymous in the book, but fits the description of Caledon, or Newmills in the same area. See William F. Kelleher, Jr, *The Troubles in Ballybogoin: Memory and Identity in Northern Ireland* (Ann Arbor, MI, 2010), p. 47.
2. *Hansard*, House of Commons,16 February 1922, vol. 150, cc 1270-1.
3. 'Dolly's Brae' is a famous loyalist song commemorating a fatal faction fight between Orange and Ribbonmen near Rathfriland, Co. Down, on 12 July 1849. *Freeman's Journal*, 3 November 1919.
4. *Derry Journal*, 28 February 1919.
5. Peter Hart, *The IRA at War, 1916–1923* (Oxford, 2003), p. 21.
6. Henry Patterson, *Class Conflict and Sectarianism: The Protestant Working Class and the Belfast Labour Movement, 1868–1920* (Newtownards, Co. Down, 1980), p. 142.
7. Department of Environment, *Conservation Caledon* (Omagh, 2003); Caledon Woollen Mills, Company, 1921–32 (PRONI, COM/40/1/C/2).

8. 'Caledon, County Tyrone', in Belfast and Ulster Towns Directory for 1910, Library Ireland, at libraryireland.com.
9. For the mill's increased order book, see *Freeman's Journal*, 31 March 1915.
10. CI, February 1919 (NAL, CO904/108).
11. Emmet O'Connor, *Syndicalism in Ireland, 1917–1923* (Cork, 1988), pp. 168–9.
12. Ibid., p. 179.
13. *Watchword of Labour*, 3 January 1920.
14. 'Monaghan Pete' is a reference to O'Donnell's success in the Monaghan Asylum Soviet: *Voice of Labour*, 8 March 1919); FR&YS Minutes, 30 April 1919.
15. IG, January 1919 (NAL, CO904/108).
16. Stronge to Montgomery, 6 February 1919 (PRONI, D627/437/52
17. Bates to Carson, 8 October 1918 (PRONI, D1507/A/28/43).
18. Coote to Montgomery, 1917 (PRONI, D627/430/18).
19. *Newsletter*, 14 July 1918; Patterson, *Class Conflict and Sectarianism*, p. 98.
20. Ronald McNeill, *Ulster's Stand for Union* (New York, 1922), pp. 111–12.
21. For Turkington's role in Fermanagh, see Jim Quinn, 'Labouring in the Margins', *Saothar 15* (1990), p. 61.
22. *Freeman's Journal*, 8 October 1919.
23. Annual Intelligence Notes for County Tyrone 1918 (NAL, CO903/19/4).
24. The CI apparently dated the dispute from the beginning of the lockout, not the strike itself (Annual Intelligence Notes for County Tyrone 1919, NAL, CO903/19/5).
25. Michael Laffan, *The Resurrection of Ireland: The Sinn Féin Party, 1916–1923* (Cambridge, 1999), p. 170.
26. Mary T. McVeigh, 'Lock Out? Caledon 1919', *Dúiche Néill* ix (1990), p. 98.
27. *Voice of Labour*, 1 February 1919; Donal Ó Drisceoil, *Peadar O'Donnell* (Cork, 2001), p. 11
28. Conor Kostick, *Revolution in Ireland: Popular Militancy, 1917 to 1923* (London, 1996), p. 70.
29. Ó Drisceoil, *Peadar O'Donnell*, p. 13.
30. The surname is incorrectly transcribed as Hawe.
31. Peadar O'Donnell, *Monkeys in the Superstructure* (Galway, 1986), p. 16.
32. *Voice of Labour*, 1 February 1919.
33. CI Tyrone, January 1919 (NAL, CO904/108).
34. *Armagh Guardian*, 21 March 1919; McVeigh, 'Lock Out?', p. 99.
35. *Derry Journal*, 26 May 1919.
36. *Armagh Guardian*, 28 March 1919; McVeigh, 'Lock Out?', p. 97.
37. *Voice of Labour*, 1 March 1919.
38. CI Tyrone, February 1919 (NAL, CO904/108).
39. *Derry Journal*, 26 May 1919.

40. Ó Drisceoil, *Peadar O'Donnell*, p. 14.
41. *Voice of Labour*, 16 March 1919.
42. *Belfast Newsletter*, 24 February 1919.
43. C. Desmond Greaves, *The Irish Transport and General Workers' Union: The Formative Years, 1909–1923* (Dublin, 1982), p. 232; *Voice of Labour*, 1 March 1919.
44. The total staff numbered 220, fifty-three of whom remained at work; the RIC apparently added the non-striking workers to the total – a mistake subsequently repeated in Westminster. CI Tyrone, February 1919, NAL, CO904/108.
45. *Voice of Labour*, 8 March 1919.
46. O'Donnell, *Monkeys in the Superstructure*, p. 13.
47. *Derry Journal*, 28 February 1919.
48. *Irish Independent*, 24 February 1919.
49. O'Donnell, *Monkeys in the Superstructure*, p. 16.
50. *Ulster Herald*, 31 May 1919.
51. *Hansard*, House of Commons Debate, 17 March 1919, vol. 113, cc 1728–9; *Tyrone Courier*, 27 March 1919.
52. McVeigh, 'Lock Out?', pp. 98–102.
53. *Watchword of Labour*, 3 January 1920.
54. *Irish Independent*, 9 June 1919; *Evening Telegraph*, 5 June 1919.
55. UULA Minutes, August 21, 1919 (PRONI, D1327/11/4/1).
56. *Voice of Labour*, 19 April 1919.
57. CI Tyrone, March 1919 (NAL, CO904/108).
58. *Voice of Labour*, 26 April 1919.
59. *Voice of Labour*, 10 May 1919.
60. *Tyrone Courier*, 9 May 1919 – quoting the *Belfast Telegraph*.
61. *Tyrone Courier*, 1 May 1919; the lodges in question were 299, 426 and 1268.
62. *Derry Journal*, 26 May 1919.
63. *Armagh Guardian*, 4 July 1919; McVeigh, 'Lock Out?', p. 104.
64. *Voice of Labour*, 31 May 1919.
65. *Voice of Labour*, 24 May 1919.
66. *Tyrone Courier*, 22 May 1919.
67. W Chaine to Carson, 17 June 1919 (PRONI, D1507/A/30/6).
68. Ruth Russell, *What's the Matter with Ireland?* (New York, 1920), pp. 152–3.
69. Fred Crawford's Diary, 28 September 1920 (PRONI, D640/11/1).
70. McVeigh, 'Lock Out?', p. 104.
71. Eric Hobsbawm, *Age of Extremes: The Short Twentieth Century, 1914–1991* (London, 1994), p. 125.
72. A. J. Gregor, *Young Mussolini and the Intellectual Origins of Fascism* (California, 1979), p. 238.
73. *Freeman's Journal*, 31 March 1915.

74. *Watchword of Labour*, 29 November 1919.
75. CI Tyrone, January 1915 (NAL, CO904/96).
76. Friends of the Somme – Mid Ulster Branch, 'Private James Goan', *Dungannon War Dead*, at dungannonwardead.com.
77. *Watchword of Labour*, 3 January 1920.
78. *Voice of Labour*, 17 May 1919.
79. O'Donnell, *Monkeys in the Superstructure*, pp. 16–17.
80. CI Tyrone, May 1919 (NAL, CO904/109).
81. *Watchword of Labour*, 13 December 1919.
82. *Freeman's Journal*, 5 January 1920.
83. *Evening Herald*, 12 May 1920.
84. The alterations are dated 1928 in anticipation of local government elections, but the village's working-class streets clearly experienced significant change in the revolutionary period (PRONI, VALB/38/8).
85. *Anglo-Celt*, 12 January 1920; *Freeman's Journal*, 5 January 1920.
86. *Belfast Newsletter*, 8 January 1920. The Spinners' Association published all correspondence in *Belfast Newsletter*, 14 January 1920.
87. O'Duffy to Collins, 10 March 1922 (NAI, DT, S 1801/A).
88. O'Duffy to Collins, 30 January 1922 (ibid.).
89. Weekly survey of the state of Ireland, 13 February 1922 (NAL, CAB 24/133).
90. Summary of Outrages in NI, 1921-22 (PRONI, HA/5/698).
91. Compensation Claim of Mrs Robert Scott, 1922 (NAL, HO 144/2235).
92. Fulton to Bates, 8 February 1922 (PRONI, HA/5/165).
93. Report of the Northern Border Commission (PRONI, HA/32/1/16).
94. Memoirs (Pre-Truce) Mr. James McKenna, formerly of North Monaghan, now residing (1970) Kilbrogan Place, Bandon, Co. Cork. "The arrest and subsequent rescue of Commandant Matt. Fitzpatrick, Clones battalion, Co. Monaghan" COFLA LOK IV.D.11 0003 05 Ee.4.5.
95. Report of the Northern Border Commission (PRONI, HA/32/1/16); Summary of outrages in Northern Ireland, March–April 1922 (PRONI, HA/5/699).
96. RUC, Belfast, 15 March 1922 (PRONI, HA/5/152); P. Finnegan, Andrew Sherry, Thomas Hegarty, File Containing Return of Persons Killed or Wounded Since 6 December 1921 in Northern Ireland, PRONI, HA/5/219; Summary of Outrages in Northern Ireland, March–April 1922 (PRONI, HA/5/699); *Tyrone Courier*, 9 March 1922.
97. Summary of Outrages in Northern Ireland, March–April 1922 (PRONI, HA/5/699); RUC, Belfast, 31 March 1922 (PRONI, HA/5/152); File Containing Return of Persons Killed or Wounded Since 6 December 1921 (PRONI, HA/5/219).
98. Summary of Outrages in Northern Ireland, March–April 1922 (PRONI, HA/5/699); RUC, Belfast, 31 March 1922 (PRONI, HA/5/152).
99. Northern Border Commission, 19 March 1922 (PRONI, HA/32/1/16).

100. RUC Report on the Political Situation at Caledon, 19 March 1922 (PRONI, HA/5/903).
101. Northern Border Commission, 27 March 1922 (PRONI, HA/32/1/16).
102. Northern Border Commission, 29 May 1922 (PRONI, HA/32/1/16).
103. James Doran, 1922–4 (PRONI, HA/5/2232).
104. RUC, Belfast, 18 April 1922 (PRONI, HA/5/152).
105. RUC, Belfast, 31 March 1922 (PRONI, HA/5/152).
106. Report of the Northern Border Commission (PRONI, HA/32/1/16).
107. Fulton to Dawson Bates, 22 March 1922, 'Steps to be taken for prevention of disturbances on border', March 1922 (PRONI, HA/5/905).
108. J. K. McClintock, 29 March 1922 (PRONI, HA/5/905).
109. Report of the Northern Border Commission, Col. Sutton, Clogher, 28 March 1922 (PRONI, HA/32/1/16).
110. RUC, Belfast, 18 April 1922 (PRONI, HA/5/152).
111. Telegram Fintona, 18 April 1922 (PRONI, HA/5/205); Persons Killed or Wounded Since 6 December 1921 in Northern Ireland (PRONI, HA/5/219); *Tyrone Courier*, 27 April 1922.
112. Charles Wickham to S. J. Watt, 30 March 1922 (PRONI, HA/5/905).
113. Report of the Northern Border Commission, Lieutenant E. F. Bolton, Clogher 9 April 1922 (PRONI, HA/32/1/16).
114. Paul Bew, Peter Gibbon and Henry Patterson, *The State in Northern Ireland, 1921–72: Political Forces and Social Classes* (Manchester, 1979), pp. 7–8.
115. Fergal McCluskey, 'Unionist Ideology in Tyrone, 1911–1914', *Clogher Record* 21: 1 (2012), pp. 65–89.
116. Bew, Gibbon and Patterson, *The State in Northern Ireland*, p. 8.
117. The concepts here rely heavily on Domenico Losurdo, *Liberalism: A Counter-History* (London, 2011), pp. 309–10.
118. Report by Gen. Ricardo, June 1922 (NAL, CO 906/27).
119. Michael Farrell, *Arming the Protestants: Formation of the Ulster Special Constabulary and the Royal Ulster Constabulary, 1920–27* (London, 1987), pp. 153, 283.
120. Report by Ricardo, June 1922 (NAL, CO 906/27).
121. Ricardo, June 1922 (NAL, CO 906/27).
122. C. Loughlin, 'The Moral Economy of Loyalty: Labour, Law and the State in Northern Ireland, 1921–39', *Labour History Review* 82: 1 (2017), pp. 1–22.
123. J. McClelland to Craig, 16 December 1925 (PRONI, PM/2/14/107).

6. Pogrom

1. Geoffrey Lewis, *Carson: The Man Who Divided Ireland* (London, 2005), p. 231.
2. Eamon Phoenix, *Northern Nationalism: Nationalist Politics, Partition and the Catholic Minority in Northern Ireland, 1890–1940* (Belfast, 1994), p. 225.
3. Roy Foster, *Modern Ireland 1600–1972* (London, 1990), p. 528.
4. Robbie McVeigh and Bill Rolston, *Anois ar Theacht an tSamhraidh: Ireland, Colonialism and the Unfinished Revolution* (Belfast, 2021), pp. 208–13.
5. Daithi Ó Corráin and Eunan O'Halpin, *The Dead of the Irish Revolution* (Yale, 2020), pp. 39; 1112.
6. Phoenix, *Northern Nationalism*, p. 251.
7. Kieran Glennon, *From Pogrom to Civil War: Tom Glennon and the Belfast IRA* (Cork, 2013), p. 263.
8. Alan F. Parkinson, *Belfast's Unholy War: The Troubles of the 1920s* (Dublin, 2004), p. 21.
9. Stronge to Montgomery, 12 March 1920, Public Record Office, Northern Ireland [PRONI], D627/435/9.
10. Parkinson, *Belfast's Unholy* War, pp. 31, 308–9.
11. T. C. Kennedy, 'War, Patriotism, and the UUC, 1914–18', *Éire-Ireland* 40 (2005), pp. 189–211.
12. Ronald McNeill, *Ulster's Stand for Union* (New York, 1922), p. 112.
13. Cabinet Conclusions, 11 November 1919, National Archives, Kew [NAL], CAB 23/37/3.
14. MacNeill, *Ulster's Stand for Union*, pp. 111–12.
15. Carson to Bates, 21 April 1919 (PRONI, D1237/18/19).
16. Geoffrey Bell, *The Protestants of Ulster* (London 1978), pp. 37–8.
17. A. T. Q. Stewart, *Edward Carson* (London, 1981), p. 107.
18. Alvin Jackson, *Home Rule: An Irish History, 1800–2000* (Oxford, 2004), pp. 133–4.
19. Graham Ellison and Jim Smyth, *The Crowned Harp: Policing in Northern Ireland* (London, 2000), p. 30.
20. Milner to Carson, 21 July 1914 (PRONI, D1507/A/6/40).
21. Alan Lester, 'Introduction: The Truth About Colonial History' in Lester, ed. *The Truth About Empire: Real Histories of British Colonialism* (London, 2024), p. 51.
22. Milner to Asquith, 18 November 1897, quoted in Saul Dubow, 'My Empire, Right or Wrong: Rhodes, Milner and the South African War', in Lester, *Truth About Empire*, p. 168.
23. Dubow, 'My Empire, Right or Wrong', p. 175.
24. John Hostettler, *Sir Edward Carson: A Dream Too Far* (Chichester, 1997), p. 307.

25. Paul Murray, *The Irish Boundary Commission and Its Origins, 1886–1925* (Dublin, 2011), p. 31.
26. Cabinet Conclusions, 19 December 1919 (NAL, CAB23/18/17); Diarmaid Ferriter, *A Nation and Not a Rabble: The Irish Revolution 1913–23* (London, 2015), p. 294.
27. Milner to Carson, 9 December 1913, Bodleian, MS 40/204–5.
28. J. O. Stubbs, 'Lord Milner and Patriotic Labour, 1914–1918', *English Historical Review*: 87: 345 (1972), pp. 717–54.
29. Robert Douglas, 'The National Democratic Party and the British Workers' League', *Historical Journal* 15: 3 (September 1972), p. 537.
30. *Meath Chronicle*, 18 October 1919.
31. *Belfast Newsletter*, 29 January 1920.
32. *Voice of Labour*, 20 April 1918.
33. Emmet O'Connor, *Syndicalism in Ireland, 1917–1923* (Cork, 1988), p. 173.
34. Emmet O'Connor, *A Labour History of Ireland, 1824–2000* (Dublin, 2011), p. 118.
35. Carson to Bates, 8 October 1918 (PRONI, D1507/A/28/43).
36. *Belfast Newsletter*, 20 January 1922.
37. *Belfast Newsletter*, 14 July 1918.
38. *Belfast Newsletter*, 6 December 1918.
39. Austen Morgan, *Labour and Partition: The Belfast Working Class, 1905–1923* (London, 1987), p. 246. Indeed, the strike's leader, Charles McKay, appears to have been a Scottish-born Catholic, as the 1911 census only lists one thirty-six-year-old – a pattern-maker from Pottinger.
40. Bates to James Craig, 31 January 1919 (PRONI, D1507/A/29/7).
41. Henry Patterson, *Class Conflict and Sectarianism: The Protestant Working Class and the Belfast Labour Movement, 1868–1920* (Newtownards, Co. Down, 1980), pp. 110–11.
42. Ibid. p. 115.
43. Bates to James Craig, 31 January 1919 (PRONI, D1507/A/29/7).
44. Bates to James Craig, 1 February 1919 (PRONI, D1507/A/29/8).
45. Eames to Bates, 28 January 1919 (PRONI, D1327/18/15).
46. Parkinson, *Belfast's Unholy War*, p. 47.
47. Matthew Hendley, 'Anti-Alienism and the Primrose League: The Externalization of the Postwar Crisis in Great Britain 1918–32', *Albion: A Quarterly Journal Concerned with British Studies* 33: 2 (2001), pp. 243–61. See also D. M. Leeson, 'British Conspiracy Theories and the Irish War of Independence', *Éire-Ireland* 56: 1 (2021), pp. 176–208.
48. PRONI, D1507/A/29/9.
49. Bates to James Craig, 1 February 1919 (PRONI, D1507/A/29/8).
50. Carson to Bates, 21 April 1919 (PRONI, D1237/18/19).
51. Bates to Captain Craig, 18 June 1919 (PRONI, D1507/A/30/3).
52. Bates to Carson, 30 June 1919 (PRONI, D1507/A/30/12).

53. Scott to Bates, undated (PRONI, D1327/18/15).
54. Thompson to Carson, 26 September 1919 (PRONI, D1507/A/31/20–1).
55. Watkins [?] to Carson, 24 July 1919 (PRONI. D1507/A/31/45–6).
56. James Craig to Crawford, 16 June 1919 (PRONI, D640/7/3).
57. PRONI, D1507/A/31/22.
58. *Belfast Newsletter*, 19 January 1920.
59. *Old Ireland*, 14 February 1920.
60. Emmet O'Connor, *Rotten Prod: The Unlikely Career of Dungaree Baird* (Cork, 2022), pp. 32–3.
61. Robinson to Bates, 30 June 1919 (PRONI, D1327/18/15).
62. *Belfast Newsletter*, 9 January 1920.
63. *Irish Times*, 19 January 1920. Identifiable 'Unionist' candidates, including the UULA's 4,699, gained 49,773 first preferences out of 89,031 votes cast. The BLP secured 12,768 votes, the Nationalist Party 10,758, and Sinn Féin 7,120.
64. Patterson, *Class Conflict and Sectarianism*, pp. 119–20.
65. *Belfast Newsletter*, 19 January 1920.
66. Carson to Bates, 29 September 1919 (PRONI, D1327/18/24).
67. Carson to Montgomery, 15 August 1919 (PRONI, D627/434/53A).
68. Montgomery to Willis, 15 June 1916 (PRONI, D627/429/35).
69. Stronge to Montgomery, 10 May 1918 (PRONI, D627/434/11).
70. Ricardo to Montgomery, 11 April 1920 (PRONI, D627/435/28).
71. 'Report on Visit to Ireland, January 1920', 4 February 1920 (NAL, CAB/24/97).
72. Carson to Bates, 26 January 1920 (PRONI, D1237/18/24).
73. Ricardo to Montgomery, 8 April 1920 (PRONI, D627/435/23).
74. Ricardo to Montgomery, 11-21 April 1920 (PRONI, D627/435/28–47).
75. Gunning-Moore to Montgomery, April 1920 (PRONI, D627/435/57B).
76. Meglaughlin to James Craig, 8 March 1920 (PRONI, D1327/18/27).
77. Montgomery to Gunning Moore, 26 April 1920 (PRONI, D627/435/58).
78. Hamilton to Bates, 15 March 1920 (PRONI, D1327/18/27).
79. Montgomery to Stronge, 5 May 1920 (PRONI, D627/435/72).
80. PRONI, D1327/18/29.
81. Parkinson, *Belfast's Unholy War*, p. 18.
82. Ronan Fanning, *Fatal Path: British Government and Irish Revolution, 1910–1922* (London, 2013), pp. 247–8.
83. UESA to Carson, 18 June 1920 (PRONI, D1507/A/35/33).
84. Michael Farrell, *Northern Ireland: The Orange State* (London, 1976), p. 26.
85. UULA, 1–3 July 1920 (PRONI, D1327/11/4/1); *Belfast Newsletter*, 12 July 1920.
86. Andrew Gailey, 'King Carson: An Essay on the Invention of Leadership', *Irish Historical Studies* 30: 117 (1996), p. 85.
87. *Belfast Newsletter*, 13 July 1920.
88. Morgan, *Labour and Partition*, pp. 267–71.

89. Patterson, *Class Conflict and Sectarianism*, pp. 126, 140.
90. Paul Bew, *Ireland: The Politics of Enmity, 1789–2006* (Oxford, 2007), p. 402.
91. Patterson, *Class Conflict and Sectarianism*, p. 115.
92. *Belfast Newsletter*, 22 July 1920.
93. UULA, 29 July 1920 (PRONI, D1327/11/4/1).
94. *Belfast Newsletter*, 31 July 1920.
95. *Belfast Newsletter*, 2 August 1920; *Irish News*, 2 August 1920.
96. UULA, 15 December 1920 (PRONI, D1327/11/4/1).
97. *Belfast Newsletter*, 3 August 1920.
98. *Belfast Newsletter*, 23 August 1920.
99. Bates to Carson, 4 August 1920 (PRONI, D1507/A/36/4).
100. UULA, 7 August 1920 (PRONI, D1327/11/4/1).
101. *Westminster Gazette*, 24 July 1920.
102. Joe Devlin secured 72.3 per cent of the vote in Belfast Falls against Éamon de Valera's 27.7 per cent.
103. Eric Mercer, 'For King, Country and a Shilling a Day: Belfast Recruiting Patterns in the Great War', *History Ireland* 11: 4 (2003), pp. 29–33.
104. Watkins [?] to Carson, 24 July 1919 (PRONI. D1507/A/31/45–6).
105. Quoted in Morgan, *Labour and Partition*, p. 270.
106. Geoffrey Bell, *Hesitant Comrades: The Irish Revolution and the British Labour Movement* (London, 2016), p. 88.
107. O'Connor, *Syndicalism in Ireland*, p. 178.
108. O'Connor, *Labour History of Ireland*, p. 119.
109. Lady Craig's diary, 14 October 1920 (PRONI, D1415/B/39).
110. *Hansard*, House of Commons, 25 October 1920, vol. 133, c. 1493.
111. *Belfast Newsletter*, 11 September 1920.
112. Kenna, *Facts and Figures*, p. 62.
113. Fred Crawford's diary, 27 September 1920 (PRONI, D640/11/1).
114. Montgomery to [?], April 1920 (PRONI, D627/439/15).
115. Michael Farrell, *Arming the Protestants: Formation of the Ulster Special Constabulary and the Royal Ulster Constabulary, 1920–27* (London, 1987), p. 15.
116. Secret Memorandum, September 1920 (PRONI, D1678/6/1).
117. Paul Bew, Peter Gibbon and Henry Patterson, *The State in Northern Ireland, 1921–72: Political Forces and Social Classes* (Manchester, 1979), pp. 7–8.
118. British Cabinet Conclusions, 23 July 1920 (NAL, CAB/24/109).
119. British Cabinet Conclusions, 30 May 1922 (NAL, CAB/23/30). A battalion contained between 500 and 1,000 soldiers; the USC had an established force of 45,250 in the summer of 1922, with 3,000 RUC. Arthur Hezlet, *The 'B' Specials: A History of the Ulster Special* Constabulary (London, 1971), pp. 88, 100.
120. *Hansard*, House of Commons, 30 March 1920, vol. 127, cc. 1125–6.

121. Cabinet Conclusions, 15 April 1922 (NAL, CAB/23/30).
122. For Craig's statement, see Brendan O'Leary, *A Treatise on Northern Ireland, Volume I: Colonialism* (Oxford, 2019), p. 340; Montgomery to Stronge, 6 April 1920 (PRONI, D627/435/21); Montgomery to Leo Maxse, 7 May 1920 (PRONI, D627/435/75).
123. *Northern Whig*, 18 May 1921.
124. *Belfast Newsletter*, 26 May 1921.
125. O'Connor to Dillon, 29 July 1921, Trinity College Dublin, MS 6744/848.
126. For statistics, see Brendan O'Leary 'A Cold House', in John Crowley et al., *Atlas of the Irish Revolution* (Cork, 2017), p. 822.
127. *Hansard*, House of Commons, 8 July 1920, vol. 131, c. 1712.
128. The metaphor comes from *1984*, but is employed by Noam Chomsky in *Because We Say So* (London, 2015).
129. The concepts here rely heavily on Domenico Losurdo, *Liberalism: A Counter-History* (London/New York, 2011), pp. 309–10.
130. Report of intelligence division, January 1924, National Archives Ireland, NEBB, 1/1/12; Free State Intelligence Division, 1924, Irish Military Archive, MS 334; Adjt. 4th ND IRA to CS GHQ, April 1924, University College Dublin Archives, Moss Twomey papers, P69/35/115.
131. *Belfast Newsletter*, 4 January 1923.
132. James Loughlin, 'Northern Ireland and British Fascism in the Inter-War Years', *Irish Historical Studies* 29: 16 (1995), p. 82.
133. Belinda Probert, *Beyond Orange and Green* (London, 1978), p. 57.
134. Bew et al., *State in Northern Ireland*, p. 16.
135. O'Connor, *Syndicalism in Ireland*, p. 101.
136. *Belfast Telegraph*, 28 April 1919.
137. Thomas Linehan, *British Fascism 1918–39: Parties, Ideology and Culture* (Manchester 2001), p. 44.
138. *Voice of Labour*, 11 September 1920.
139. Theodore Allen, *The Invention of the White Race*, Vol. 1 (London, 1994), xviii.

7 The 'Miracle of Coalisland'

1. *Northern Whig*, 20 January 1923.
2. *Northern Whig*, 30 March 1923.
3. Archdale Memo, 11 April 1923 (Public Records Office of Northern Ireland [PRONI] CAB 9F/64/1; FIN18/3/75), also quoted in Patrick Buckland, *The Factory of Grievances* (Dublin, 1979), p. 124.
4. Ronan Fanning, 'Anglo-Irish Relations: Partition and the British Dimension in Historical Perspective', *Irish Studies in International Affairs* 2: 1 (1985), p. 13.

5. *Tyrone Courier*, 18 June 1914.
6. *Hansard*, House of Commons Debate, 16 February 1922, vol. 150, c. 1270.
7. Paul Murray, *The Irish Boundary Commission and Its Origins, 1886–1925* (Dublin, 2011), p. 314.
8. Buckland, *Factory of Grievances*, p. 23.
9. Government of Northern Ireland, *Violence and Civil Disturbances in Northern Ireland in 1969: Report of Tribunal of Inquiry* (Belfast, 1972), Paragraph 138.
10. Michael Farrell, *Arming the Protestants: Formation of the Ulster Special Constabulary and the Royal Ulster Constabulary, 1920–27* (London, 1987), pp. 43–4.
11. Highly confidential Memoranda, September 1920 (PRONI, Newton family papers, D1678/6/1).
12. *Mid-Ulster Mail*, 2 August 1924.
13. R. B Staples, 'Irish Coal and Iron' 1920 (PRONI, D1567/F/12/2).
14. Ibid.
15. *Northern Whig*, 6 September 1923.
16. Staples, 'Irish Coal and Iron'.
17. Brian Feeney, *Antrim, 1912–25* (Dublin, 2021), p. 18.
18. Kelly to Parr, 23 September 1925 (PRONI COM/13/1/55); Belfast Cabinet Conclusions [BCC], 1 December 1926 (PRONI, CAB4/182).
19. Kelly to Pollock, 7 November 1922 (PRONI, FIN18/3/75).
20. Information from Coalisland Museum and Heritage Centre, *A History of Coalisland Weaving Company*, n.d. – pdf available at coalisland-lnp.com.
21. *Mid-Ulster Mail*, 2 August 1924.
22. 1926 Census County Tyrone Report (Belfast, 1928), p. 77.
23. McCluskey, *Tyrone, 1912–25*, pp. 131–6.
24. Buckland, *Factory of Grievances*, p. 123.
25. Durham to Kelly, 2 November 1922 (PRONI, FIN18/3/75).
26. Pollock to Kelly, 9 November 1922 (PRONI, FIN18/3/75).
27. Memorandum by Minister of Commerce, April 1923 (PRONI, FIN18/3/81).
28. McKeown to Pollock, 14 November 1922 (PRONI, FIN18/3/75).
29. Christopher Norton, 'Creating Jobs, Manufacturing Unity: Ulster Unionism and Mass Unemployment 1922–34', *Contemporary British History* 15: 2 (2001), p. 11.
30. Paul Bew, Peter Gibbon and Henry Patterson, *Northern Ireland 1921–1994: Political Forces and Social Classes* (London, 1995), p. 56.
31. Duggan to Ulster Bank, 2 July 1924 (PRONI, 18/3/81).
32. BCC, 10 January 1923 (PRONI, CAB4/98).
33. BCC, 2 October 1923 (PRONI, CAB4/88).
34. Kevin Matthews, *Fatal Influence: The Impact of Ireland on British Politics* (Dublin, 2004), p. 103.

35. D. P. Jordan, 'The Economics of Devolution: Evidence from Northern Ireland 1920–1972', PhD dissertation, Queens University, Belfast (2001), pp. 96–7.
36. BCC, 28 October 1925 (PRONI, CAB4/153) and 15 December 1925 (PRONI, CAB4/156).
37. *Donegal News*, 17 May 1924.
38. Irish Independent, 23 May 1924.
39. *Freemans Journal*, 26 July 1924; *Irish News*, 8 January 1927.
40. *Mid-Ulster Mail*, 2 August 1924.
41. *Northern Whig*, 24 July 1924.
42. *Ballymena Telegraph*, 26 July 1924.
43. *Irish News*, 16 July 1924.
44. Matthews, *Fatal Influence*, p. 105.
45. HC Deb. Vol. 180, Col. 1651–1686, 23 February 1925; Matthews, *Fatal Influence*, p. 204.
46. Ibid., pp. 106–7; Arthur Hezlet, *The 'B' Specials: A History of the Ulster Special Constabulary* (London, 1972), p. 93.
47. Hezlet, *'B' Specials*, p. 110.
48. Confidential report by Major Robert Stevenson, 30 June 1922 (NAL, CO906/27).
49. Ibid.
50. Divisional Commissioner's Office, Belfast, 16 May 1922, Divisional Commissioner's Bi-monthly Reports (PRONI, HA/5/152); *Ulster Herald*, 13 May 1922.
51. *Tyrone Courier*, 11 May 1922.
52. Report, D.I. Walshe Dungannon, 6 May 1922, 'Charles Lavelle and Peter Hagan, Both from Coalisland Shot Dead at Annagher, Co. Tyrone: Special Inquiry in Lieu of Inquest' (PRONI, HA/5/921).
53. *Voice of Labour*, 5 November 1921.
54. IRA 2nd Northern Division, 3rd brigade, 1st Battalion (Coalisland), B Company (Edendork) Irish Military Archives MA-MSPC-RO-392, p. 10.
55. See 1901 and 1911 censuses.
56. *Voice of Labour*, 26 November 1921.
57. *Workers' Republic*, 25 March 1922.
58. *Voice of Labour*, 10 February 1923.
59. *Belfast Telegraph*, 27 February 1923; *Mid-Ulster Mail*, 3 May 1923.
60. *Voice of Labour*, 10 February 1923.
61. *Voice of Labour*, 17 February 1923.
62. *Voice of Labour*, 24 February 1923.
63. *Voice of Labour*, 1 April 1922.
64. *Voice of Labour*, 4 March 1922.
65. *Voice of Labour*, 10 March 1923.
66. *Mid-Ulster Mail*, 16 June 1923.
67. *Freeman's Journal*, 30 July 1923.

68. *Mid-Ulster Mail*, 28 April 1923.
69. McClung to Dawson Bates, 20 July 1923 (PRONI, HA5/1289).
70. RUC IG to MHA, 24 July 1923 (PRONI, HA5/1289).
71. MHA to McClung, 25 July 1923 (PRONI, HA5/1289); Robert McClung to MHA, 26 July 1923 (PRONI, HA5/1289).
72. *Mid-Ulster Mail*, 1 September 1923.
73. Ibid.
74. *Belfast Newsletter*, 2 October 1923.
75. RUC IG to MHA, 14 October 1924 (PRONI, HA5/1289).
76. *Belfast Newsletter*, 12 April 1924; *Belfast Telegraph*, 15 April 1924.
77. RUC IG to MHA, 11 April 1924 (PRONI, HA5/1349).
78. *Portadown Times*, 16 May 1924.
79. *Belfast Newsletter*, 12 April 1924.
80. Stephen Broadberry and Carsten Burhop, 'Real Wages and Labor Productivity in Britain and Germany, 1871–1938: A Unified Approach to the International Comparison of Living Standards', *Journal of Economic History* 70: 2 (June 2010), p. 420; 'Rates of Wages of Typical Classes of Workers in Certain Industries: 1914, 1920, 1925', cited in *Hansard*, House of Commons Debate, 30 July 1925, vol. 187, cc 671–3W.
81. RUC to MHA, 18 April 1924 (PRONI, HA5/1349).
82. *Belfast Newsletter*, 17 April 1924.
83. *Portadown Times*, 16 May 1924.
84. *Belfast Newsletter*, 24 May 1924.
85. *Belfast Telegraph*, 26 May 1924.
86. *Mid-Ulster Mail*, 31 May 1924; *Portadown Times*, 13 June 1924.
87. RUC IG to MHA, 27 May 1924 (PRONI, HA5/1307).
88. *Mid-Ulster Mail*, 4 August 1923.
89. Sam Kyle to MHA, 27 September 1924 (PRONI, HA5/1289).
90. *Northern Whig*, 27 June 1924.
91. *Freeman's Journal*, 12 July 1924; *Donegal News*, 12 July 1924.
92. RUC IG to MHA, 28 June 1924 (PRONI, HA5/1361).
93. *Northern Whig*, 30 June 1924.
94. *Northern Whig*, 30 June 1924.
95. *Irish Worker*, 26 July 1924.
96. *Voice of Labour*, 12 July 1924.
97. RUC IG to MHA, 8 July 1924 (PRONI, HA5/1361).
98. W. McKenna to Cavanagh, 12 August 1924 (PRONI, HA/5/1556).
99. *Voice of Labour*, 12 July 1924.
100. *Irish News*, 30 July 1924.
101. Duncan Report, 5 March 1925 (PRONI, COM59/1/11).
102. RUC IG to MHA, 29 October 1924 (PRONI, HA5/1349).
103. *Irish News*, 5 November 1924.
104. RUC IG to MHA, 5 November 1924 (PRONI, HA5/1349).
105. RUC to MHA, 29 November 1924 (PRONI, HA5/1349).

106. *Belfast Newsletter*, 9 November 1924; *Donegal News*, 15 November 1924; *Belfast Newsletter*, 29 October 1924.
107. *Derry Sentinel*, 2 December 1924.
108. RUC IG to MHA, 17 December 1924 (PRONI, HA5/1349).
109. *Irish News*, 24 September 1924.
110. Duncan Report, 5 March 1925 (PRONI, COM59/1/11).
111. *Irish News*, 15 July 1926.
112. Coalisland Collieries to Ministry of Commerce, 31 May 1926 (PRONI, COM59/1/11).
113. A. H. Steele, 16 April 1926 (PRONI, COM59/1/11).
114. *Irish News*, 8 January 1927.
115. Buckland, *Factory of Grievances*, p. 125.
116. Inter-cabinet Minute, 2 March 1937 (PRONI, FIN18/3/81) and 1 January 1940 (PRONI, FIN18/3/81).
117. *Mid-Ulster Mail*, 6 December 1924.
118. Hezlet, *'B' Specials*, pp. 120–1.
119. MHA Minute Sheet, 25 January 1926 (PRONI, HA5/1298).
120. Wickham to MHA 22, January 1926 (PRONI, HA5/1298).
121. MHA to Wickham, 4 February 1926 (PRONI, HA5/1298).
122. Wickham to MHA, 13 February 1926 (PRONI, HA5/1298).
123. Quoted in D. G. Pringle, 'Electoral Systems and Political Manipulation: A Case Study of Northern Ireland in the 1920s', *Economic and Social Review* 11: 3 (April 1980), p. 196.
124. Norton, 'Creating Jobs, Manufacturing Unity', p. 11.
125. David McKittrick and David McVea, *Making Sense of the Troubles: A History of the Northern Ireland Conflict* (London, 2002), p. 15.
126. *Hansard*, 20 March 1934, Parliamentary Debates, Northern Ireland House of Commons, Vol. XVI, Cols. 617–18.
127. *Hansard*, 24 April 1934, Parliamentary Debates, Northern Ireland House of Commons, Vol. XVI, Cols. 1,091–5.
128. The phrase is Howard Zinn's.
129. Bernadette Devlin, *The Price of My Soul* (New York, 1969), pp. 94–6.
130. E. P. Thompson, *The Making of the English Working Class* (London, 1963), p. 27.

Conclusion

1. *Irish Worker*, 14 March 1914.
2. Emmet O'Connor, *Rotten Prod: The Unlikely Career of Dungaree Baird* (Cork, 2022).
3. Darlington is describing the pre-war Labour Unrest here. See Ralph Darlington, *Labour Revolt in Britain, 1910–1914* (London, 2023), pp. 30–1.

4. Richard Hyman, *The Workers' Union* (Clarendon, 1971), p. 112.
5. Quoted in O'Connor, *Rotten Prod*, pp. 32–4.
6. Emmet O'Connor, *Syndicalism in Ireland, 1917–1923* (Cork, 1988), p. 110.
7. Olivier Coquelin, 'Cleeve's Soviets: "Socialism from Below" in Revolutionary Ireland, 1920–1922', in F. Devine and F. Mac Bhloscaidh, *Bread Not Profits: Provincial Working-Class Politics During the Irish Revolution* (Dublin, 2022), pp. 45–59.
8. O'Connor, *Syndicalism in Ireland*, p. 65.
9. Ibid., p. 186; 23 April 1918 – against conscription; Limerick Soviet – linked to British Military rule in April 1919; 12-13 April 1920 – in support of hunger strikers; and the March 1922 – general strike against 'militarism'.
10. Kieran Allen, *1916: Ireland's Revolutionary Tradition* (London, 2016), p. 211.
11. Quoted in Dónal Ó Drisceoil, 'Losing a War it Never Fought: labour, socialism and the War of Independence', in J. Crowley et al, *The Atlas of the Irish revolution* (Cork, 2017), p. 451.
12. O'Connor, *Syndicalism in Ireland*, p. 100.
13. *Manchester Guardian*, 24 February 1922.
14. Fergus Campbell, *Land and Revolution: Nationalist Politics in the West of Ireland, 1891–1921* (Oxford, 2008), p. 227.
15. Memo to Army Inquiry 1924, 11 January 1923 (UCDA Mulcahy Papers P/7/C/21).
16. Quoted in Kieran Allen, *Fianna Fáil and Irish Labour, 1926 to present* (London, 1997), p. 24.
17. O'Connor, *Rotten Prod*, p. 98.
18. Mike Davis, *Old Gods, New Enigmas: Marx's Lost Theory* (London, 2025), p. 17.
19. James Hinton, *The First Shop Stewards' Movement* (London, 1973), p. 57, quoted in Davis, *Old Gods*, p. 95.
20. Eric Hobsbawm, *The Age of Capital: 1848–1875* (London, 1975), p. 225, quoted in Davis, *Old Gods*, p. 96.
21. David R. Roediger, *The Wages of Whiteness* (London/New York: 1991), p. 116.
22. Quoted in John Gray, *City in Revolt: James Larkin and the Belfast Dock Strike of 1907* (Belfast, 1985), p. 18.
23. For the Outdoor Relief Strikes, see Seán Mitchel, *Struggle or Starve: Working-Class Unity in Belfast's 1932 Outdoor Relief Riots* (Chicago, 2017).
24. Ronald Storrs, *The Memoirs of Sir Ronald Storrs* (London, 2008), p. 364.
25. Alvin Jackson, *Home Rule: An Irish History, 1800–2000* (Oxford, 2004), pp. 153–4.
26. Paul Murray, *The Irish Boundary Commission and Its Origins, 1886–1925* (Dublin, 2011), p. 31.

27. J. O. Stubbs, 'Lord Milner and Patriotic Labour, 1914–1918', *English Historical Review*: 87: 345 (1972), pp. 717–54.
28. Crawford Diary, 9 August 1920 (PRONI, D640/11/1).
29. Geoffrey Bell, *Hesitant Comrades: The Irish Revolution and the British Labour Movement* (London, 2016) p. 86.
30. O'Connor, *Rotten Prod*, p. 71.
31. Londonderry to McKeown [?], 9 September 1922 (PRONI, D3099/2/7/43).
32. Theodore Allen, *The Invention of the White Race: Volume One* (London, 1994), xviii.
33. Des Bell and Liam O'Dowd, eds, *Northern Ireland Beyond 100* (Cork, 2024), pp. 56–7.
34. Gray, *City in Revolt*, p. 209; Emmet O'Connor, *Big Jim Larkin: Hero or Wrecker?* (Dublin, 2015), p. 33; Darlington, *Labour Revolt*, pp. 61–2.
35. Ruth Russell, *What's the Matter with Ireland?* (New York, 1920), p. 146.
36. Darlington, *Labour Revolt*, p. 61.
37. Ibid., p. 99.
38. Ibid.
39. Robert Fisk, *The Great War for Civilisation* (London, 2005), p. 375.
40. See Ian Cobain, 'The Evaporation of Hatred', *Dublin Review of Books*, February 2025.
41. Russell, *What's the Matter with Ireland?*, p. 149.
42. Mitchell, *The Ghost Limb: Alternative Protestants and the Spirit of 1798* (Belfast, 2022), pp. 3–4.
43. Ibid., pp. 222–3.

Index